A HISTORY OF THE ARYA SAMAJ

Dayananda Sarasvati, Swami

A HISTORY OF THE ARYA SAMAJ

[An Account of its Origin, Doctrines and Activities with a Biographical Sketch of the Founder]

By

LAJPAT RAI

Revised, expanded and edited by Sri Ram Sharma

ORIENT LONGMANS
BOMBAY CALCUTTA MADRAS NEW DELHI

ORIENT LONGMANS LIMITED
Regd. Office : 3/5, ASAF ALI ROAD, NEW DELHI 1
NICOL ROAD, BALLARD ESTATE, BOMBAY 1
17, CHITTARANJAN AVENUE, CALCUTTA 13
36-A, MOUNT ROAD, MADRAS 2
1/24, ASAF ALI ROAD, NEW DELHI 1

LONGMANS, GREEN AND CO LTD
48, GROSVENOR STREET, LONDON W. 1
*Associated companies, branches and representatives
throughout the world*

First published in India 1967

© *Orient Longmans Limited 1967*

PRINTED IN INDIA
BY S. C. GHOSE AT CALCUTTA PRESS PRIVATE LTD.
1 WELLINGTON SQUARE, CALCUTTA- 13.

EDITOR'S PREFACE

WHILE the birth centenary of Lala Lajpat Rai was being celebrated in 1965, it was decided to publish some of his works. The Central Centenary Committee published two volumes of his writings. The Bombay Centenary Celebration Committee published two volumes, one of appreciations of Lala Lajpat Rai and his work, another of selections from his writings. Orient Longmans Limited, the associates of the original publishers of his *The Arya Samaj*, decided to publish a revised and expanded edition of the book and requested me to undertake the task of revising, editing and expanding it.

In bringing out this revised edition, the text has been thoroughly revised, additional notes have been added where necessary. Citations of authorities have been checked and provided where needed. The division of the book into three parts has been discarded and the arrangement of chapters recast. I have omitted the text of the Vedic mantras in Devnagri characters as it could not be of any interest to non-Sanskritists. Three appendixes have been added. The first, "Swami Dayananda and the Vedas", reproduces an article contributed by Aurobindo Ghosh to the *Vedic Magazine*, Hardwar. The second, "A Red Letter Day", reproduces an article I contributed to the *Indian Express*, on the D.A.V. College Foundation Day (1 June). The last chapter was originally written by me for a seminar held in 1964 by the Delhi University on Indian Thought in the Nineteenth Century and Its Impact on Contemporary Civilization. The third appendix tries to throw some light on the author's own part in Indian politics which led to his deportation. The Bibliography has been revised and brought up to date.

I am grateful to the editorial department of Orient Longmans Ltd. for their help in bringing out this revised edition.

Despite much that has since been written on the Arya Samaj, this book continues to provide an overall view of the Arya Samaj, a critical biography of Swami Dayanand and an analytical account of the work it has been doing till

1914 when the book was first published. Its history since then has been mostly one of expansion of the tasks it had then undertaken. I have traced the outlines of that story till the death of Mahatma Hansraj in 1942 in *Mahatma Hansraj: A Maker of Modern Punjab*. The Bibliography includes some of the recent works that cover the post-1914 period.

Following the author's plan, I have confined the Bibliography to works in English alone.

I have left the concluding chapter as the author wrote it. To revise it or to bring it up to date would have been a sacrilege which I thought I should not be guilty of.

I am thankful to the Servants of the People Society for their permission to bring out this edition in its revised and expanded form.

SRI RAM SHARMA

EDITOR'S PREFACE

WHILE the birth centenary of Lala Lajpat Rai was being celebrated in 1965, it was decided to publish some of his works. The Central Centenary Committee published two volumes of his writings. The Bombay Centenary Celebration Committee published two volumes, one of appreciations of Lala Lajpat Rai and his work, another of selections from his writings. Orient Longmans Limited, the associates of the original publishers of his *The Arya Samaj*, decided to publish a revised and expanded edition of the book and requested me to undertake the task of revising, editing and expanding it.

In bringing out this revised edition, the text has been thoroughly revised, additional notes have been added where necessary. Citations of authorities have been checked and provided where needed. The division of the book into three parts has been discarded and the arrangement of chapters recast. I have omitted the text of the Vedic mantras in Devnagri characters as it could not be of any interest to non-Sanskritists. Three appendixes have been added. The first, "Swami Dayananda and the Vedas", reproduces an article contributed by Aurobindo Ghosh to the *Vedic Magazine*, Hardwar. The second, "A Red Letter Day", reproduces an article I contributed to the *Indian Express*, on the D.A.V. College Foundation Day (1 June). The last chapter was originally written by me for a seminar held in 1964 by the Delhi University on Indian Thought in the Nineteenth Century and Its Impact on Contemporary Civilization. The third appendix tries to throw some light on the author's own part in Indian politics which led to his deportation. The Bibliography has been revised and brought up to date.

I am grateful to the editorial department of Orient Longmans Ltd. for their help in bringing out this revised edition.

Despite much that has since been written on the Arya Samaj, this book continues to provide an overall view of the Arya Samaj, a critical biography of Swami Dayanand and an analytical account of the work it has been doing till

1914 when the book was first published. Its history since then has been mostly one of expansion of the tasks it had then undertaken. I have traced the outlines of that story till the death of Mahatma Hansraj in 1942 in *Mahatma Hansraj: A Maker of Modern Punjab*. The Bibliography includes some of the recent works that cover the post-1914 period.

Following the author's plan, I have confined the Bibliography to works in English alone.

I have left the concluding chapter as the author wrote it. To revise it or to bring it up to date would have been a sacrilege which I thought I should not be guilty of.

I am thankful to the Servants of the People Society for their permission to bring out this edition in its revised and expanded form.

Sri Ram Sharma

ERRATUM

For the *Dayanand Dalituddhar Mandal*, p. 121, n. 5 and p. 126, n. 7 read the *Dayanand Salvation Mission*.

CONTENTS

		Page
Editor's Preface		v
Introduction		1
I. Early Life		7
II. Fighting For Truth		26
III. Founding of the Arya Samaj and Death		40
IV. The Teachings of Dayanand		49
V. Dayanand's Translation of the *Vedas*		66
Appendix—*Dayananda and the Vedas*		71
VI. Religious Teachings		79
VII. Religious Ideals and Aims		99
VIII. Social Ideals and Aims		113
IX. Shuddhi Work of the Arya Samaj		120
X. Philanthropic Activities		129
XI. Educational Work		135
Appendix I—A Red-Letter Day		152
Appendix II—Educational Institutions of Higher Learning under the D.A.V. College, Trust and Management Society		155
XII. Organization of the Arya Samaj		156
XIII. The Arya Samaj and Politics		160
Appendix		174
XIV. Conclusion		177
XV. The Arya Samaj and Its Impact on Contemporary India		188
Bibliography		205
Index		207

INTRODUCTION

Great is Thy power, O Indra we are Thine. Grant,
O Bounteous Lord, the prayer of this Thy adorer.

R. i, 57, 5

It was in 1907 that the Arya Samaj first attracted notice outside India. Since then hardly a book has been published in the English language, dealing with Indian movements or with Indian conditions of life, which does not speak of the Arya Samaj. Liberal and Labour writers have spoken of it in terms of appreciation and sympathy, while a few Conservative Imperialists have condemned it as anti-British. Missionaries have also written of it, either as fair critics or in a spirit of rancour. Before 1907, the Arya Samaj had very few books in English dealing with its doctrines. With the exception of a few tracts by the late lamented Pandit Gurudatta Vidyarthi and a few tracts by Bawa Chhajju Singh, there was hardly anything which could be presented to a non-Indian student of the Arya Samaj.[1] The founder had written in Sanskrit or Hindi only.[2] The bulk of the literature produced by his followers was also either in Sanskrit, Hindi or Urdu. It is true that two English translations of the *Satyarath Prakash*—one by Master Durga Prasad, the other by Mr. Chiranjiva Bharadwaja—existed even before 1907, but both lacked absolute accuracy and were otherwise unsuitable for foreign students.[3]

The translation of Indian ideas and Indian sentiments into an occidental language, indeed, is an extremely difficult task. High proficiency in both languages is essential for even moderate success; and even then sometimes an exact rendering of Indian terms into English is well-nigh impossible. Take, for instance, the Sanskrit word, "Dharma". The English language possesses no word which can accurately convey the meaning to an

---

[1] Since 1914 several works on the Arya Samaj in English have been published. See Bibliography—Editor.

[2] His collected works would cover some 150,000 pages of octavo size—Ed.

[3] Lala Ganga Prashad, M.A. has published a new, more accurate and readable translation of the *Satyarath Prakash* in English—Ed.

Indian. Under the circumstances, translation from Hindi into English is of doubtful utility.

In spite of this difficulty, the demand for the Arya Samaj literature in English has been growing, and more than once it has been suggested to me that I should do something to meet that demand. The kind friends who suggested this did not perhaps know that I lacked qualifications for the work even more than those did who had attempted to give English renderings of the *Satyarath Prakash*. There have been and are abler men in the Arya Samaj who could acquit themselves creditably at this task. Some of them, unfortunately, have been removed from among us by death; others, though willing, are otherwise engaged and cannot find the time necessary to do justice to the work; still others have neither time nor inclination for the effort. The Gurukula section of the Arya Samaj have been trying to do something in the matter, but so far nothing tangible has resulted. The fact is that the Arya Samajes have so much to do for their own people that they have scarcely any time or funds to spare for those who do not know our language. For the present their hands are too full.

Until recently, the Arya Samajes were quite content to continue their work of reform among their own people, and had no desire to attract the notice of the outside world. They have been drawn into the world arena much against their will. Circumstances have forced their hands, and they have learnt in the school of adversity and by bitter experience that quiet, unassuming work is liable to serious misconstruction and misrepresentation. In these days of world-movements, no organization, however modest in its aims, can afford to be misrepresented and misunderstood—much less a movement which in its conception is not modest, neither in its aims and ideals, nor in its scope. So long as the Arya Samaj was attacked in India alone, it could afford to ignore those attacks. The people among and for whom it worked knew its worth, and no amount of interested criticism or ignorant misrepresentation could do it any harm. The Arya Samaj cared not for the foreigner, neither for his conversion nor for his opinion. It was not seeking recognition, either by Government or by learned societies. But when, in 1907, it found that its exclusiveness and self-reliance were misunderstood and that it ran the risk of being condemned unheard, it raised its voice in protest, and invited Europeans to visit its institutions, stay in them, and see for themselves the truth. Since then, some of the quiet workers have even gone out of their way to put their case before the Government, the learned world, and the English Press in India and in England. In self-defence, some of the busiest of Arya Samaj workers have had to find time to write in the English language of its principles, its teachings, its aims and its work. Still later, Lala Munshi Rama, the leader of the Gurukula section of the Arya Samaj, has published several speeches and tracts in the English language explaining the aims and objects of the Samaj and the Gurukula, as also have some of his colleagues, notably Professors Ram Deva and Bal Krishna. Among others who have written in English on this subject may be mentioned Rai Thakar Datta and Lala Ralla Ram, besides Professor Diwan Chand, M.A., of the Dayananda Anglo-Vedic College. Nevertheless, the need of a work which would give a general idea of the movement, its history, and its activities, for use both in India and abroad, has been felt very keenly. At one time it was hoped that the late Lala Dwarka Dass, M.A., who combined in his person a profound knowledge of Western thought with an equally profound knowledge of Hindu thought, would supply the need; but, unfortunately, that hope was frustrated by his death in October, 1912.

The present work is an attempt to meet the need we have explained. No one is more conscious of its defects than the writer himself, who can lay no claim either to profound knowledge or to excellence in style. His sole claim for being heard on the subject is that he has been in the movement ever since he was a boy of eighteen (A.D. 1882); that he has given the best part of his leisure time to the movement; that he has taken the lead in organizing several of its activities; that he owes a great deal of what may be considered good in him to its influence; and that the Samaj has passed through a serious political crisis on account of his connection with it In the absence of abler and better qualified hands, having time and inclination to devote to the work, he has tried to do it from a sense of duty to and love for the Arya Samaj.

For the work itself no claim to originality is made; in fact, it is more of the nature of a compilation. This explains the presence of so many lengthy quotations in the body of the book. The object of these is to state the position of the Samaj in the words of its leaders, who naturally are the best exponents of its doctrine and its views.

The chapters on the life of Swami Dayananda are based on *The Life and Teachings of Swami Dayananda*, by Bawa Chhajju Singh, who for fifteen years or more edited the official organ, in the English language, of the Samaj. In his turn he had drawn upon, among other sources, one of the biographies of Swami Dayananda, written by the present author himself, in 1898 in Hindustani. On the teachings of the Samaj, the following books, besides the Life aforementioned have been consulted:— (1) *A Handbook of the Arya Samaj*, published by the Tract Department of the Provincial Assembly of the Arya Samajes in the United Provinces of Agra and Oudh; (2) *Teachings of the Arya Samaj*, by Bawa Chhajju Singh; and (3) Printed Lectures of Lalas Hansraj and Munshi Ram, the leaders of the two sections. Invariably I have given in a footnote the reference to the work from which I have borrowed anything bodily. By good fortune I have been able to reproduce the original article which appeared in *The Christian Intelligencer* in 1870, giving an account of the disputation held at Benares, in November, 1869, between Swami Dayananda and the Kashi Pandits. Bawa Chhajju Singh had had to retranslate into English the vernacular translation given in my work in 1898. For this valuable contribution my best thanks are due to Mr. Porter, the Librarian of the Church Missionary Society, London, for having lent me the volume containing the article.

In giving an account of the various institutions managed and controlled by the Arya Samaj, I have endeavoured to use the language of the official reports or of the pamphlets issued under the authority of the managers, as in the case of the Gurukula at Kangri. My position in relation to the two colleges of the Arya Samaj, the Dayananda Anglo-Vedic College of Lahore and the Gurukula at Kangri, is perhaps unique. For the first I feel the love of a parent, for the second that of a lover. Yet I am not in full agreement with either scheme, and have had my differences with both. For this reason I have felt it advisable

INTRODUCTION

to give the account of these two institutions in the language of their founders, which course has necessitated giving somewhat lengthy quotations, the substance of which could be condensed into much smaller space. Similarly, I have exercised scrupulous care in describing the politics of the Samaj and in giving the position of its critics, by quoting the original documents. With these exceptions, I take sole responsibility for the opinions expressed in this work.

If the fact be considered that I have played some part in making the Samaj what it is, I shall perhaps be excused if I venture to recommend this book to those who, within a brief space, wish to make acquaintance with the society and its founders, and have a bird's eye view of its activities in the past. This book is meant for circulation both in and outside India—a fact which has contributed not inconsiderably to its bulk. Certain matters have been dealt with in detail for the benefit of non-Indians which might well have been omitted from a book intended for the use of Indians only; and *vice versa*. There is another matter which I should like to mention in connection with the preparation of this book: viz. that the whole of it was conceived, sketched and written in the course of not more than eight weeks, in London, far from the scene of the activities covered by it: and without the inestimable advantage of consultation with the leaders of the Samaj. My constant endeavour has been to take a detached, unbiassed view of all things: but I do not know if I have been quite successful in doing so, since it must be admitted to be difficult to take a detached view of affairs in which one has been so intimately involved. This work is the first of its kind, and might be improved in subsequent editions, if it should be so fortunate as to find favour with those for whom it is meant.

The Veda-mantras scattered through the book have been selected from Lala Gokal Chand's *Message of the Vedas*, or from Bawa Chhajju Singh's *Teachings of the Arya Samaj*. In the absence of any qualifications for translating the mantras for myself, I have adopted their translations, which I believe to be correct and very near to the translations made by Western scholars.

My acknowledgments are due to the authors from whose works I have largely quoted, and also to the editors of the monthly and other periodicals which I have used. I am, besides, very grateful to Professor Sidney Webb, LL.D., for having read my manuscript and written for it a preface. It is to his learned wife and himself that I am indebted for the encouragement which has stimulated me to write this book, and it is they who impressed upon me the necessity for such a work in the interest of the Arya Samaj. My thanks in addition are due to my friend. Mr. W. F. Westbrook, for having read the manuscript and made valuable suggestions.

LAJPAT RAI

London
October 13, 1914

Chapter I

EARLY LIFE

Agni gives to the worshipper a son, the best, of the highest fame, of deep devotion, of an unconquerable spirit, and the bringer of glory to his parents.

—R. v, 25, 5

1. Parentage and Birth

Morvi is a small and prosperous town in Kathiawar, Gujerat, a short distance from the North-Western coast of the Indian Peninsula, the headquarters of the native State of that name under the Kathiawar agency of the British Government of Bombay. Dayanand's family belonged to the State, and his father held a post of some responsibility and position in the Government. His family were land-owners and were considered wealthy enough to engage in money-lending. They were Brahmins of the highest order, learned in Vedic lore and held in great respect on that account.

Dayanand's father had the reputation of being a rigid, austere Brahmin, thoroughly orthodox and uncompromising in his religious beliefs and practices. Nothing would induce him to tolerate even the slightest departure from the letter of the law, as laid down in books or handed down by tradition, as regards ritual observances and religious practices. He was a man of fervent faith, iron will, and dour temper. Dayanand's mother, on the other hand, was the personification of sweetness, gentleness, and goodness. She was a typical Indian lady, unlettered and uneducated in the sense that she was never taught reading and writing, but possessed all the qualities of a good mother and a capable and efficient housewife. We do not know of how the couple lived and got on together, but there is no reason to suppose that they were in any way incompatible: since in India, similar marriages, arranged by the parents in the early childhood of the contracting parties, are not inevitable failures. It is not rare to find husband and wife forming a complete whole by the fusion of the different qualities and temperaments peculiar to each, in a way complementary to each other. Swami Dayanand thus had the twofold advantage of inheriting a strong will from his father and a benevolent disposition from his mother. He was born in 1824, (Hindu era, 1881 *Vikram*), in his parents' home.

2. *Education and the Dawn of Enlightenment*

We have it on the authority of Dayanand himself that his instruction commenced at the age of five, and that in his eighth year he was invested with the sacred thread.

This investiture is a sort of baptism which is conferred on every Hindu child, born of "twice-born" parents. From now on begins his life as a *Brahmchari* (i.e. Brahminical student). The most suitable age for this ceremony is eight in the case of children of Brahmin parentage, and twelve for others. For the former, the reading of the alphabet begins at five. Children may be invested with the sacred thread then or afterwards, but not later than the eighth year. With the investiture the child is admitted into the formal life of a student and becomes "twice-born" himself and entitled to wear the symbolic thread as well as read the *Vedas*. The investiture imposes upon him the vow of chastity, purity, and poverty for the duration of his student career, which generally lasts until he is twenty-five, but may, in exceptional cases, be extended to forty-eight. It also imposes the obligation of daily worship, daily recitation of the *Vedas*, daily performance of Homa, the service of the Guru or spiritual teacher, and the strictest purity of thought, word, and deed consistent with a life of strict simplicity, verging on austerity. Like everything else Hindu, this institution has lost its soul and at the present day is more or less an empty formality, a relic of days of yore, and a reminder of ancient beliefs: yet it is encircled by a halo of great sanctity, and is considered to be a momentous event in the life of a Hindu child—all the more if he be a Brahmin, the highest caste. It is performed more or less ceremoniously, according to the means and resources of the parents, and is an occasion of great rejoicing and festivity, accompanied by extensive charity.

According to the letter of the law, the investiture must be followed by the removal of the child from the parental home and his admission into the family of his teacher, where he must remain until his education is completed. His successful departure from his teacher's home is heralded by his graduation, which entitles him to the status of a householder.

In educated Brahmin families, the father, if qualified, imparts his knowledge to his son and thereby avoids violation of the law, but otherwise the law is observed in its breach. We have no means of ascertaining what happened in the case of young Mulshankar (Dayanand's original name), but from what we have heard about the relations of Dayanand with his father, and of the latter's strict orthodoxy, we have reason to believe that the father assumed the role of teacher, and thus took into his own hands the twofold authority of father and teacher. So far the case resembles that of John Stuart Mill. But Dayanand was a born rebel, and it did not take him very long to revolt against paternal authority, which aimed at imposing upon the son his authority in all matters, even those that concerned the soul of his son and pupil. Dayanand's father was a devout worshipper of Shiva, one of the three highest gods in the Hindu Pantheon. In different parts of India, Shiva is worshipped in various forms: in some places as a symbol of creation, in others as a symbol of destruction.

Among other duties, Hindu worship entails keeping a certain number of fasts during the year on days considered to be sacred. *Shivaratri* is one of these, when every pious Shiva-worshipper is expected to fast for about thirty-six hours, or even more. Dayanand was fourteen when his father insisted on his keeping the fast, in orthodox fashion. The mother did not relish the idea, but had perforce to yield when Dayanand himself expressed his willingness to obey his father.

None could have foreseen that Dayanand's father's piously intended insistence upon his son's earning religious merit at the tender age of fourteen by observing the fast of *Shivaratri*, was to result in such a tremendous change in the mind of Dayanand turning him into the most virulent and successful opponent of image-worship of his times. In the words of Dayanand's biographer, as the fateful evening set in, the father and son wended their way to the temple on the outskirts of the village, where the rules to be observed with the worship were duly explained to him. One of these required the devotee who kept the fast to keep awake the whole night, repeating prayers before the image of the god, since otherwise the fast would bear no fruit. Worship began with the chanting of hymns, the whole congregation joining in the singing. The first quarter of the night passed off very well, the entire congregation displaying great fervour and enthusiasm, such as is born of deep (though blind) religious faith. In the second quarter fervour began to wane, but still they abided by the letter of the law. As soon, however, as midnight was past, the worshippers began to feel that nature was rather too powerful to be resisted even by blind faith. Dayanand's father was one of the first to give in, and the officiating priest followed suit. The boy of fourteen, however, was resolved not to yield. He had no desire to lose the merit to be gained by keeping the fast in strict accordance with the letter of the law. He used every device to ward off sleep, and succeeded where his father had failed. His hard-won success was fruitful indeed, though in a way quite different from the one expected by his father.

He was still engaged in struggling against sleep and muttering his prayers, when suddenly occurred a common and insignificant incident which changed the course of his life. A mouse crept up on the body of Shiva, and assured that the image was quite harmless, began to nibble at the offerings placed before the image by the devotees as a token of their adoration of the god. This launched the boy on a train of earnest thought. He had been informed that the god was omnipotent and omniscient; that the image represented him in all his glory; that it was God Himself; and that it had the power to bless or curse men. What he saw, however, was quite inconsistent with these statements. The image was evidently an inanimate object which could not even protect itself from the impertinence of a mouse! This, then, could not be the right way to worship, and the image could not be Shiva himself, as was taught by the priesthood.

The boy had been gifted with a logical mind, and though

young, possessed the courage born of true enlightened scepticism. The thought struck him like a thunderbolt and, with this scepticism obsessing him, he could no longer pay homage to the image as before. He would not, however, go to sleep, nor could he steal away without first rousing his father and attempting to have his doubts set at rest. The father was at first annoyed both at being disturbed and at the boy's audacity. Dayanand was not to be put off so lightly, but persisted and eventually got the only answer which a thoughtful and intelligent image-worshipper has for this fateful question. He said that the image was not the personification of the god. It merely represented him for the purpose of worship, and, "he being worshipped through it, he is as much pleased as though he were actually present in the image and were himself adored." Dayanand's father vouchsafed this explanation, but at the same time soundly berated his son for his habit of raising doubts and asking questions. He did not like it. He insisted on unquestioning obedience; but this the boy was not prepared to give. His father's explanation did not satisfy him, so he quietly asked permission to go home. This permission the father grudgingly accorded, being reluctant to restrain his son by force, but at the same time reminded Dayanand of the obligation that his fast must not be broken before sunrise. Dayanand, however, had already taken his own decision. He had dispensed with image worship and all its ritual. He went home, broke his fast, and went to sleep.

When the father returned home in the morning and found his son sound asleep, he remonstrated, and was furious with the mother. On the boy's getting up, he scolded him interminably. Dayanand, however, was none the worse for the scolding; he quietly turned to his studies, and went his own way regardless of the paternal wishes. Henceforth, naturally, relations with his father were strained, and he had to depend on the goodwill and sympathy of an uncle who was better able to understand him and to sympathize with the trend of his mind.

We have related this incident at some length to furnish a forecast of the developed mind of Swami Dayanand, the reformer, and also to explain the iconoclasm of his nature. A born rebel like Dayanand who at the age of fourteen set aside the authority of his father with a resolution rare even in adults was not likely, in the years to come, to submit to the tyranny of society and traditional custom after he had resolved to play the man and to burst the bonds of religious prejudice and superstition which held captive the minds and so detrimentally affected the character of his countrymen. The Arya Samajists, all over the country, celebrate the night of *Shivaratri* as the anniversary of Dayanand's enlightenment, and even the non-Arya Samajists join in the celebration with pride and pleasure.

To return to Dayanand's early years. The education which he imbibed had not much of what is understood by that term in the West. Dayanand's father was a Sam-Vedi Brahmin, the loftiest among the Brahmins. The highest Brahmins of the Deccan and Western India are distinguished by and named after the particular *Veda* which has been specially studied and honoured in their family for generations. The *Vedas* are four in number, corresponding to the four castes. Among them the *Sama-Veda* ranks highest, corresponding to the Brahmin of Varnas (the caste system). The *Yajura* comes next, then the *Rig*, and lastly the *Atharva*. All the four *Vedas* are studied, but families are honoured and respected according to the *Veda* which has received their special attention. In the troubled times of Muslim domination and amid the turmoil emanating from frequent political changes, it was considered wiser to memorize the *Vedas* rather than run the risk of their being lost to humanity. Dayanand's family was of the highest class, being Sam-Vedis; but we do not know why, in the case of Dayanand himself, his education began with the *Yajur-Veda*. Before he was fourteen, he knew the whole *Yajur-Veda* by heart and also portions of the other three *Vedas*, besides having studied some minor works on Sanskrit grammar. The Brahmins, not affected by modern educational trends, begin with the text of the *Vedas* and the rules of grammar which are committed to memory. Explanation of the rules of grammar and their application follows; but in the vast majority of cases, the *Vedas* remain stored in the memory without the scholar ever learning their meaning. Other pieces of Sanskrit literature, both prose and poetry, are taught and followed by standard works on logic, philosophy, philology, law, ethics, religion, ritual, rhetoric, etc.

EARLY LIFE

On these well-established lines Dayanand continued his studies and made considerable progress. He was an intelligent, earnest, and diligent student. But, unlike the average boy, he was something more than a student. He was in quest of enlightenment. He wished to penetrate to the core of things. The death of a beloved sister launched him on an inquiry as to the cause of death. His grief for her loss was too deep for tears. It plunged him into meditation on death as apart from life: what it meant, and how it could be overcome.

The youthful inquirer kept on with his studies, brooding on the problem of life and death; but ere long he was destined to witness what tended still more to intensify his desire to fathom the mystery. He was nineteen when his beloved uncle, who had so often rocked him in his lap, and who had, when he grew up, so often shared his confidence and striven to help him when he was in trouble, was laid low by the same disease that had proved fatal for his sister. The malady was of a virulent type, and baffled the skill of the physician. While the expiring man lay on his death-bed, he was gazing at Dayanand with the fondness of the most devoted parent, his eyes brimming with tears. Dayanand could not meet the gaze of this angel among men, and withal a person of vast learning, without bursting into tears; he wept so much that his eyes became swollen. The end came at last, and the house was once more a house of mourning.

Dayanand moved around distracted, asking his friends and the learned Pandits of his acquaintance if they could inform him how death could be overcome. The reply was that yogabhyas (contemplation or communion) was the way to secure it. Dayanand thought over the answer, and reached the conclusion that in order to learn yoga he must leave home. The world and its attractions were transient and valueless when compared with the bliss of salvation. Dayanand thought in the strain of the Divine verse:

"Whoever thoroughly understands the nature of the visible creation and of the imperishable atom from which the visible creation springs at one and the same time, the same shall, by virtue of his knowledge of the primal atom, triumph over death, and shall obtain beatitude by virtue of his knowledge of the visible creation and by reason of his virtuous activity in that creation." *Yajur*, xl, 14

The nature of the aspirations which now filled Dayanand's breast was not long in becoming known to his father and mother. They were alarmed, particularly the latter, and sought means for preventing their son from carrying out his purpose.

3. *Flight from Home*

The remedy that appeared feasible was the usual one, familiar to mankind from days of old, of creating more intimate interests which would prevent him from leaving home, and weave a web of affection round his person. Parents all over the world and in all ages have considered marriage to be the best remedy to wean young minds from ascetic lines of thought. Buddha's parents tried the same remedy, so did the parents of Nanak. These, however, were gentler spirits than Dayanand. They could not resist the will of their parents, who consequently succeeded in their immediate object, though failing ultimately. Dayanand objected to the scheme of his parents and declined to be married. He was by this time a youth of nineteen, and the intervention of friends led to the marriage being postponed for a year. This respite quickly passed, and his parents insisted on his marriage. For a time he acceded to their demands and requested that he be sent to Banaras to complete his studies.

Banaras, the sacred Kashi, is the Rome of the Hindus. It is also their Oxford. It attracts earnest students of Sanskrit literature, of Hindu theology, and of Hindu philosophy, from all parts of India. In pre-British days its charm was even greater, since no Hindu considered his education complete, entitling him to be called a scholar, without a course of study at Banaras.

Under ordinary circumstances, the idea proposed by Dayanand would have appealed to the parents of a promising student, since a course of study at Banaras raises the scholar to the dignity of an authority on Hindu Shastras, whose counsel would be sought and respected by prince and commoner alike. Dayanand's parents, however, having reason to suspect the workings of their son's mind, and not wishing to lose him

EARLY LIFE

altogether, refused to grant his request. A compromise was eventually arrived at and Dayanand was allowed to proceed to a neighbouring village and pursue his studies with a learned theologian there. In the course of his studies he confided in the teacher who, in his turn, considered it obligatory to inform Dayanand's parents. At this, they recalled him, intending to terminate his procrastination by fastening upon him, once for all, the matrimonial bond.

But they had not fully gauged the determination of their son. A week or so before the wedding day, he left home. His father pursued him, but failed to trace him. In less than three days after leaving home, Dayanand was stripped of all the valuables he had on his person, as well as the money in his pocket. He became a Sadhu, changed his name, assumed ochre-coloured garments, and began to search for a suitable Guru (a spiritual teacher), who could initiate him in the way of solving the mystery of life and death for himself and attaining moksha (i.e. liberation or beatitude).

A few days elapsed before Dayanand's father obtained a clue to his son's whereabouts from an acquaintance who had seen him in his new garb. This time the pursuer had more success and effected the desired capture. Dayanand was confined for the night in a room, with a guard posted at the door. The captive, however, resolved to escape, and did so that very night! By dawn he had put several miles between himself and his father, whom he never saw again.

This was his final separation from home and all that the word implies. It was casting himself adrift from worldly ties. He felt filial sorrow for his mother, who loved him devotedly, but he had to fulfil a mission; and even as early as 1903 *Vikram* (about 1845 or 1846) he could visualize it, though faintly, in his mind's eye. He was leaving home to make all India his abode. He was forsaking his kindred to succour humanity and the cause of truth.

From whatever we know of him he never did regret the step he had taken: a step which alone enabled him to serve his people, his country and his God as greatly as he did. It was the logical conclusion of the step taken seven years ago when he revolted against his father's misuse of parental authority in attempting to dictate on matters affecting his innermost beliefs.

4. *Pursuit of Knowledge and Truth*

For full fifteen years, from 1845 to 1860, young Dayanand wandered north, south, east, and west, almost all over India, in quest of knowledge and truth. During these wanderings he tapped the highest and the purest sources of knowledge. He moved from place to place inquiring about scholars of renown, men of wisdom and ascetics (Sadhus) of great religious merit. Whenever he met one from whom he could imbibe any knowledge, he halted and sat at his feet. With some he studied philosophy, with others the *Vedas*. It was in the course of these wanderings that he acquired the theory and practice of Yoga. There was scarcely a Hindu place of pilgrimage throughout India which he did not visit. Some, favoured as centres of learning, he visited again and again. In search of teachers of fame and yogis of merit he penetrated the innermost recesses of the Himalaya, the Vindhya, and the Aravali, the three important mountain ranges in India. He crossed and recrossed the valleys of the noblest of Indian rivers, the Ganges, the Jamuna, and the Narbadda, and mounted the highest accessible summits of the hills in the vicinity of the sources of those rivers. It is a distinguishing feature of the Hindu religion that its holiest places are noted for their natural beauty, the grandeur of their scenery, and the purity of their waters. These include some, or rather the majority of the most sublime and lofty peaks of the Himalayas accessible to man, of which some can be approached only at certain times of the year, and are open at the most for a month to four or five months only. The valleys of majestic rivers are the favourite resorts of Hindu scholars, saints, who sometimes get no cooked food for months. All these places were visited by Dayanand, and every nook and corner of them was as familiar to him as the lanes of his native village. He loved nature and drank deeply from her inexhaustible sources.

It was in these surroundings of sublime beauty that he practised Yoga. It was there in direct communion with nature that he turned his thoughts to God, and meditated on the deepest problems of life and death, spending long periods in an atmosphere of purest bliss and unalloyed contentment. It was here that he made the acquaintance of the best, the noblest, and the purest of Hindu saints, who led a life of uninterrupted meditation and discipline, having subordinated their senses to their intellect and their intellect to their spirit. For days he ate nothing but wild fruits; for months he lived on milk only, and sometimes for years at a stretch he spoke no language but Sanskrit. He delved deeply into the mysteries of nature and tapped all sources of knowledge. He despised nobody from whom he could acquire knowledge, either in the way of book learning, religious insight, or spiritual exercises. He attended all religious assemblies and participated in all the discussions and debates for which religious India and Hindu fraternities are renowned. Occasionally he followed the rivers (particularly the Ganges in the north and the Narbadda in the south) right up to their sources, braved every danger and trained himself to a life of hardship and privation.

Travelling in the lofty Himalayas, particularly along the banks of the rivers, is ever dangerous, but in those days devoid of railways, roads, camping places, rest-houses, and perhaps very scanty shelter even in the lower ranges of the hills, the drawbacks and perils of travelling are better imagined than described. Dayanand, however, was never hindered by them; he was preparing himself for a life in which he was to face dangers and difficulties even in the midst of civilization. These were the disciplinary and probationary years which adequately equipped him to cope with the life awaiting him in the years to come, but about which he could not at the time have had the slightest presentiment.

For a short period after his flight from home he passed as a Brahmachari (student), the first stage of a Hindu's life, but within a few years was formally initiated into the order of Sannyasis. According to the most approved authorities there are four stages of a Hindu's life. The first is that of Brahmcharya (i.e. studentship); the second is that of Grihastha (i.e. the life of a householder, or, say, married life); the third is that of Banprastha (i.e. of retirement from active life and of meditation); the fourth is that of Sannyas (i.e. complete renunciation and a life dedicated to service). The duties and obligations of the first three stages must be duly discharged before one can be qualified to enter the fourth and the last stage, which entitles one to the highest respect which society can offer and the most implicit trust which society and state can repose in any one of its members. In the case of individuals possessing extraordinary ability and character, the shastras permit admission into the fourth order directly at the close of the first stage, whenever they are considered suitable for that honour by one or more members of the fraternity.

None but a Sannyasi can admit another into that order, and the rules on this point are so rigid that even in this age of licence and degeneration Dayanand had great difficulty in securing admittance into the order. He was refused more than once, but his perseverance was soon rewarded, and within a few years of his departure from home he gained admittance into the highest order of Sannyasis; such was the estimate of his character formed by the man officiating at his initiation.

A Hindu Sannyasi is prohibited from cooking food for himself. He must not have money or valuables in his possession. He is not allowed to own more than absolutely necessary apparel. He is forbidden to acquire money or engage in any profitable business whatsoever but must restrict himself to study, contemplation, or service. He must not deck out his person, but must lead a life of perfect self-denial and perpetual spiritual discipline. He may be of service to others, but not on payment or compensation. He belongs to no caste and is entirely free from all the restrictions of caste. He must not eat meat, but can accept vegetarian food from the hands of any caste, creed or colour. He must not enjoy the company of women longer than may be strictly necessary in discharging his duty as a religious preacher. He must not abide very long at one place, nor make a home for himself. He may accept no gifts with the exception of food, essential clothing and footwear.

It was this life to which young Dayanand pledged himself of his own free will before he was twenty-five years old, and not a soul, not even his bitterest enemies (for of enemies he had enough and to spare), could assert that he ever broke his oath. Opponents have criticized his teaching vehemently; they have queried his motives and abused him; but not a breath of suspicion has ever fallen on the purity of his life and character. We may summarize the notable characteristics of Dayanand's life during the period of which we are writing, under three heads:

I. Dayanand was not of those who accept knowledge easily from authority. He would take nothing which could not be verified or demonstrated. An incident which occurred during this period of his life may serve as an illustration. One day when wandering in the valley of the Ganges, he noticed a corpse afloat in the river. At the time he had with him some books on anatomy and physiology. The sight of a corpse at once suggested the idea of testing by actual observation the accuracy of the facts cited in the books. He was in a jungle, far from human habitation, and not likely to be disturbed. He salvaged the body, cut it open and examined it. He found that what was taught in the books was not true. So into the river went the books to keep company with the body.

II. Never for a moment did he falter or turn his gaze from the ideal to which he aspired. In India there are innumerable religious shrines and temples, the heads of which live in a luxurious state because of hereditary wealth. They own large endowments in land and revenues which are attached to their shrines and are the recipients of constant offerings from their disciples and devotees. Being a handsome young man of good physique, intelligent, well read and well versed in religious polemics, more than one mahant (as the heads of the institutions or fraternities are termed) wished to make him a chela, or spiritual heir, and offered to nominate him as their successor, but on all such occasions Dayanand refused, stating that his goal was different and that he was not seeking wealth or power.

III. During this period, he met numbers of Sadhus and Pandits, some good, some bad, some noble, some ignoble. Some attracted him, others repelled him. He met a few whom he regarded with the highest respect, and at whose feet he sat for long in a spirit of perfect reverence and true homage; but <u>he did not meet a single one who attained his ideal of a Guru (spiritual teacher)</u>. Born rebel as he was, he could not accept as his models the blind followers of authority or slaves of tradition; nor did he care for a life of mere renunciation or just meditation. Encircled by ignorance, prejudice, superstition, misery and tyranny, he did not desire a life of soulless bliss and peace. He was a passionate lover of liberty. In his wanderings through that beautiful and noble land of his—land of the loftiest thoughts, the purest ethics and the noblest traditions—he found everything chaotic. Even the repositories of the sacred lore of the Aryas, the representatives of the authors of the *Upanishads* and the Darshanas, the descendants of Manu and Yajnyavalka, were steeped in ignorance and superstition.

The religion which once permitted freedom of thought and conscience to every individual, in which divergence of opinion was not only tolerated but respected; which imposed on each the duty of reading and understanding the *Vedas* for himself; which taught that everyone was the master of his own soul, directly responsible for his thoughts and deeds to his God, and entitled to receive inspiration by direct communion with that never failing source of spiritual replenishment and uplift, the Maker of the Universe—this magnificent religion had been reduced to a soul-destroying system of blind faith in authority. Those who had acknowledged no mediators and gloried in their freedom from spiritual or religious bondage, had created thirty million gods, and had accepted as their saviours an equal number of Brahmins by caste. He found that in a land of eternal sunshine, physical, intellectual, and spiritual, everything was submerged in darkness. Light and knowledge had deserted the country. Even the best, the purest, and the loftiest among men were only moonlike. The sun had set, perhaps never to rise again. His heart bled to observe that a land once noted for freshness and vigour of intellect and force of mind was so stale, shallow, and feeble in its intellectual and mental products. It grieved his soul to see that his people had lost all originality of thought, and that the descendants of the boldest intellectual pioneers that the world ever produced had stagnated in intellectual bondage and spiritual bankruptcy. He observed that the élite of the Hindus had cultivated a morbid and contemptible craving for peace; that instead of battling with the passions and lower instincts and blazing a new trail by their success, they were fleeing out of sheer cowardice. He aimed at conquest, and he sought a guide, a friend and a teacher who would, by practice as well as precept, indicate the way. He wished to overcome death by vanquishing ignorance, superstition and fear and at the same time put others in the way of acting likewise. He had conferred with the Himalayas, with their eternal snows and cloud-draped peaks; he had conversed with the Ganges and the Narbadda; he had penetrated the innermost sanctuaries of the dense and almost inaccessible jungles and forests of the plains; he had slept in the top of the tallest Himalayan deodar; he had courted the embraces of the hardest of primeval rocks and the caresses of the swiftest of waters: all these friends of his youth and companions of his errant years had advised him not to seek the peace of repose or the lassitude of an inactive life. They had imbued him with the desire for increasing activity; they had infused him with the strength of their simple but unshaken faith in duty and in service; they had added to the purity, loftiness, and strength of his soul. The soil had been well-prepared. The seed had been sown. It required only to be watered by a vigilant gardener able to appreciate the potentialities of the soil and the inherent strength of the seed. In due course he found the man he wanted, the Guru whom he had sought all these years, the teacher, guide and philosopher who was to water the seed already sown.

5. *Virjananda Saraswati*

Swami Virjananda Saraswati, at whose feet Dayanand completed his education, was a Sannyasi of the order to which Dayanand belonged. He had been bred in the school of adversity. Dayanand had left his home because his parents loved him too well. He had departed at the comparatively advanced age of twenty-one, of his own choice, to the great sorrow and disillusionment of his parents. Poor Virjananda, on the other hand, was just a child of eleven when circumstances cast him adrift on the world, without anyone to cherish him. He was an orphan. Brothers are, as a rule, kinder in India, but in this case the nagging, shrewish tongue and the nasty temper of his brother's wife proved too much even for the child of eleven. What added to the sadness of his orphanhood was the fact that <u>he was totally blind</u>, having lost his sight at the age of five through a virulent attack of smallpox. He was too spirited, however, in spite of his blindness and his orphanhood, to endure the tyranny of his brother's wife, He left his brother's house with a heart brimful of sorrow. The death of his parents had deprived him of the ties and associations which render a home so attractive and sweet. On leaving his brother's house he repaired to Haridwar on the banks of the Ganges, one of the most beautiful spots in northern India, where the Ganges flows from the hills and extends in the plains. This is one of the most sacred sites of the Hindus and a favourite resort of Sadhus, Sannyasis, and Pandits.

The Ganges, indeed, is an object of adoration and love to every Hindu. Hundreds and thousands visit it, year in, year out; a great number traversing thousands of miles barefoot and following the river to its source high up in the Himalayas. Its banks are studded with temples and other places conducive to study and contemplation. A Hindu who dies on its banks is supposed to enter heaven straightaway. The pious Hindu's reasons for this exaggerated notion of the river's sanctity are partly based on his love of nature, whose grandeur and beauty fills him with ecstatic love of, and boundless admiration for, his Creator.

The water of the Ganges is perhaps unsurpassed in the world for purity, sweetness, and wealth in salts. It can be stored for years without losing its freshness. Gallons of it are kept in Hindu households to be used on occasions of religious celebration or even of worldly importance. People swear by it as they would swear by their gods. No Hindu dare utter a falsehood with the water of Ganges (Gangajali, as it is called) in the hollow of his hand. Scores of learned Sadhus, Yogis, and Pandits dwell on its banks. Some of the best and most profound Sanskrit scholars have been educated here, and in their turn imparted their knowledge, without remuneration, to all who came in quest of it. Charging a fee for imparting knowledge, especially if it relates to the spirit, is a grievous sin. The donor and the recipient alike must give and receive it in a religious spirit, as performing an obligation both sacred and pleasing.

EARLY LIFE

The teacher and the pupil, the Guru and the Chela, are maintained alike by private philanthropy. There are numerous eating places, where cooked food is available twice daily for the mere asking to those who are engaged in the sanctified work of teaching and learning, or in religious contemplation and meditation. This stream of charity never fails, not even when millions are perishing elsewhere in India from famine due to failure of the monsoon. Permanent endowments, landed and house properties of immense value, are attached to these institutions. If and when they fail, further donors come forward and guarantee their continuity.

Sadhus and Sannyasis, Yogis and teachers of sanctity, usually abide in isolated straw huts, but the general body of students and pilgrims dwell in commodious buildings built of brick and mortar erected for their convenience by donations from pious benefactors! This system has evolved and matured from time immemorial and has survived undisturbed for generations. But there are always some who come never to depart, unless it be merely a migration to another place of learning of equal or greater facilities. They are life-long students, as well as teachers in their turn.

Such is the place in which Virjananda sojourned when misfortune forced him to leave home; and well may the country that nurtured him be proud of the decision which he took at such a tender age. He departed never to return. In a few years he assimilated all that the best and the most learned in Haridwar could teach him. He was an apt pupil, gifted with a wonderful memory, which his blindness had magnified considerably. The reputation and esteem which he acquired by his scholarship and character were so high that a Sannyasi of high ability and profound austerity admitted him into the highest order of his class, his blindness notwithstanding. Later in life Virjananda migrated to Mathura another holy place, famous as the birthplace of Lord Krishna, one of the greatest and wisest of Hindu heroes, accorded the honour of Divinity. It was here that Dayanand encountered him.

It was a fusion of two kindred souls. Virjananda had outgrown his education. His hatred of image-worship, of superstition, of the pettiness of current Hindu life, and of the traditional system of teaching, kindled in him a consuming fire. He had the intolerance of the true iconoclast. By dint of incessant labour and constant concentration of mind, he had mastered both the Sanskrit language and its literature, and all the intellectual treasure contained therein. He had an intuitive faculty of separating the chaff from the grain. He dissected and analysed everything within range of his observation and study, and could, therefore, put his finger on the weak points of the prevalent Hindu thought and religion. Moreover, he was morally fearless. He expressed what he thought—he uttered what he believed. His denunciation of the popular gods, the popular modes of worship, and the popular method of teaching, was trenchant and merciless.

Yet, such was the prestige of his character, his reputation and his learning, that, despite his blindness, students flocked to him, though few could remain long enough to receive the full benefit thereof, since he was rather short-tempered. Nor did he ever suffer privation. Hindus of wealth and position might dislike his denunciation of what they believed and practised, but they attended to his wants and kept him amply provided with the necessities of life.

Three ruling chiefs of Rajputana, on various occasions became his pupils. One continued his studies for fully three years; but when, one day, he played truant, the Swami abandoned him without notice and returned to Mathura. Another, the ruler of a first class principality, requested him to compile an easy grammar—which the Swami declined to do. He considered this as a slur on the ancient Rishis who had left monumental works on the subject. This was the man with whom Dayanand completed his education.

Dayanand had already been studying for more than thirty years and he now required just a finishing touch from the hands of a master spirit. For two years and a half he waited on Virjananda, ministered to him with filial love, and learned all that Virjananda had to teach. Virjananda was a man of hot temper and sometimes treated his pupils harshly. Once he actually inflicted corporal punishment on Swami Dayanand; yet the latter did not forsake him, and duly finished his course. Then Virjananda informed him that he had nothing more to teach him.

Their farewell was memorable for both the pupil and the teacher. It was then that Swami Virjananda demanded the customary fee which in days of old every Brahmchari must pay his Guru on his departure. Virjananda was aware that Dayanand possessed nothing of worldly value that he could offer him, nor did he himself care for any such gifts. What he asked of his pupil was a pledge to devote his life to disseminating truth, to waging unremitting warfare against the falsehood of the prevailing Hindu faith (faith mainly based on the *Puranas*), and to establish the right method of education, as was in vogue in pre-Buddhist times.

Dayanand gave this pledge willingly, and with a solemn joy: and never was a pledge adhered to more loyally and faithfully!

Chapter II

FIGHTING FOR TRUTH

May we be fearless from friends and from the unfriendly, fearless from whom we know and whom we know not, fearless in the night and fearless in the daytime! May all the directions be friendly to us!

Ath. xix, 15,6

1. First Years of Public Life

The first few years of Dayanand's public life were more or less devoted to preparation for the stupendous task which he had set himself. During these years he reviewed and revised what he had read, and disciplined himself in the methods of public life. He visited some of the most important towns of the North-Western Province, but sojourned most of the time on the banks of the Ganges and in its vicinity. Everywhere his outspoken views, his bold utterances, his then novel exposition of the Hindu religion and his profound scholarship attracted hundreds of his countrymen to his discourses. Grammar and a knowledge of the *Vedas* were his strong points. Many came to cross swords with him, but stayed to admire and follow. He held numerous discussions with the high and the low, students and scholars, theologians and sceptics, Sadhus and Pandits. He spoke in Sanskrit, since Sanskrit was the language of the learned. Wherever he went he stirred up commotion in the Hindu world. The Hindu theologians, whose deepest and most vital interests were so adversely touched by his teachings, were up in arms. They not only abused and threatened him, more than once they even conspired to assassinate him. In the course of five years, no fewer than four attempts were made on his life. Yet there was a charm about his life, his habits and manners, which gained him friends and protectors. He never stooped to prosecute his persecutors. On one occasion, when a man had tried to poison him and was arrested by the police, he would not prosecute and thus secured the miscreant's release.

In orthodox circles he achieved fame in a brief space of time. High and low, rich and poor, all classes flocked to him and drank in his discourses gazing at him with mingled awe, respect, and admiration. In certain places the public discussions were presided over by the highest ranking British officers in the district, this being considered the most effective way of maintaining order.

In the first five years of his mission he had numerous admirers but few adherents and followers. Yet among the latter were some of the most wealthy traders and landholders of the districts visited by him.

It was true that he was very learned, and few could venture to oppose him in controversy. The traits that drew his hearers were boldness, courage, and his attacks on popular beliefs and practices. Never before had they encountered such a man. In a section of the country hundreds of miles away from his native province, whose language he could not use freely and effectively, to whose people he was a stranger, with no friends to depend on or to protect him, he forged ahead and assailed some of the most cherished beliefs with a scathing vehemence that itself—apart from the force of his arguments—terrified his opponents. People looked on this fiery teacher askance and with awe. The worst, or perhaps the best, of it was that he discoursed with so much authority and directness, with so much erudition and confidence, with so much cogency of reasoning and force of logic, that the very first onslaught abased the opponent. The expounders of popular religion and the repositories of the Hindu faith stood aghast. The assault was so sudden and so furious that stronghold after stronghold capitulated without the assailant being any the worse for his exploits.

Orthodox leaders appealed to Kashi, the Rome of Hinduism. They were confident that there the invader would meet adversaries worthy of his steel and be laid low. Dayanand, too, well knew that unless he reduced Kashi to submission and won a decisive battle there, all the victories so far achieved would be futile. So, before the sixth year of his public career was at an end, he reached Kashi, and under the shade of a tree, began to preach and express his views on religion, philosophy, and grammar. Soon afterwards a public discussion was announced. It was attended by thousands. Ranged on one side were 300 leading Hindu scholars and theologians of Banaras; on the other, Dayanand, with but a few laymen to make a show of support. The meeting was presided over by no less a personage than the Maharaja of Banaras. At the close of the discussion both sides claimed victory; but what really did happen may be gleaned from the following account which was published in a Christian Missionary Journal, evidently written by a European missionary:

A Hindoo Reformer[1]

"The fame of the reformer who lately put the whole city of Benares in commotion seems to have gone abroad. Some account, therefore, of him and his views, and the public disputation held with him, from one who was present at the disputation, and met and conversed with the reformer several times before and after that event, will perhaps be not uninteresting to the readers of the *Intelligencer*.

"The name of the reformer is Dayanand Saraswati Swami. He is a native of some village in Guzerat; the name of the place he will not disclose to any one, from a fear that his father, who declares him to be mad, will come and take him forcibly away, as he already once did on a previous occasion. He is a fine-looking man, large but well proportioned; his face, especially, expressive of much intelligence. His outward appearance is that of a Sanyasi or religious beggar: almost entirely naked and besmeared with the sacred bhasma (ashes of cow-dung). He speaks Sanskrit fluently, though not in very polished style, and in a few instances not quite correctly.[2] He is a good reasoner and pretty fair in controversy, at least so far that he generally allows his opponent to state his case without interruption; but extremely authoritative in all his positions. His case and mind is made up, and, believing his acquaintance with the *Vedas* to be superior to that of any of his adversaries, he will listen with a kind of contemptuous

---

[1] The spelling of this writer is preserved, but some of his accents are omitted—Author.

[2] "For example, he denied that the verbal root *man*, to believe, may form the I. pers. plur. pres. *manmahe*, besides the forms *manumahe* and *manyamahe*."

FIGHTING FOR TRUTH

courtesy to anything that they may have to bring forward, and often, especially in the case of inferior pandits, only answer by an authoritative assertion of the contrary. He is well versed in the *Vedas*, excepting the fourth or *Atharva Veda*, which he had read only in fragments, and which he saw for the first time in full when I lent him my own complete MS. copy. It should be remembered, however, that the Brahmans understand by the *Vedas* a great deal more than we do, namely, not only the hymns generally known as the four *Vedas*, but also the theological treatises in prose appended to the former, —called the *Brahmanas* and *Upanishads*, etc. —He devoted himself entirely to the study of the *Vedas* from his eleventh year, and thus he is more practically conversant with them than most, if not all, of the great pandits of Benares, who generally know them only at second-hand, or even less. At any rate, and this is the most remarkable feature distinguishing him from other pandits, he is an independent student of the *Vedas*, and free from the trammels of traditional interpretation. The standard commentary of the famous Sayanacharya is held of little account by him. It can be no wonder, therefore, that his Vedic studies, conducted in that spirit, led him to the conviction that almost the whole of the (comparatively) modern Hinduism is in entire and irreconcilable contradiction with the *Vedas* and the Hinduism of Vedic times, about 2,000 years ago. Being of an active character, he determined not to keep his conviction to himself, but to impart it to his countrymen, and try to effect an entire reform of Hindu society. Briefly, his object is to replace Hindu society exactly into the same state as it was about 2,000 years ago, when, as yet, none of the six philosophical systems existed, nor any of the eighteen *Puranas*, the sources of modern Hinduism with its castes and idolatry; but when the *Vedas* and Vedic usages reigned supreme, and when one God only was adored, and the *Vedas* only were studied, and the sacrifice of the *homa* only, with its elaborate ceremonial, was performed by the priest for himself and the soldier and the peasant. At least, this is the fond dream of the reformer. But history never travels back in this manner; no nation, especially not one like the Hindus, can or ever will retrace its steps to live again in a state of things of 2,000 years ago. Hence this attempt at reform must fail. But he may prepare the way for another reform; he may possibly convince the Hindus that their modern Hinduism is altogether in opposition to the *Vedas*, a fact of which most of them are profoundly ignorant, and the few who know or suspect it find it convenient to shut their eyes to it. If once they become thoroughly convinced of this radical error, they will no doubt abandon Hinduism at once, for they cling to it only because they believe that it has the sanction of immemorial antiquity and of the earliest forefathers of their race, who are believed to have communed with the Eternal One Himself. They cannot go back to the Vedic state; that is dead and gone, and will never revive. Some thing more or less new must follow. We will hope it may be Christianity, but, whatever it may be, anything seems better than the present intellectually and morally monstrous idolatry and caste. I confess, however, that I am not sanguine that the efforts of the reformer will effect even this preparatory step to reform. He travels up and down the banks of the Ganges, and stops here and there in the large towns to disseminate his views, but, as far as I could ascertain, he seems to have met nowhere with much success except in Furruckabad, near Cawnpore, where, indeed, if report is to be trusted, his success has been complete. The Brahmins of that place in a body are said to have declared for him, and to have cleared the temples of all idols. It is certain that a very rich Mahajan of that place has become a convert to his views, and has established a school where the reformed Hinduism is taught; and there is not much doubt that his influence will have effected the conversion of all those needy Brahmins who depend on him for their sustenance. But beyond this probably the report is exaggeration. His appearance in Benares was certainly a failure. Nevertheless the commotion caused by it at first was great, and though it now, to outward appearance,[3] seems to have quite subsided, some of the ferment is still active under the surface; and, if it were judiciously worked by the Mission, and indirect support given to the cause of the reformer, it seems not improbable that the result, of which his attempt failed at first, might yet be accomplished.

"The date of his arrival in Benares I do not know. It must

[3] This evidently was written five or six months after the event.—Author.

have been in the beginning of October: I was then absent.
I first saw him after my return in November. I went to see
him in company with the Prince of Bhaurtpore and one or
two pandits. The excitement was then at its height. The
whole of the Brahmanic and educated population of Benares
seemed to flock to him. In the verandah of a small house
at the end of a large garden near the monkey tank, he was
holding daily levees from early in the morning till late in the
evening, for a continuous stream of people who came, eager
to see and listen to, or dispute with the novel reformer. It
does not appear, however, that the heads of the orthodox
party or the pandits of the greatest repute ever visited him,
unless they did it secretly. The intensity of the excitement
at last induced the Raja of Benares, in concert with his court
pandits and other men of influence, to take some notice of
the reformer, and to arrange a public disputation between
him and the orthodox party, in order to allay the excitement
by a defeat of the reformer. They were quite sanguine as
to his defeat; but I fear there was a determination from the
beginning that they would win the day by any means, whether
foul or fair. The disputation took place on the 17th of November, in the place where the reformer had taken up his abode;
it lasted from about 3 to 7 p.m. The Raja himself was present
and presided. Even the great Vedantist, the head it seems
of the orthodox party, Vishudananda Gour Swami, who is
said never to have left his dwelling before—of course an
exaggeration—condescended to emerge for once from his
place of meditation on the banks of the Ganges to assist with
his learning the failing wits of the defenders of orthodoxy,
and to give additional authority to the anticipated defeat
of the reformer—a clear proof that the reformer was thought
a formidable enemy. All the most reputed pandits were
there, and a large concourse of other people, learned and
unlearned, but all of the respectable class. A detachment of
policemen also were present, who guarded the entrance to
the garden against a dense crowd outside, which in vain
strove to get admittance; but they were also intended, I
suspect, to protect the lonely reformer in case any act of
violence should be attempted against him by his enraged
adversaries. But nothing of the kind occurred; all went off

quietly, except that, at the last, when the assembly broke up, the orthodox party loudly jeered the poor reformer in token of their ill-gotten victory. But, whether gotten ill or well, their victory had certainly the result they desired. The change was very remarkable in the state of things before and after the disputation. As quickly as the excitement had arisen before, so quickly it subsided afterwards. Whereas, before, multitudes flocked to see him, those who came afterwards might be easily counted. The reformer himself was practically excommunicated, and any one who would visit him after his refutation was threatened with the same measure. Immediately after the disputation, a written defence was sent by the reformer to his opponents, but I believe no notice was taken of it. Then an account of his doctrines was prepared by the reformer and printed about a month afterwards. At the same time also a public challenge to his opponents to answer his pamphlets was issued by him. But again no notice was taken of it by the orthodox party. The reformer still remained till towards the end of January. Then he left Benares to visit the Mela at Allahabad, and to try to influence the multitude assembled there. The last time I saw him, he had not made up his mind whether he should return to Benares after the Mela or visit some other place. Since his departure the orthodox party have also brought out a pamphlet on the disputation and the questions between themselves and the reformer in general. The doctrines of the reformer may be referred chiefly to the following three heads: the extent of the Hindu Canon, the truth of idolatry, and the mythology and the question of caste; connected with these, however, there are many minor points.

"The first of the three forms the foundation of his whole reform. The only writings which he acknowledges as Shastras are the following twenty-one: 1-4, the four *Vedas;* 5-8, the four *Upavedas;* 9-14, the six *Vedangas;* 15, twelve *Upanishads;* 16, the *Sarirakasutras;* 17, the *Katyayanasutras,* etc.; 18, the *Yogabhashya;* 19, the *Vakovakya;* 20, the *Manusmriti;* and 21, the *Mahabharata.*[4] Of these the *Vedas* are acknowledged on

[4] "The four *Vedas* are the *Rigveda,* the *Yajurveda,* the *Samaveda,* and the *Atharvan Veda,* including their respective Brahmanas. The four Upavedas are the *Ayurveda* on medical science, including two books; the Dhanurveda, military science; the Gandharvaveda on musical science; and the Arthaveda on mechanical science;

account of their being the utterance of God Himself, and the others as being directly founded on the *Vedas* or expressly mentioned in them. Whatever else is considered as shastras by the orthodox Hindus, notably the six Darsanas or philosophical systems and the eighteen *Puranas*, he repudiates as false, because their contents are contradicted by the *Vedas* or because they are not mentioned in them. Starting from this premise, he rejects everything in modern Hinduism which is either directly contradicted in the *Vedas* or not expressly sanctioned in them.

"It will be seen from this statement that there is no difference between him and the orthodox pandits as to the principle of the Canon; for both agree in this, that the *Vedas* only are authoritative, and that whatsoever is opposed to them is false; the difference really arises in the previous question: what are the *Vedas*? Dayanand acknowledges only the present *Vedas*, and what can be proved from them; the other pandits, on the contrary, believe and assert the previous existence of many other Vedic writings, which they say have perished, and which, they assume, contained the complete proof for every shastra and everything in Hinduism which cannot be supported by the now existing *Vedas*. Such a position, of course, is very difficult to be proved. But some European scholars think that the pandits are to be believed; among them is Max Muller. His argument is briefly this:[5] the assertion of lost *Vedas* was first made during the Buddhistic controversy to vindicate a Vedic origin to some parts of Brahmanism; now, as the assertion is incapable of proof, the Buddhists might easily have made use of it to support their own tenets: it is therefore a dangerous weapon, and, it is thought, would not have been used by the advocates of Brahmanism, unless

the six Vedangas are the Siksha on pronunciation; the Kalpa on ceremonial; the Vyakarana or Grammar of Panini; the Commentary of Patanjali (*Mahabhashya*); the *Nirukta* or etymological vocabulary; the Chhanda on prosody; and the Juotisha on astronomy and astrology, including only one book; the *Bhrigu Sanhita*. The twelve *Upanishads* are: *Isa, Kena, Katha, Prasna, Mundaka, Mandukya, Taitareya, Aitereya, Chhandogya, Brihadaranyaka, Svetasvatara*, and *Kaivalya*. There exist many more *Upanishads* which are acknowledged by orthodox pandits; but they are all rejected by Dayanand. The *Mahabharata* is not acknowledged by him in its entirety; but many portions are declared by him spurious, among others, if I mistake not, the famous *Bhagavadgita*. This list of shastras here given may be relied upon as correct, as the reformer wrote them down for me on a paper with his own hand."

[5] See his *Ancient Sanskrit Literature*, pp. 106-7.

it had been true. I doubt, however, whether this is a sound argument. As there was no proof for some things in the existing *Vedas*, there was only this alternative left to the advocates of Brahmanism, either to admit that there was no Vedic proof, which would have been suicidal, or to assert the previous existence of lost Vedic writings, whether or not there was any foundation for it, although this was dangerous. There can be no hesitation as to which of these alternatives they would choose. Dayanand denies altogether the possibility of a loss of any *Vedas*.[6] But, be that as it may, it must be evident to any unprejudiced inquirer, that even if other Vedic writings existed formerly, their general tenor must have been similar to those still existent, and that they would nowise have given support to modern Hinduism.

2. Idolatry and Mythology

"The former the reformer rejects entirely, not only as a harmless error, but as positively sinful. He further rejects polytheism. There is only one God with all those attributes generally ascribed to Him by monotheists. He is the creator first of the *Vedas*, then of the world, hence the *Vedas* are eternal as compared with the world; but non-eternal as compared with God. The names of God are manifold: He is named in the *Vedas* Vishnu, Atma, Agni, etc., according as one aspect of the Divine nature is prominently remembered. Though God is distinct from the world—for Dayanand rejects the Vedantic and ordinary Hindu pantheism—yet He is also immanent in the world as the principle of its life and existence. As such, God is to be viewed as Agni (life) and hence to be worshipped by means of Agni (fire). But he must not be misunderstood: when he says that God in the world is Agni, he does not mean by Agni fire, but something which may best be expressed by soul or vital principle, or principle of existence; again, he does not mean to say that the ordinary Agni (fire) is a representation of God, but, as being the clearest manifestation of God-Agni, it is the fittest ceremonial means of worshipping God; fire is not to be wor-

---

[6] I am afraid this is not quite correct. Dayanand denied that any Vedas had been lost, but he maintained that much Vedic literature had been lost—Author.

shipped, but to be used as a means in the worship of God. The worship or service of God consists chiefly in the following three acts: first and foremost the study of the *Vedas* with a view to the knowledge of God; then the observance of the moral laws as the will of God; thirdly, the worship of God by fire or the homa-sacrifice. The observance of these is the means of salvation. Incarnations (avataras) for the salvation of mankind never took place, nor can they ever take place; it is incompatible with the nature of God to become incarnate. Hence Dayanand rejects the Hindu avataras as much as the Christian incarnation; that is to say, he rejects them as avataras of God. If such avataras really took place, they were avataras of devatas, and not of God.[7] Vishnu, Siva, Brahma, if there be such beings, are only devatas, i.e. superior created beings or angels, not Divine beings. Thus he rejects also most, if not all, of the mythology of the *Puranas*, especially the fables about Krishna.

3. Caste

"This the reformer considers only as a political institution made by the rulers for the common good of society, and not a natural or religious distinction. It is not a natural distinction; for the four castes were not created by God as distinct species of men; but all men are of equal nature, of the same species; and brothers. It is not a religious institution, for the salvation of men and their fate in the other world does not depend upon its observance. The castes are simply different professions or guilds (adhikaras), established by the state to guard against confusion and mutual interference, and for the better accomplishment of the different works. Some men, specially fitted for the work, were set aside by the state for the prosecution of worship, science, and literature (the Brahmans); others to guard the outward peace and internal order of the state (the Kshattriyas); others to carry on trade and till the ground (the Vaisyas); again, others to do all the meaner kinds of labour (the Sudras). Each class was made up into a guild and furnished with its rights and privileges

---

[7] This is wrong. Dayanand never asserted that any *incarnation* of devatas ever took place. The writer probably refers to an assertion of Dayanand that all beings are subject to the law of transmigration of souls.—Editor.

and made hereditary. But, as the whole classification is a creation of the state, any Sudra, who is deserving of the promotion, can be made by the state a Vaisya or Kshattriya or Brahmana, if he qualifies himself for the work of the respective class. Likewise any Brahmana, who deserves the degradation, can be made by the state a Sudra. In fact, any Brahmana who is disqualified for his work, becomes at once a Sudra *de jure*, and a Sudra, who qualifies himself for it, becomes at once a Brahmana *de jure;* though neither can become so *de facto* also either by his own will or the will of others, as long as the state does not make him so. This last limitation obviously makes his theory impracticable. The state will not concern itself nowadays with the regulation of such guilds, to degrade a disreputable Brahmana into a Sudra or reward a clever Sudra with Brahmanhood. He ought to leave that to the spontaneous action of society regulating itself.[8]

"The public disputation took place on 17th November in the house where the reformer was staying. As soon as the Raja of Benares arrived, the discussion commenced by Dayanand asking Pandit Taracharana, the Raja's court pandit, who had been appointed to defend the cause of orthodoxy, whether he admitted the *Vedas* as the authority. When this had been agreed to, he requested Taracharana to produce passages from the *Vedas* sanctioning idolatry, Pashanadipujana (lit. worship of stones, etc.). Instead of doing this, Taracharana for some time tried to substitute proofs from the *Puranas*. At last Dayanand happening to say that he only admitted the *Manusmriti*, *Sarirakasutras*, etc. as authoritative because founded on the *Vedas*. Vishudananda, the great Vedantist interfered, and, quoting a Vedanta Sutra from the *Sarirakasutras*, asked Dayanand to show that it was founded on the *Vedas*. After some hesitation Dayanand replied that he could do this only after referring to the *Vedas*, as he did not remember the whole of them. Vishudananda then tauntingly said, if he could not do that he should not set himself up as a teacher in Benares. Dayanand replied, that none of the pandits had the whole of the *Vedas* in his memory. Thereupon Vishudananda and several others asserted that they knew the whole of the *Vedas*

---

[8] That he does. See his *Satyarath Prakash.*—Author.

by heart. Then followed several questions, quite unconnected with the subject of the discussions, but put by Dayanand to show that his opponents had asserted more than they could justify. They could answer none of his questions. At last some pandits took up the thread of the discussion again by asking Dayanand whether the terms *pratima* (likeness) and *purti* (fulness) occurring in the *Vedas* did not sanction idolatry. He answered that, rightly interpreted, they did not do so. As none of his opponents objected to his interpretation, it is plain that they either perceived the correctness of it, or were too little acquainted with the *Vedas* to venture to contradict it. Then Madhavacharya, a pandit of no repute, produced two leaves of a Vedic Ms., and, reading a passage[9] containing the word '*Puranas*', asked to what this term referred. Dayanand replied: it was there simply an adjective, meaning 'ancient,' and not the proper name. Vishudananda challenging this interpretation, some discussion followed as to its grammatical correctness; but at last all seemed to acquiesce in it. Then Madhavacharya produced again two other leaves of a Vedic MS., and read a passage[10] with this purport that upon the completion of a yajna (sacrifice) on the tenth day the reading of the *Puranas* should be heard, and asked how the term '*Purana*' could be here an adjective. Dayanand took the MS. in his hands and began to meditate what answer he should give. His opponents waited about two minutes, and, as still no answer was forthcoming, they rose, jeering and calling out that he was unable to answer and was defeated, and went away. They might certainly have allowed him a little more time, but it is evident that he was puzzled as to an answer; and the answer which he afterwards published in his pamphlet that to the word '*Purana*' was to be supplied vidya (science), meaning purani Vidya, that is, the Veda is not very satisfactory. There can hardly be much double that the eighteen *Puranas* are really referred to in that passage; but, as it is out of a Brahmana of the Samaveda, and that contains many modern additions, its value would after all be not much in the eyes of non-Hindus, and, I suspect, even of Dayanand; for he once admitted to me that the Brahmanas did contain modern inter-

---

[9] "Brahmananitihasak puranani".
[10] "Vajnasanaptoi Satyan dasame divase purananam patham srinuyat."

polated portions, and that any passage sanctioning idolatry was to be considered, as such, as a spurious portion.

"The reformer is not unacquainted with Christianity. He has read the Gospels, though I do not think very carefully. I had some conversation with him about it. But at present his mind is too much occupied with his own plans of reformation to give any serious thought to the investigation of the claim of another religion."[11]

For a long time a heated controversy raged in the Press, both Indian and Anglo-Indian, about the disputation. The matter was so important and of such great interest from a public point of view that even the *Pioneer*, the leading semi-official Anglo-Indian paper of Allahabad, threw open its columns to correspondence on the subject. The event was the central topic throughout India, and aroused enormous interest.[12]

From this date may be reckoned the effective beginning of Dayanand's mission for a reformed Hindu Church, free from cant, superstition, and popular error.

From Banaras the Swami trekked on eastward and in due course reached Calcutta, the then capital of India and headquarters of the British Government in India. The Brahmo Samaj extended cordial welcome, and some of its leaders conferred with him with the intention of winning his co-operation in their movement; but the Swami could not give up his faith in the infallibility of the *Vedas* and the doctrine of transmigration of souls, the two cardinal principles which differentiate the Arya Samaj from the Brahmo Samaj. His visit to Calcutta, however, brought him into personal contact and intimate touch with the leaders of the English-educated community. Babu Keshub Chunder Sen, the respected leader of the Brahmo Samaj, advocated the supreme importance of carrying on his propaganda in the popular language, a practical suggestion that was readily and gratefully accepted by the Swami. It was put into force at once. This single step entailed

[11] From the *Christian Intelligencer*, Calcutta, March, 1870, p. 79.
[12] A number of tracts were published by partisans and non-partisans giving their versions of what had actually happened and of the merits of the matters in dispute. Partisans and non-partisans were all agreed that Dayanand was a great scholar and that his knowledge of Sanskrit was unique. Swami Dayanand himself published a tract on the subject which covers 16 pages in his collected works—Editor.

a colossal difference in favour of his mission, since it brought him into direct touch with the bulk of his countrymen, both educated and uneducated, who did not know Sanskrit and could not understand him without the aid of translators and interpreters. In Calcutta he made the acquaintance of Maharishi Debendranath Tagore, the father of Rabindranath Tagore, whose Brahmoism had more in common with the faith of Dayanand than the religious beliefs of the other leaders of the Brahmo Samaj.

After spending another two years in the dissemination of his doctrines, Dayanand proceeded to Bombay, where eventually his mission was to take an organized form.

Chapter III

FOUNDING OF THE ARYA SAMAJ AND DEATH

Walk together, speak together, let your minds be all alike.
May the purpose be common, common the assembly, common the mind: so be their thoughts united. I lay before you a common object, and worship with your common oblation.
May your decisions be unanimous, your minds being of one accord. May the thoughts of all be united so that there may be a happy agreement among all.

R. x, 191, 3, 4.

1. Constitution of the Arya Samaj

The first Arya Samaj was established at Bombay on 10th April, 1875, with the following principles and rules representing both its creed and its constitution:

"2. The (Arya) Samaj shall regard the *Vedas* alone as independently and absolutely authoritative. For purposes of testimony and for the understanding of the *Vedas*, as also for historical purposes, all the four Brahmanas—*Shathpatha*, etc., the six Vedangas, the four Upavedas, the six Darshanas, and 1,127 Shakhas or expositions of the *Vedas*, shall by virtue of their being ancient and recognized works of Rishis, be also regarded as secondarily authoritative, in so far only as their teaching is in accord with that of the *Vedas*.

"3. There shall be a principal Arya Samaj in each province, and the other Arya Samajes shall be its branches, all connected with one another.

"5. The principal Samaj shall possess various Vedic works in Sanskrit and Aryabhasha (Hindi) for the dissemination of true knowledge, and it shall issue a weekly paper under the name of *Arya Prakash*, also an exponent of the Vedic teaching. The paper and the books shall be patronized by all Samajes.

"8. The members of the Samaj shall be men of truth, of

FOUNDING OF THE ARYA SAMAJ AND DEATH

upright policy and principles, of pure character, and of philanthropic impulses.

"9. The members shall give their spare time to the earnest service of the Samaj. Those that have no family to care for should, in particular, be always striving to promote the well-being of the society.

"10. Every eighth day the President, the Secretary, and other members of the Samaj shall come together in the Samaj Mandir.....

"11. Having assembled together, they should be calm and composed in their minds, and in a spirit of love, and free from bias, they may ask questions and obtain answers from each other. This done, they shall sing the hymns of the *Sama Veda* in praise of God, and songs bearing on the true Dharma, to the accompaniment of musical instruments. The mantras shall be commented upon and explained, and the lectures delivered on similar (Vedic) themes. After this there shall be music again, to be followed by an exposition of mantras and speeches.

"12. Every member shall cheerfully contribute a hundredth part of the money he has earned honestly and with the sweat of his brow, towards the funds of the Samaj, the Arya Vidyala and the *Arya Prakash* paper. If he contributes more, the greater shall be his reward. The money thus contributed shall be used for the purposes specified and in no other way.

"13. The more an individual bestirs himself for the fund of the Samaj for the purposes specified, and for the diffusion of a knowledge of the teachings of the Arya Samaj, the more honour shall he receive for his energy and zeal.

"14. The Samaj shall do *stuti, prarthana,* and *upasana* (i.e. shall glorify, pray to and hold communion with the one only God), in the manner commended by the *Vedas*. They believe God to be formless, almighty, just, infinite, immutable, eternal, incomparable, merciful, the father of all, the mother of the entire universe, all-supporting, all truth, all intelligence, all happiness, and the supreme and the only lord of the universe; as also all-pervading and the knower of all hearts, indestructible, deathless, everlasting, pure and conscious; as endless, the bestower of happiness, the giver of righteousness, wealth, comfort and salvation;—to speak of Him as endowed with such and similar other qualities and attributes, is to do his *stuti* (i.e. to glorify and praise Him). Asking His help in all righteous undertakings, is identical with *prarthana* (i.e. praying to Him), and to become absorbed in the contemplation of His Essence, which is absolute Happiness, is termed *upasana* (i.e. holding communion with Him). He alone shall be adored, and naught besides.

"15. The Samaj shall perform Vedic sanskars (ritual), such as Anteshthi (the death ceremony), etc.

"16. The *Vedas* and the ancient Arsha Granthas shall be studied and taught in the Arya Vidyala, and true and right training, calculated to improve males and females, shall be imparted, on Vedic lines.

"17. In the interests of the country, both kinds of reform shall receive thorough attention in the Samaj, spiritual as well as worldly. There shall be uplifting in both directions for the promotion of purity; indeed, the welfare of entire mankind shall be the objective of the Samaj.

"18. The Samaj shall believe only in what is right and just, i.e. in the true Vedic Dharma, free from prejudice, and tested by all tests laid down by the ancient authorities by which truth is distinguished from falsity.

"19. The Samaj shall send learned men, of approved character, everywhere to preach truth.

"20. In the interests of the education of both males and females, separate schools shall be established, if possible, in all places. In the seminaries for females the work of teaching and that of serving the students shall be carried on by females only, and in the schools for males the responsibility of doing the same shall lie with males. Never shall this rule be infringed. . . . .

"22. The President and the other members of the Samaj shall, for the maintenance of mutual goodwill, keep their minds wholly divested of all feelings of pride, hate, anger, etc., and, with such vices shut out, they shall, being free of enmity and pure of heart, love one another, even as each loves his own self.

"23. When deliberating on a subject, that which has been, as the fruit of this deliberation, ascertained to be in thorough accord with the principles of justice and universal benevolence, and absolutely true, the same shall be made known to the members and believed in by them. Acting thus is termed rising above bias or prejudice.

"24. He alone who conforms his conduct to the principles specified, and is righteous and endowed with true virtues, shall be admitted to the higher circle of the Samaj, while he who is otherwise shall be but an ordinary member of the Samaj. But the individual who openly appears to be utterly depraved and debased shall be expelled. Such a step, however, shall not be dictated by prejudice; on the contrary, everything shall be done after due deliberation by the exalted members of the Samaj, and not otherwise.

"27. Whenever an occasion for giving charity arises, as, for instance, in connection with a marriage, the birth of a son, or a death in the family, and so on, the Arya Samajist concerned shall be expected to make a donation to the Samaj.

"28. Whenever an addition is made to the principles or rules above laid down, or whenever any of these is altered or amended, such an addition, alteration or amendment shall invariably be the result of thorough deliberation on the subject by the exalted Sabhasads of the Samaj, after due and proper notice to all concerned."

Note: We have omitted a few unimportant Articles.

Here again, as also at Poona, Dayanand came into close contact with the educated among the Hindu community, i.e. with those who had received their education in the schools and colleges and at the universities established and patterned on the European model. But the next step in the evolution of the Arya Samaj did not take place till two years later, in Lahore, the capital of the Punjab, in Northern India. Here the Samaj took final shape, which it preserves to this day: the principles were finally revised, and the constitution reframed and finally settled. All the Arya Samajes in India or elsewhere accept these principles and are governed by this constitution. There has been no modification in the former, but the latter may have been adapted in minor particulars to local conditions. We will discuss both in greater detail later.

2. Death

The rest of his life—from 1877 to October, 1883—was spent by the Swami in preaching and teaching and in writing books, as well as establishing and organizing Arya Samajes throughout India. The only province which the Swami could not traverse was Madras.

In the Punjab, the United Provinces of Agra and Oude, and in Rajputana and Gujerat, he met with the greatest success. In these provinces a network of Arya Samajes had been established before his death, but the progress since made may be inferred from the fact that the membership of 243,000 in 1911 was two and a half times what it was in 1901, and six times that of 1891. Some of the noblest and highest in the land accepted his faith, and became his disciples and pupils: for example, the Maharana of Udaipur, the most ancient and respected of the Hindu chiefs.

Maharana Sajjan Singh studied Hindu law and Hindu jurisprudence with Dayanand, and association with the latter had temporarily a very chastening influence on the otherwise, dissolute prince. It was at Jodhpur, the capital of the only other Hindu state, that he succumbed to a fatal illness. He had gone there in response to an invitation from the Maharaja, who was anxious to become his disciple and study with him. To their mutual misfortune, but also to the greater misfortune of the country, the Swami took very strong exception to the Maharaja's keeping a concubine, a Musulman woman who naturally regarded him with violent aversion. It is the current rumour that she contrived to have a subtle poison mixed with his food, resulting in mortal illness. The Maharaja, of course, was guiltless of complicity in this alleged crime, and was genuinely grief-stricken when apprised of the Swami's malady. He did everything in his power to obtain for the patient the best available medical aid and every comfort that money could procure. But there was no improvement and the Swami succumbed and passed away at Ajmere, in British territory, whither he had been removed by his friends a few days before.

This sad event occurred on 30th October, 1883. Those who were at his deathbed are unanimous in testifying to his perfect calmness at the time of death.

It was at Jodhpur that Maharaja Pratap Singh, the brother of the ruling chief (to become General Sir Pratap Singh G.C.S.I., G.C.V.O., K.C.B. etc. later on), became his disciple —an event which he always cited with pride.

The amount of obloquy and persecution to which Swami Dayanand was exposed in his lifetime may be gathered from that fact that numerous attempts were made on his life by the orthodox Hindus; assassins were hired to kill him; missiles were thrown at him during his lectures and disputations; he was dubbed a hired emissary of the Christians, an apostate, an atheist, and so forth. The spirit in which he faced this fierce opposition may be judged from the following anecdote which we cull from Madame Blavatsky's account of him in her *Caves and Jungles of Hindusthan*.

"One is inclined to think that this wonderful Hindu bears a charmed life, so careless is he of raising the worst human passions, which are so dangerous in India. At Benares, a worshipper of the Shiva, feeling sure that his cobra, trained purposely for the mysteries of a Shivaite pagoda, would at once make an end of the offender's life, triumphantly exclaimed: 'Let the god Vasuki (the snake god) himself show which of us is right'."

"Dayanand jerked off the cobra twisting round his leg, and with a single vigorous movement crushed the reptile's head. 'Let him do so', he quietly assented, 'your god has been too slow. It is I who have decided the dispute. Now go', added he, addressing the crowd, 'and tell every one how easily perish all false gods'. Truly, a marble statue could not be less moved by the raging wrath of the crowd. We saw him once at work. He sent away all his faithful followers, and forbade them either to watch over him or to defend him, and stood alone before the infuriated crowd, facing calmly the monster, ready to spring upon him and tear him to pieces."

In the same work, Madame Blavatsky pays the following compliment to his learning and scholarship:

"It is perfectly certain that India never saw a more learned Sanskrit scholar, a deeper metaphysician, a more wonderful orator, and a more fearless denunciator of any evil, than Dayanand, since the time of Shankaracharya."[1]

One more testimony to his erudition and we have concluded our account of the Swami's life. This is a grudging admission of his great powers by his opponents among the orthodox Hindus; we give it in the words of Professor Max Muller:

"At a large convocation at Calcutta, about 300 Pandits from Gauda, Navadipa, and Kasi discussed the orthodoxy of his opinions......But, although the decision was adverse, the writer of the report adds: the mass of young Hindus are not Sanskrit scholars, and it is no wonder that they should be won over by hundreds to Dayanand's views, enforced as they are by an oratorical power of the highest order, and a determined will force that breaks down all opposition."[2]

His death elicited the highest tributes from all classes and creeds, Indian and non-Indian, Hindus, Musulmans, Christians, and Parsis. The greatest among his contemporaries wrote about or lauded him in the highest terms and deplored his premature death: among these we may mention the late Sir Syed Ahmad Khan, leader of the Indian Moslems; Colonel Olcott, President of the Theosophical Society, and Madame Blavatsky, its founder. But the most characteristic tribute emanated from Professor Max Muller, who compared him with Dr. Pusey of England, and wrote a remarkably eulogistic notice on the man and his work.[3]

"Deeply read in the theological literature of his country.... he was opposed to many of the abuses that had crept in, as he well knew, during the later periods of the religious growth of India, and of which, as is now well known, no trace can be found in the ancient sacred texts of the *Brahmans*, the *Vedas*....In his public disputations with the most learned

---

[1] The famous founder of the Vedantic school of Indian thought, of whom Max Muller and other German scholars have spoken in the highest terms of praise, and who flourished in A.D. 800.

[2] *Biographical Essays*, Max Muller, 1884, pp. 179-80.

[3] Ibid. p. 167.

Pandits at Benares and elsewhere, he was generally supposed to have been victorious, though often the aid of the police had to be called in to protect him from the blows of his conquered foes."

We append as a fitting conclusion to this chapter a few passages from a lengthy tribute which appeared in the official organ of the Theosophical Society, *The Theosophist:*

"A master spirit has passed away from India. Pandit Dayananda Saraswati...is gone; the irrepressible, energetic reformer, whose mighty voice and passionate eloquence for the last few years raised thousands of people in India from lethargic indifference and stupor into active patriotism, is no more....

"*De mortuis nil nisi bonum.* All our differences have been burnt with the body.....We remember only the grand virtues and noble qualities of our former colleague and teacher, and late antagonist. We bear in mind but his life-long devotion to the cause of Aryan regeneration; his ardent love for the grand philosophy of his forefathers; his relentless, untiring zeal in the work of the projected social and religious reforms; and it is with unfeigned sorrow that we now hasten to join the ranks of his many mourners. In him India has lost one of her noblest sons. A patriot in the true sense of the word, Swami Dayananda laboured from his earliest years for the recovery of the lost treasures of Indian intellect. His zeal for the reformation of his mother-land was exceeded only by his unbounded learning. Whatever might be said as to his interpretation of the sacred writings, there can be but one opinion as to his knowledge of Sanskrit, and the impetus to the study of both received at his hands. There are few towns and but one province we believe—namely, Madras— that Pandit Dayanand did not visit in furtherance of his missionary work, and fewer still where he has not left the impress of his remarkable mind behind him. He threw, as it were, a bomb-shell in the midst of the stagnant masses of degenerated Hinduism, and fired with love for the teachings of the Rishis and Vedic learning the hearts of all who were drawn within the influence of his eloquent oratory. Certainly there was no better or grander orator in Hindi and Sanskrit than Dayanand throughout the length and breadth of this land.

"As soon as the sad rumour was confirmed, Colonel Olcott, who was then at Cawnpore, paid a public tribute to the Swami's memory. He said that whatever might have been our rights or wrongs in the controversy, and whatever other pandits or orientalists could say against the Swami, there was room for no two opinions as to his energetic patriotism or of the nationalising influence exerted upon his followers. In Pandit Dayanand Saraswati there was a total absence of anything like degrading sycophancy and toadyism towards foreigners from interested motives.

"Truly, however heretical and blasphemous might have appeared his religious radicalism in the sight of old orthodox Brahminism, still the teachings and Vedic doctrines promulgated by him were a thousand times more consonant with Shruti or even Smriti than the doctrines taught by all other native Samajes put together. If he merged the old idols into One Living Being, Ishwara, as being only the attributes and powers of the latter, he yet had never attempted the folly of forcing down the throats of his followers the hybrid compound of a Durga-Moses, Christ-and-Koran, and Buddha-Chaitnya mixture of the modern reformers. The Arya Samaj rites certainly make the nearest approach to the real Vedic national religion."

Chapter IV

THE TEACHINGS OF DAYANAND

He hath paid Sacrifice, toiled in worship and offered gifts to wealth-increasing Agni, him the displeasure of the mighty moves not; outrage and scorn affect not such a mortal.

R. vi, 3, 2

1. His Attack on Mythological Hinduism and Caste

In the preceding chapters we have given a résumé of the chief incidents of Swami Dayanand's life, in order to provide the reader with a comprehensive idea of the prevalent conditions under which he lived and of the environment in which he was born, bred, and educated. No one can appreciate the magnitude of the task that the Swami had set himself to achieve, or of his successful efforts, unless fully acquainted with what Hindu religion and Hindu society embodied at the outset of Dayanand's career. When we use the past tense we do not mean to imply that the Hinduism of the uneducated masses is very materially different from what it was. There is no doubt that since then a great change has come over orthodox Hinduism by its contact with Western thought, and still more by the constant probing it has been subjected to in the light of the aggressive propaganda of the Arya Samaj. Not only have the educated classes (though still orthodox) changed their point of view, but even the extremely ignorant and superstitious masses are not what they were when Dayanand was born. Yet, in general, what we are going to say about the Hinduism of Dayanand's time is perhaps equally true of present-day Hinduism. The principal difference lies in what was of universal application then has had its scope constricted and narrowed by general education as well as by the propaganda of reforming bodies like the Arya Samaj.

In propounding a general idea of popular Hinduism in contrast with the beliefs and teachings of Dayanand, we will begin with the personal authority of the priest, to which class Dayanand himself belonged by right of birth. Hindu priests are called Brahmins. When Dayanand reached years of discretion he found that the Brahmin was the *summum bonum* in Hindu religion, and the ordinary individual of no consequence. Every Brahmin represented God himself, and was the sole exponent of the divine wishes and commands. His word was law, and could only be flouted on pain of eternal damnation. A Brahmin was neither selected nor appointed, nor ordained. He was just that by accident of birth, and his authority as a priest was quite apart from his educational or other qualifications. He alone could define religion. He alone could lay down what every man should believe and how he should act. The right of independent judgment was non-existent. The Brahmin alone knew, or was assumed to be conversant with the Scriptures although, in reality, not even one in a thousand was acquainted with the *Vedas*. But then, everything in Sanskrit was as sacred as the *Vedas*. The lightest word of a Brahmin was the essence of the *Vedas*, be it from the *Puranas*, or from the Epics, or even from an ordinary Sanskrit poem or drama. But it was of no consequence even if the Brahmin was totally ignorant of Sanskrit. The mere fact of his birth was supposed to endow him with divinity. Such was the dominant influence of the Brahmins on the great mass of Hindus when Dayanand was born that the recognition of the sacred status of the Brahmin was the primary test of Hinduism. Hinduism is so vast a conglomeration of creeds, dogmas, beliefs, rituals and customs that the Census authorities, at least in 1911, considered the worship of the Brahmin to be the *sine qua non* of this faith. In his report for the United Provinces of Agra and Oude for the year 1911, Mr. Blunt says:

"Though it is legitimate to assert that the Brahmins' influence on the growth of Hinduism has been overrated, at the expense of more natural causes, it is impossible to overrate their omnipotence in matters of religion and the completeness of their rule over the members of the Hindu system. The mediaeval Popes were spiritual despots: but, compared with the autocracy of the Brahmans, they were mere constitutional monarchs......The Brahman may not be God, but he is at all events Godlike, a subject not only of veneration but of actual worship." He thus comes to the conclusion that "the first great criterion by which a Hindu is determined" is that "every Hindu must acknowledge the Brahmin's superiority and his omnipotence in spiritual and social matters."

This is undoubtedly a correct description of the conditions existing a century ago, or even in certain regions 50 years ago; but it does not hold good today. At present there must be hundreds of thousands of Hindus, both in and outside the Arya Samaj, to whom this criterion would not apply. The "divine right" by birth of the Brahmin is fast vanishing. The monopoly of the Brahmin in administering religious sacraments and in performing religious ceremonies is being slowly but perceptibly undermined. Even in illiterate circles his authority is under fire.

Yet in the second half of the nineteenth century the description we have quoted above was literally true. The recognition of the authority of the mere Brahmin was the focus of the Hindu religion. It was this central authority that ruled and controlled the whole system of Hindu life; its pantheon of gods and goddesses, its dogmas, its philosophy, its rituals, its social economy and all that pertained thereto.

The organization of Roman Catholicism fades into insignificance when compared with the marvellously intricate and rigid organization of Hinduism effected by the Brahmins. It was the greatest organization the world had ever known. It encompassed the minutest details of individual and social life. The Brahmin's eye overlooked practically every waking moment of a Hindu's existence. There was nothing, however, sinful, monstrous, or atrociously vicious, which a Hindu could not do so long as a Brahmin could be prevailed upon to set matters right by processes of expiation promulgated by him and known to him alone. Various rites and ceremonies had been devised and used as accessories to this procedure for atonement. Multitudinous and mysterious were the ways and practices whereby "forgiveness of sins and redemption, coupled with the guarantee of a passport to heaven after death, were brought about." The simple and spiritual religion of the *Vedas*, the philosophical teaching of the *Upanishads*, had been superseded by what was only an "affair of temples and material sacrifices, of shows and processions, of festivals spread over the whole year in honour of innumerable deities," accompanied by all the paraphernalia of "bells and candles and vestments and ceremonials and incantations and tunes, unintelligible to those who heard them", and in some cases even to those who uttered them.

With a keen eye, bent upon discovering the origin of things and tracing their successive developments, with an intuitive faculty for driving at the root of the matter, Dayanand saw that the authority of the Brahmin was the pivot and the core of the whole system. Neither by habit nor by training was he prone to diplomacy or duplicity: subtlety of speech or action was alien to his nature. He felt the supreme importance of speaking the truth, the naked truth, and the whole truth. He therefore went straight to the point, attacked the central fortification of the citadel, and aimed at shaking it to the foundations. He questioned the authority of the Brahmin merely from right of birth. The Brahmin relied on Manu for his rights and privileges, and the Swami proved, on the authority of Manu himself, that a Brahmin must be versed in the *Vedas*, above avarice and completely composed in his demeanour: and that a Brahmin who did not reach that standard did not deserve to be treated and respected as such. He quoted chapter and verse in support of his contention, and demonstrated from those very books which the Brahmins relied on, how in ancient times persons not born of Brahmin parents acquired the position of Brahmins by learning and piety, and how those born of Brahmin parents were relegated to lower positions in accordance with their personal qualifications. He denied the right of any human being to control the free judgment of his fellow-men or women, in matters relating to the soul. He held that the Brahmin by birth was just an ordinary man who, on account of his hereditary characteristics had, perhaps, a better opportunity of becoming a veritable Brahmin than others not so born but with an equal right to become Brahmins if they could manage to acquire the necessary qualifications. He denied that even a real Brahmin could be worshipped in the sense in which God is worshipped. He was nothing more than a leader, a teacher, a preceptor, a guide and a philosopher. He denounced the worship of gods and goddesses, and preached that only the Supreme Being, the Primal Cause of the Universe, the Universal and All-pervading Spirit, should be worshipped, and none else; that God and God's word revealed at the beginning of the world were the only final and infallible authorities in religion; that all truth, purity and goodness emanated from God; that no one had any right to intervene between man and God; and that it was the right and duty of every man to seek inspiration and illumination from God Himself, and to live in the consciousness of a personal and direct relationship with Him.

From time immemorial, the Brahmins had monopolized the study of the *Vedas*. For a Sudra to hear a Vedic verse was the most heinous sin. The other castes were privileged, in theory, to hear and study the *Vedas* but in practice no Brahmin ever taught the *Vedas* to any but a born Brahmin. As a matter of fact, however, even among Brahmins the *Vedas* were known in parts only and to few—say, proportionately one in ten thousand in Upper India and one in a thousand in the south. All the four *Vedas* had been studied by a very few only; even their knowledge went no further than the text. The majority of them understood no more than a few verses required for ritual purposes, or forming part of the daily prayers. The great bulk of Brahmins were as ignorant of the *Vedas* as were the other Hindus. Even ceremonies were not necessarily performed along with Vedic texts. Formulae and texts had been culled from later literature and the essential ceremonies were performed with their help. As for interpreting the *Vedas*, only one man had ventured to do so within the 1,500 years immediately preceding the birth of Swami Dayanand, and he had achieved nothing more than the compilation of an enormous commentary based on current and traditional interpretation. To attempt an independent interpretation of the *Vedas* was an act of supreme audacity, tantamount to blasphemy, for which no human punishment was deemed adequate.

Pharisees sprung up who organized the most subtle and exacting ecclesiasticism ever invented by the genius of man, relegating religion to dead dogma and dry formality, and sealing off the windows to the souls of the nation. It is true that all this was done in the name and on the ostensible authority of the great teachers of antiquity. The caste, the law, and the authority had become omnipotent.

Into these surroundings came Dayanand with a clear vision of the original truth and of its vast possibilities for his people in particular and for humanity in general. He began in right earnest, and, with marvellous insight, attacked straightway the root cause of the evil—the unquestioned authority of the mere Brahmin by birth. His educated countrymen had evidently informed him about the Popes of Rome, and he applied that name to the Brahmins of India and denounced them with all the vehemence of an intensely vehement nature.

2. *The Right to Study the Scriptures*

To ensure abiding success for his crusade, it was incumbent that the restrictions imposed by the ecclesiastical system on the study of the Hindu Scriptures—the *Vedas*—should be removed, and the huge mass of literature, the outcome of centuries, should be divested of all authority excepting in so far as it adhered to the revealed literature. The Brahmins had invested with divine authority everything written or composed by them: Dayanand exposed the subterfuge and lifted the veil. He called upon all people, regardless of caste and creed, to study the *Vedas*, and conceded to every human being the right of personal interpretation of the *Vedas*, provided they were given their etymological and philosophical meanings and conformed to the ancient and approved canons of understanding and interpreting them. This was verily a revolution which, by one master stroke, shattered the shackles which Hindus had borne for centuries. Discarding tradition and custom, he began to interpret the *Vedas* for himself. His knowledge of Vedic literature was almost unsurpassed among his contemporaries. Thus he was in a position to justify all his sayings not merely by reason and logic alone, but most of all, by profuse quotations from sacred literature—the *Brahmans*, the *Upanishads*, and the *Sutras*.

It may be difficult for us to visualize that in the second half of the nineteenth century the *Vedas* were a sealed book in India, and no one could even read them, much less quote them in open debate attended by all communities, Hindus and non-Hindus alike. At present the *Vedas* are being read, studied and commented upon by all classes and castes of Hindus. This is the greatest service rendered by Dayanand to the cause of religious and intellectual as well as social freedom in India, and this alone entitles him to be called the saviour of Hindu India.

3. The Key to the Vedas: Canons of Interpretation

Swami Dayanand did not acknowledge the existing commentaries on the *Vedas* to be binding on any body. Those of Sayana[1] and Mahidhar he summarily rejected. The latter he regarded as deliberately and viciously perverse in his interpretation of the *Vedas*, and the former misguided and prejudiced. His interpretation and commentary aimed at the justification of the prevailing theology and its concomitant institutions.

Sayana lived and wrote when the sun of Hindu greatness had long set; when Hindu life and institutions suffered perversion at the hands of an exacting priesthood, possibly with an eye to defending it from the inroads of a strong, proselytising creed like Islam. It was a logical conclusion of Dayanand's teachings on the *Vedas* that he should provide a key to unlock their hidden treasures, so that his hearers might be assisted in their studies. This he accomplished by explaining the rules of Vedic interpretation and insisting on Vedic language being understood in the spirit of Vedic times.[2] The Sanskrit of the *Vedas* is mainly obsolete and quite unlike modern Sanskrit as written and read within the last 2,500 years. Even the grammar has undergone considerable changes. Modern grammar is of little help in understanding the sense of the *Vedas*. The *Vedas* should be studied in the light of

---

[1] European scholars speak of Sayana as "A mere drag on the progress of Vedic Scholarship."—*Sacred Books of the East*, Vol. XXXII., *Vedic Hymns*, p. xxxii. Mahidhar is hardly relied upon by European scholars.

[2] Speaking of the difficulties of understanding the *Vedas*, Prof. Max Muller says: "Though we may understand almost every word, yet we find it so difficult to lay hold of a connected chain of thought and to discover expressions that will not throw a wrong shade on the original features of the ancient words of the Veda."—*Sacred Books of the East*, Vol. XXXII, p. xxxii.

Vedic grammar and with the aid of literature devoid of all modernity.

The first canon for the interpretation of Vedic terms laid down by admittedly the greatest authority on the subject, Yaska, the author of *Nirukta*, is that the Vedic terms are all "yaugika".[3]

Patanjali, the author of the most authoritative and universally accepted commentary on Vedic grammar, supports that view. Pandit Gurudatta Vidyarthi, in his learned brochure *The Terminology of the Vedas*, to which Professor Max Muller refers approvingly in his monumental work on Vedic Hymns (*Sacred Books of the East*, Vol XXXII), has declared that all the Rishis and Munis of ancient India—i.e. all the ancient authors and commentators—were unanimous on this point.[4] In his *History of Ancient Sanskrit Literature*, Professor Max Muller has concurred, at least as regards certain portions of the *Vedas*. "But there is a charm," says he, "in these primitive strains discoverable in no other class of poetry. Every word retains something of its radical meaning, every epithet tells; every thought, in spite of the most intricate and abrupt expression, is, if we once disentangle it, true, correct and complete."[5]

Further in the same work, Max Muller says: "Names...... are to be found in the Veda, as it were, in a still fluid state. They never appear as appellations, nor yet as proper names; they are organic, not yet broken or smoothed down."[6]

Pandit Gurudatta indicates how this simple rule was ignored by Sayana and the European scholars thus fostering the idea that the *Vedas* inculcate the worship of innumerable gods and goddesses, called *devatas*. "This word, *devata*," says the Pandit, "is a most fruitful source of error, and it is very necessary that its exact meaning and application should be determined. Not understanding the Vedic sense of this word, *Devata*, and easily

---

[3] A yaugika term is one that has a derivative meaning, that is, one that only signifies the meaning of the root together with the modifications effected by the affixes. In fact, the structural elements of which the word is compounded afford the whole and the only clue to the true signification of the word. The word is purely connotive.—Pandit Gurudatta Vidyarthi, *Terminology of the Vedas*, Chicago Edition, p. 7.

[4] *Vedic Terminology*, p. 8.
[5] Max Muller's *History of Ancient Sanskrit Literature*, p. 553.
[6] Ibid. p. 755.

admitting the popular superstitious interpretation of a belief in mythological gods and goddesses, crumbling into wretched idolatry, European scholars have imagined the Vedas to be full of the worship of such material and have degraded its religion even below polytheism and perhaps at par with atheism, calling it 'henotheistic'. He again quotes the ancient authorities on the true meaning of the word *devata*, when used in connection with Vedic texts, and demonstrates by several examples how European scholars have misunderstood and misinterpreted the *Vedas* through ignorance and neglect of these authorities. The discussion is concluded by the following observations, which are well worth quoting in full:

"We have seen that Yaska regards the names of those substances whose properties are treated of, in the mantra, as the *devatas*. What substances, then, are the *devatas*? They are all that can form the subject of human knowledge. All human knowledge is limited by two conditions, i.e., time and space. Our knowledge of causation is mainly that of succession of events. And succession is nothing but an order in time. Secondly, our knowledge must be a knowledge of something, and that something must be somewhere. It must have a locality of its existence and occurrence. Now to the essentials of knowledge. The most exhaustive division of human knowledge is between objective and subjective. Objective knowledge is the knowledge of all that passes without the human body. It is the knowledge of the phenomena of the external universe....In speaking of subjective knowledge, there is, firstly, the ego, the human spirit, the conscious entity; secondly, the internal phenomena of which the human spirit is conscious." These latter are again divided into "deliberate activities" and "vital activities," and it is concluded that, since our prior analysis of the knowable leads to six things, time, locality, force, human spirit, deliberate activities and vital activities, these are fit to be called *devatas*: and, if the account of the *Nirukta* concerning Vedic *devatas* be accepted as true, the Vedas should be understood to inculcate these six things as *devatas* and no others." We have given this lengthy quotation as making clear the position of Swami Dayanand with regard to the true canons of Vedic interpretation.[7]

[7] As an instance of the perversity of the missionary mind in reading mytho-

For over 2,500 years had these canons been neglected, resulting in a hopeless welter of confusion as to the religion of the *Vedas*. The cry of "Back to the *Vedas*!" would have been meaningless but for the supplying of this key to unlock the treasures concealed there. We are therefore disposed to conclude that this was the most important of the Swami's teachings, the keystone of the structure he erected.

We are aware that both Hindu and European scholars take strong exception to his commentary on and interpretation of the *Vedas*. They consider it "more ingenious than ingenuous,"[8] but the Swami's claim to be a great scholar and a great reformer does not rest upon the accuracy of his voluminous Commentary on the *Vedas*. What matter for us are the principles he has enacted: (a) the right of every human being to read and interpret the *Vedas* for himself and for others; (b) the duty of every Arya to do so; and (c) the canons of its interpretation, as stated above. This alone would have entitled him to a niche in the Temple of Fame: But he did much more.

4. *The World-Apostle of Hinduism*

For the first time in the history of Hinduism since its fall, a Hindu scholar, born of Brahmin parents, opened the sealed gate of Hinduism to the rest of mankind.[9] This followed as a logical consequence of his position in relation to the *Vedas*. The *Vedas* were the Word of God; they had been revealed in the beginning of creation, for the good of the race; they alone were the primeval revelation. It was therefore the right of every human being to know them. He maintained that the *Vedas* themselves said so, and that it was the duty of everybody who knew the *Vedas* to disseminate his knowledge throughout the world for the benefit of mankind. The Christians believed in the eternal damnation of those who would not accept Christ as their Saviour. They claimed the monopoly of salvation for a belief in Christ and the Holy *Bible*. The Hindus advanced

---

logical gods and goddesses in the *Vedas*, reference may be made to a paper written by Mr. Griswold, M.A., of Lahore, wherein he presumes to differ from Yaska, the author of *Nirukta*, the greatest authority on Vedic interpretation.

[8] *United Provinces Report for 1911* by Mr. Blunt, p. 133.

[9] Cf. however, *Foreign Elements in the Hindu Population*, D. R. Bhandarkar and *Conversion and Reconversion to Hinduism During the Muslim Period*, Sri Ram Sharma.

neither of these claims for the *Vedas*. They hold that salvation could be attained by different paths, that a good Muslim, a good Christian, or one who was neither, stood as much chance of being saved as a good Hindu. Salvation, according to them, depended on genuine knowledge followed by exemplary conduct. They did not maintain that one must be a Hindu to fulfil either condition. The modern Hindus, however, implicitly believed, and the vast bulk of them still do that a Hindu could be one by birth only, and that none born outside the pale of Hindu society could ever become a Hindu. "Hinduism," says Sir Alfred Lyall in his *Asiatic Studies*, Part I, "is a matter of birth right and inheritance... A man does not become a Hindu, but is born into Hinduism." Hindu society was thus a constantly diminishing entity. It was a self-contained community—a charmed circle, barred against all outsiders. Swami Dayanand broke that bar and cast open the closed portals. The Arya Samaj was intended to be, and is, essentially a Hindu organization—Hindus and non-Hindus are unanimous on that point. Yet it is open to every one, regardless of caste, colour or nationality who subscribes to its principles and desires to be enrolled as a member. Once a member, he has all the rights and privileges of one, be he a Hindu or not. How this principle has worked in practice will be related in another chapter.

5. *Dayanand's Beliefs*

As for the remainder of Dayanand's religious teachings, we shall render them in his own words. At the end of his great work, called *Satyarath Prakash* (lit. "The True Exposition"), he summarizes his beliefs categorically, with a short explanatory preface from which we quote the following passages:

"I believe in a religion based on universal and all-embracing principles which have always been accepted as true by mankind, and will continue to command the allegiance of mankind in the ages to come. Hence it is that the religion in question is called the Primeval Eternal Religion, which means that it is above the hostility of all human creeds whatsoever.

"My conception of God and all other objects in the Universe is founded on the teachings of the Veda and other true Shastras, and is in conformity with the beliefs of all the sages, from Brahma down to Jaimini. I offer a statement of these beliefs for the acceptance of all good men. That alone I hold to be acceptable which is worthy of being believed in by all men in all ages. I do not entertain the least idea of founding a new religion or sect. My sole aim is to believe in truth and help others to believe in it, to reject falsehood and to help others in doing the same.........He alone is entitled to be called a man who possesses a thoughtful nature and feels for others in the same way as he does for his own self, does not fear the unjust, however powerful, but fears the truly virtuous, however weak. Moreover, he should always exert himself to his utmost to protect the righteous, and advance their good, and conduct himself worthily towards them, even though they be extremely poor and weak and destitute of material resources. On the other hand, he should constantly strive to destroy, humble and oppose the wicked, sovereign rulers of the whole earth and men of great influence and power though they be. In other words, a man should, as far as lies in his power, constantly endeavour to undermine the power of the unjust and to strengthen that of the just. He may have to bear any amount of terrible suffering, he may have even to quaff the bitter cup of death in the performance of this duty, which devolves on him on account of being a man, but he should not shirk it."

We proceed to give his beliefs in the order in which he has recorded them:

"I. He, who is called Brahm or the most High; who is Parmatma, or the Spirit who permeates the whole universe; who is Truth, Intelligence, and Happiness; Whose nature, attributes and characteristics are holy; Who is omniscient, formless, all pervading, unborn, infinite, almighty, just, and merciful; Who is the author of the universe, sustains and dissolves it; Who awards all souls the fruits of their deeds in strict accordance with the requirements of absolute justice; and Who is possessed of other like attributes—even Him I believe to be the Lord of creation.

"2. The four *Vedas*, the repository of Knowledge and Religious Truth, are the Word of God. They comprise what is known as the Samhita—Mantra Bhag only. They are absolutely free from error, and the supreme and independent authority in all things. They require no other book to bear witness to their Divine origin. Even as the sun or a lamp is, by its own light, an absolute and independent manifester of its own existence—yea, it reveals the existence of things other than itself—even so are the ·Vedas.

"The commentaries on the four *Vedas*, viz. the *Brahmanas*, the six Angas, the six Upangas, the four Up-Vedas, and the eleven hundred and twenty-seven Shakhas, which are expositions of the Vedic texts by Brahma and other great Rishis—I look upon as works of a dependent character. In other words, their authority is to be followed only so far as they conform to the teachings of the *Vedas*. Whatever passages in these works are opposed to the Vedic teaching, I reject them entirely.

"3. That which inculcates justice and equity, which teaches truthfulness in thought, speech and deed—in a word, that which is in conformity with the Will of God, as embodied in the *Vedas*, even that I call Dharma. But that which is intermixed with what is partial, which sanctions injustice, which teaches untruthfulness of thought, speech or deed—in brief that which is in antagonism to the Will of God, as embodied in the *Vedas*, that I term Adharma.

"4. The immortal, eternal Principle which is endowed with thought and judgment, with desire and hate, which is susceptible of pleasure and pain, whose capacity for knowledge is limited—even that is 'Soul'.

"5. God and Soul are two distinct entities. Each has certain attributes which are not and cannot be predicable of the other, and each performs certain functions which the other does not and cannot perform. They are, however, inseparable one from the other, being related to each other as the pervader and the pervaded, and have certain attributes in common. Even as a material object is, was and shall always be, distinct from the space in which it exists and as the two cannot, were not, and shall never be, one and the same, even so God and the Soul are to each other. Their mutual relation is that of the pervader and the pervaded, of father and son. This worships and that is worshipped.

"6. Three things are eternal, namely God, Soul, and Prakriti —the material cause of the universe. These are also known as the eternal substances. Being eternal, their essential qualities, their functions, and their natures are eternally the same.

"7. Substances, properties, and functions, which result from combination, cease to exist on dissolution. But the power or force, by virtue of which a substance unites with another or separates from it, is eternally inherent in the substance, and this power will compel it to seek similar unions and disunions in future. The unions and disunions, as well as the power by virtue of which they take place, are also eternal, in consequence of the regularity of their succession.

"8. That which results from a combination of primary elements, compounded together consistently with a thorough and complete knowledge of the distinctive properties of every separate element and with all the perfection of design—even that, in all its infinite variety, is called creation.

"9. The purpose of creation is the essential and natural exercise of the creative energy of the Deity. A person once asked some one: "What is the purpose of the eyes?' 'Why, to see with, to be sure,' was the reply. The same is the case here. God's creative energy must have play, and the souls must reap the fruits of their karma.

"10. The creation has a Creator. The existence of a design in the universe as well as the fact that dead unconscious matter is incapable of forming itself into seed or any other thing endowed with life and vitality, shows that it must have a Creator.

"11. The earthly bondage of the soul has a cause. This cause is ignorance, which is the source of sin as, among other things, it leads man to worship things other than the Creator and obscures his intellectual faculties, whereof pain and suffering is the result. Ignorance is termed bondage, as it involves the Soul in pain which everybody wants to escape but which he must suffer if he is ignorant.

"12. The emancipation of the soul from pain and suffering of every description, and a subsequent career of freedom in the all-pervading God and His immense creation, is termed Salvation. Salvation lasts for a period only, on the expiration of which the saved soul again assumes a body.

"13. The means of salvation are the worship of God or the contemplation of His nature and attributes with concentrated attention, the practice of virtue, the acquisition of true knowledge by the practice of Brahmcharya, the company of the wise and learned, the love of true knowledge, purity of thought, active benevolence, and so on.

"16. The 'caste' of an individual is determined by merit and sterling worth only..................

"20. Devas (gods) are those who are wise and learned; asuras, those who are foolish and ignorant; rakshas, those who are wicked and sin-loving; and pishachas, those whose mode of life is filthy and debasing.

"21. Devapuja (or the worship of the gods) consists in showing honour and respect to the wise and learned, to one's father, mother and preceptor, to the preachers of the true doctrine, to a just and impartial sovereign, to lovers of righteousness, to chaste men and women.

"23. The *Puranas* (ancient commentaries on the *Vedas* and other works on theology) are the *Aitreya Brahmanas* and similar compositions by the great Rishis like Brahma and others. In Itihas or history I include Kalpa, Gatha, and Narashansi. The *Bhagwat* and other books of that sort are not the *Puranas*.

"25. An energetic and active life is preferable to passive acquiescence in the decrees of fate, inasmuch as destiny is the consequence of acts. A life of virtuous activity will secure the soul a good destiny, as a life of wickedness will produce the opposite result. Hence acts, being the makers of destiny, virtuous activity is superior to passive resignation.

"26. The most approved behaviour of one man towards his fellow-creatures lies in his treating everyone according to his worth, in his treating him as he would wish himself to be treated by others, in sympathizing with him, from the core of his heart, in his joys and sorrows, in his losses and gains.

"27. Sanskar, or sacrament, is that which contributes to man's physical, mental and spiritual improvement. The sanskars are sixteen in number. Their due and proper observance is obligatory on all. Nothing should be done for the departed after the remains have been cremated.

"28. The performance of yajna is most commendable. It consists in showing honour and respect to the wise and learned, in the proper application of the principles of chemistry and other physical sciences to the affairs of life, in the dissemination of knowledge, in the performance of Agnihotra, which, by contributing to the purification of the air and water, and the healthy growth of vegetables, directly tends to promote the well-being of all sentient creatures.

"39. All truth must satisfy five tests: (1) It must not militate against the nature and attributes of God; (2) it must not be opposed to the teaching of the *Vedas;* (3) it must stand the test of the well-known eight kinds of proofs based on natural laws; (4) it must have the sanction of 'apt purshas' (i.e. men learned, true and holy); and lastly (5) it must be in consonance with the dictates of one's own conscience. Every doctrine must be subjected to these five tests, and accepted if it fulfils them......

"41. The soul is a free agent—at liberty to act as it pleases, but it is dependent on God's grace for the enjoyment of the fruit of its actions. God is free as well as just.

"42. Swarga (heaven) represents the state of happiness.

"43. Narka (hell) represents pain and suffering.

"46. When, according to the rules prescribed by the Shastras, a person bestows, as the result of reciprocal affection, his or her hand upon one of the opposite sex and in a public manner, he or she is said to contract marriage.

"48. Stuti (or praise) is the enumeration of Divine attributes and qualities, with a view to fix them in the mind and realize their meaning. Among other things it inspires us with love towards God.

"49. Prarthana is praying to God for the gift of knowledge and similar other blessings which result from a communion with Him. Its principal fruit is humility and serenity of mind. Prayer does not dispense with effort.

"50. Upasna is conforming, as far as possible, in purity and holiness to the Divine Spirit. It is feeling the presence of the Deity in the Soul by the realization of His all-pervading nature. Upasna extends the bounds of our knowledge.

"51. Sagun Stuti is praising God by the enumeration of the qualities and attributes which He possesses, but Nirgun Stuti is praising God by those qualities and attributes which are foreign to His nature.

"Sagun Prarthana is praying to God for virtuous qualities; but Nirgun Prarthana is imploring the Deity to cast out from us that which is evil.

"Sagun Upasna is the realization, in the soul, of the presence of God as possessing the attributes which are inherent in Him, while Nirgun upasna is the realization, in the soul, of the presence of God as distinct from what is foreign to His nature."

We have omitted some articles as unimportant, or because they were included elsewhere.

But Swami Dayanand was something more than a religious propagandist. He was a social reformer too, and a true patriot. His opinions on social and political issues will be reviewed in succeeding chapters, when we proceed to discuss the social work of the Arya Samaj and its politics.

Chapter V

DAYANAND'S TRANSLATION OF THE VEDAS

He who does not know the Vedas, does not know Him who is great.

Taitreya Brahman, iii, 12, 9

As for Dayanand's translation of the *Vedas* being "ingenious", it should be borne in mind that it is no mean task to assess the real sense of the *Vedas*, much less to interpret it. In 1869, when Professor Max Muller published the first edition of his *Vedic Hymns,* Part I, he characterized his work as one of "deciphering", and more than twenty years later, when publishing the second and revised edition, he reiterated: "I hold that they (i.e. the first translators) ought to be decipherers."[1] Referring to his adversaries in the field of translating the *Vedas* (a host of German professors), he says: "There is another point also on which I am quite willing to admit that my adversaries are right. 'No one who knows anything about the *Veda*', they say, 'would think of attempting a translation of it atpresent. A translation of the *Rig-Veda* is a task for the next century."[2] In another place he says:[3] "If by translation we mean a complete, satisfactory and final translation of the whole of *Rig-Veda,* I should feel inclined to go even further than Professor von Roth. Not only shall we have to wait till the next century for such a work, but I doubt whether we shall ever obtain it."[4] Then he compares his own translation of the 165th Hymn of the first Mandala of the *Rig-Veda* with that of Professor von Roth, and concludes that a comparison like this "will disclose the unsettled state of Vedic scholarship, but the more fully this fact is acknowledged the better, I believe, it will be for the progress of our studies. They (i.e.

---

[1] *Sacred Books of the East,* Vol. XXXII, "Vedic Hymns", Part I, Introduction, p. ix.
[2] Ibid. p. xi.
[3] Ibid. p. xxi.
[4] "The *Veda,* I feel convinced, will occupy scholars for centuries to come, and maintain its position as the most ancient of books in the library of mankind."— Max Muller in *The Sacred Books of the East,* Vol. XXXII, "Vedic Hymns", p. xxxi.

the translations of the *Vedas* by European scholars) have suffered more than anything else from the baneful positivism which has done so much harm in hieroglyphic and cuneiform researches. That the same words and names should be interpreted differently from year to year is perfectly intelligible to everyone who is familar with the nature of the decipherments. What has seriously injured the credit of the studies is that the latest decipherments have always been represented as final and unchangeable...... When we come to really difficult passages, the Vedic hymns often require a far greater effort of divination than the hymns addressed to Egyptian or Babylonian deities."

Max Muller certainly vents a crying grievance when he complains of the "baneful positivism" of European scholars as to interpretations which are little better than guess-work; yet his own conclusions on the *Vedas* and on the religion of which they are the vehicle, are open to similar criticism. The conclusions of European scholars on ancient civilizations are vitiated also, in many cases, by their judging these older civilizations by Christian or other modern standards, which they assume to be true and permanent. They forget that all standards are mutable—that the one whose permanence they tacitly assume is dissolving here and reforming there before their very eyes. While we are deeply grateful to the Western scholars for the time and labour they have lavished on Vedic research, which is likely to be of the greatest possible value to the rising generation of Indians who are devoting themselves to the study and interpretation of the *Vedas*, we cannot but remark that their hasty conclusions as to the religion of the *Vedas* caused immeasurable and unnecessary harm by creating a mass of prejudice against the Vedic religion among the earlier generations of educated Hindus. The missionary propagandists in their zeal for conversion, in their anxiety to show the superiority of the Christian *Bible*, condemned the *Vedas* in the most forceful language at their command. For this purpose they even transgressed the rules of fair play and honest controversy by quoting the conclusions of European scholars on the Vedic religion and Vedic culture without furnishing the accompanying qualifications, and without affording the reader any idea of the unsatisfactory character of the translations on which those conclusions were based, though well known to and acknowledged by themselves. It is not surprising, therefore, that misled by these garbled quotations, some educated Indians rejected the *Vedas*, and accepted Christian thought, though not the Christian religion, particularly in Bengal and Bombay.

Swami Dayanand made it his mission to dam the flow of this anti-Vedic and anti-Hindu current by showing that the conclusions of European scholars were defective, and often influenced by their conscious or unconscious Christian bias. In any case, in the language of the European scholars themselves, their translations are only provisional. Swami Dayanand was not conversant with any European language, not even English. His criticism of Max Muller, etc., in his commentaries on the *Rig-Veda*, is therefore based on information provided by friends who were acquainted with English.

In his wake, Pandit Gurudatta Vidyarthi, an erudite scholar of modern science and modern thought, and also of Sanskrit, examined some of the conclusions of the European translators in the light of Sanskrit grammar and philosophy and literature, and proved how misleading and erroneous they were.[5]

Those who may be disposed to sit in judgement on Swami Dayanand and to dissert on the merits of his translation of or *Commentaries on the Vedas* would do well to bear in mind:

(a) That this was his first attempt.

(b) That all this great work was accomplished within the brief span of not even seven years. The first instalment, or the first part of his Commentaries, containing an exposition of a few Mantras only, was published at the end of 1876, and he died on 30th October, 1883.

(c) That this period was the busiest of his life, when most of his time was engaged in propaganda work. It was during this period that he established the Arya Samajes, conducted public and private discussions, refuted criticism of his views and writings, and, besides the commentaries on the *Vedas*, wrote and published a number of other books in Sanskrit and

---

[5]See his lectures on Prof. Sir Monier Williams's *Indian Wisdom*, and his articles on European Scholars and the *Vedas* in his *Collected Works*.

Hindi. Moreover, he devoted some of his time to teaching. We have already mentioned that several princes studied under him, but among his pupils were also included priests, Sadhus and laymen.

(d) That he had to accomplish most of his work single-handed. He employed Pandits to write from his dictation, to translate his Sanskrit into Hindi and then to make fair copies for the press. But beyond that he had no aid from anyone in his translation of the *Vedas*, for the simple reason that no one knew the *Vedas* well enough to be of any help. Those who had a smattering of knowledge deemed it sacrilegious to attempt a translation.

(e) That he had no time to revise and to reconsider.

Under the circumstances, what he achieved was more than creditable, and verily deserves our unstinted praise. The Arya Samaj does not claim infallibility for his translation, nor did he. But his honesty of purpose is visible on every page of his work, in that, unlike most of the European translators of the *Vedas* (Max Muller excepted), he is not content with vouchsafing his own empirical view of the text, but in almost every instance has supplemented it with reasons and explanations and often by quotations from ancient authors credited with a superior and deeper knowledge of the *Vedas* because of the proximity of their times to the Vedic period of Indian civilization.

His translation of the text is always preceded by a full analysis of the grammatical and etymological construction of the words composing a verse. Then follows the meaning of every word; then the translation of the whole, and finally the commentary and its general sense as he understood it.

All this appears in his own language, Sanskrit, which was translated into Hindi for him by the Pandits whom he employed for that purpose. It was the most audacious act of his life to have issued a translation of the *Vedas* in Hindi, the vernacular of North India, since such a translation had never even been attempted before. This fact should be the conclusive proof of the transparency and honesty of his motives.

Dilating on his own efforts to understand and then translate the *Vedas* for the public, Prof. Max Muller says that it is a mere beginning, "a mere contribution towards the better understanding of the Vedic hymns," and he felt convinced that on many points his translation would yield to correction and be replaced sooner or later by a more authoritative one. "There are", continues he, "as all Vedic scholars know, whole verses which as yet yield no sense whatever. There are words the meaning of which we can but guess."[6]

All that we claim for Dayanand's translation of the *Vedas* is that, from the Hindu point of view, it is the best and the most scholarly translation of that ancient book so far offered to the public; yet, that Dayanand has only blazed the trail for the coming generations as to how they should approach the *Vedas*—how they should interpret them. It would necessitate centuries of toil and constant care before anything like a complete and thoroughly intelligent translation of the *Vedas* would be available. Generations of learned Hindus will need to devote their entire lives to the study of the *Vedas* in a spirit of reverent humility, fully resolved to master all difficulties, before these ancient scriptures surrender even a fraction of their treasures of beauty and of truth.

---

[6]*Sacred Books of the East*, Vol. XXXII, "Vedic Hymns", Part I, p. xxxii.

APPENDIX

DAYANANDA AND THE VEDA

DAYANANDA accepted the Veda as his rock of firm foundation, he took it for his guiding veiw of life, his rule of inner existence his inspiration for external work, but he regarded it as even more, the word of eternal Truth on which man's knowledge of God and his relations with the Divine Being, and with his fellows can be rightly and securely founded. This everlasting rock of the Veda, many assert, has no existence, there is nothing there but the commonest mud and sand, it is only a hymnal of primitive barbarians, only a rude worship of personified natural phenomena, or even less than that, a liturgy of ceremonial sacrifice, half religion, half magic, by which superstitious animal men of yore hoped to get themselves gold and food and cattle, slaughter pitilessly their enemies, protect themselves from disease, calamity and demoniac influences and enjoy the coarse pleasures of a material Paradise. To that we must add a third view, the orthodox, or at least that which arises from Sayana's commentary, this view admits, practically, the ignobler interpretation of the substance of the Veda and yet—or is it therefore?—exalts this primitive farrago as a holy Scripture and a Book of Sacred Works.

Now this matter is no mere scholastic question, but has a living importance, not only for a just estimate of Dayananda's work but for our consciousness of our past and for the determination of the influences that shall mould our future. A nation grows into what it shall be by the force of that which it was in the past and is in the present and in this growth there come periods of conscious and subconscious stock-taking when the national soul selects, modifies, rejects, keeps out of all that it had or is acquiring whatever it needs as substance and capital for its growth and action in the future: in such a period of stock-taking we are still and Dayananda was one of its great and formative spirits. But among all the materials of our past, the Veda is the most venerable and has been directly and indirectly the most potent. Even when its sense was no longer understood, even when its traditions were lost behind Pauranic forms, it was still held in honour, though without knowledge, as an authoritative revelation and an inspired Book of Knowledge, the source of all sanctions and the standard of all truth.

But there has always been this double and incompatible tradition about the Veda that it is a book of ritual and mythology and that it is a book of divine knowledge. The Brahmanas seized on the one tradition, the Upanishads on the other. Later, the learned took the hymns for a book essentially of ritual and works, they went elsewhere for pure knowledge, but the instinct of the race bowed down before it with an obstinate inarticulate memory of a loftier tradition. And when in our age the Veda was brought out of its obscure security behind the purdah of a reverential neglect, the same phenomenon re-appears. While Western scholarship extending the hints of Sayana seemed to have classed it forever as a ritual liturgy to Nature-Gods, the genius of the race, looking through the eyes of Dayananda, pierced behind the error of many centuries and again the intuition of a timeless revelation and a divine truth was given to humanity. In any case, we have to make one choice or another. We can no longer securely enshrine the Veda wrapped up in the folds of an ignorant reverence or guarded by a pious self-deceit. Either the Veda is what Sayana says it is, and then we have to leave it behind for ever as the document of a mythology and ritual which have no longer any living truth or force for thinking minds, or it is what the European scholars say it is, and then we have to put it away among the relics of the past as an antique record of semi-barbarous worship; or else it is indeed Veda, a book of divine knowledge, and then it becomes of supreme importance to us to know and to hear its message.

It is objected to the sense Dayananda gave to the Veda that it is no true sense but an arbitrary fabrication of imaginative learning and ingenuity, to his method that it is fantastic and unacceptable by the critical reason, to his teaching of a revealed Scripture that the very idea is a rejected superstition impossible for any enlightened mind to admit or to announce sincerely. I will not now examine the solidity of Dayananda's interpretation of Vedic texts, nor anticipate the verdict of the future on his commentary, nor discuss his theory of revelation. I shall only state the broad principles underlying his thought about the Veda as they present themselves to me. For, in action and thought of a great soul or a great personality the vital thing to my mind is not the form he gave to it, but in his action the helpful power he put forth and in his thought the helpful truth he has added or it may be, restored to the yet all too scanty stock of our human acquisition and divine potentiality.

To start with the negation of his work by his critics, in whose mouth does it lie to accuse Dayananda's dealings with the Veda of a fantastic or arbitrary ingenuity? Not in the mouth of those who accept Sayana's traditional interpretation. For, if ever there was a monument of arbitrarily erudite ingenuity, of great learning divorced, as great learning too often is, from sound judgment and sure taste and a faithful critical and comparative observation, from direct seeing and often even from plainest common-sense or of a constant fitting of the text into the Procrustean bed of preconceived theory, it is surely this commentary, otherwise so imposing, so useful as first crude material, so erudite and laborious, left to us by Acharaya Sayana. Nor does the reproach lie in the mouth of those who take as final the recent labours of European scholarship. For if ever there was a toil of interpretation in which the loosest rein has been given to an ingenious speculation, in which doubtful indications have been snatched at as certain proofs, in which the boldest conclusions have been insisted upon with the scantiest justification, the most enormous difficulties ignored and preconceived prejudice maintained in face of the clear and often admitted suggestions of the text, it is surely this labour, so eminently respectable, otherwise for its industry, good will and power of research, performed through a long century by European Vedic scholarship.

What is the main positive issue in this matter? An interpretation of the Veda must stand or fall by its central conception of the Vedic religion and the amount of support given to it by the intrinsic evidence of the Veda itself. Here Dayananda's view is quite clear, its foundation inexpungable. The Vedic hymns are chanted to the One Deity under many names, names which are used and even designed to express His qualities and powers. Was this conception of Dayananda's arbitrary conceit fetched out of his own too ingenious imagination? Not at all; it is the explicit statement of the Veda itself; "One existent, sages" not the ignorant, mind you, but the seers, the men of knowledge—"speak of in many ways, as Indra and Yama, as Matariswan, as Agni." The Vedic Rishis ought surely to have known something about their own religion more, let us hope, than Roth or Max Muller, and this is what they knew.

We are aware how modern scholars twist away from the evidence. This hymn, they say, was a late production, this loftier idea which it expresses with so clear a force rose up somehow in the later Aryan mind or was borrowed by those ignorant fire-worshippers, sun-worshippers, sky-worshippers from their cultured and philosophic Dravidian enemies. But throughout the Veda we have confirmatory hymns and expressions; Agni or Indra or any other is expressly hymned as one with all the other gods. Agni contains all other divine powers within himself, the Maruts are described as all the gods, one deity is addressed by the names of others as well as his own, or, most commonly, he is given as Lord and King of the universe, attributes only appropriate to the Supreme Deity. Ah, but that cannot mean, ought not to mean, must not mean the worship of One; let us invent a new word, call it henotheism and suppose that the Rishis did not really believe Indra or Agni to be the Supreme Deity but treated any god or every god as such for the nonce, perhaps that he might feel the more flattered and lend a more gracious ear to so hyperbolic a compliment! But why should not the foundation of Vedic thought be natural monotheism rather than this new fangled monstrosity of henotheism? Well, because primitive barbarians could not possibly have risen to such high conceptions and, if you allow them to have so risen, you imperil our theory of evolutionary stages of human development and you destroy our whole idea about the sense of the Vedic hymns and their place in the history of mankind. Truth must hide herself, common sense disappear from the field so that a theory may flourish? I ask, in this point, and it is *the* fundamental point, who deals most straightforwardly with the text. Dayananda or the Western scholars?

But if this fundamental point of Dayananda's is granted, if the character given by the Vedic Rishis themselves to their gods is admitted, we are bound, whenever the hymns speak of Agni or another, to see behind that name present always to the thought of the Rishi the one Supreme Deity or else one of His powers with its attendant qualities or workings. Immediately the whole character of the Veda is fixed in the sense Dayananda gave to it, the merely ritual, mythological, polytheistic interpretation of Sayana collapses, the meteorological and naturalistic European interpretation collapses. We have instead a real Scripture of the world's sacred books and the divine word of a lofty and noble religion.

All the rest of Dayananda's theory arises logically out of this fundamental conception. If the names of the god-heads express qualities of the one Godhead and it is these which the Rishis adored and towards which they directed their aspiration, then there must inevitably be in the Veda a large part of psychology of the Divine Nature, psychology of the relations of man with God and a constant indication of the law governing man's Godward conduct. Dayananda asserts the presence of such an ethical element, he finds in the Veda the law of life given by God to the human being. And if the Vedic godheads express the powers of a supreme Deity who is Creator, Ruler and Father of the universe, then there must inevitably be in the Veda a large part of cosmology, the law of creation and of cosmos. Dayananda asserts the presence of such a cosmic element, he finds in the Veda the secrets of creation and the law of Nature by which the Omniscient governs the world.

Neither Western scholarship nor ritualistic learning has succeeded in eliminating the psychological and ethical value of the hymns, but they have both tended in different degrees to minimise it. Western scholars minimise because they feel uneasy whenever ideas that are not primitive, seem to insist on their presence in these primeval utterances; they do not hesitate openly to abandon in certain passages interpretations which they adopt in others and which are admittedly necessitated by their own philological and critical reasoning because, if admitted always, they would often involve deep and subtle psychological conceptions which *cannot* have occurred to primitive minds! Sayana minimises because his theory of Vedic discipline was not ethical righteousness with a moral and spiritual result but mechanical performance of ritual with a material reward. But in spite of these efforts of suppression, the lofty ideas of the Veda still reveal themselves in strange contrast to its alleged burden of fantastic naturalism or dull ritualism. The Vedic godheads are constantly hymned as Master of Wisdom, Power, Purity, purifiers, healers of grief and evil, destroyers of sin and falsehood, warriors for the truth; constantly the Rishis pray to them for healing and purification, to be made seers of knowledge, possessors of the truth, to be upheld in the divine law, to be assisted and armed with strength, manhood and energy. Dayananda has brought this idea of the divine right and truth into the Veda; the Veda is as much and more a book of divine Law as the Hebrew Bible or the Zoroastrian Avesta.

The cosmic element is not less conspicuous in the Veda; the Rishis speak always of the worlds, the firm laws that govern them, the divine workings in the cosmos. But Dayananda goes farther; he affirms that the truths of modern physical science are discoverable in the hymns. Here we have the sole point of fundamental principle about which there can be any justifiable misgivings. I confess my incompetence to advance any settled opinion in the matter. But this much needs to be said that his idea is increasingly supported by the recent trend of knowledge about the ancient world. The ancient civilisations did possess secrets of science, some of which modern knowledge has recovered, extended and made more rich and precise but others are even now not recovered. There is then nothing fantastic in Dayananda's idea that Veda contains truth of science as well as truth of religion. I will even add my own conviction that the Veda contains other truths of a Science, the modern world does not at all possess, and in that case Dayananda has rather understated than overstated the depth and range of the Vedic wisdom.

Objection has also been made to the philological and etymological method by which he arrived at his results, especially in his dealings with the names of the godheads. But this objection, I feel certain, is an error due to our introduction of modern ideas about language into our study of this ancient tongue. We moderns use words as counters without any memory or appreciation of their original sense: when we speak we think of the object spoken of, not at all of the expressive word which is to us a dead and brute thing, mere coin of verbal currency with no value of its own. In early language, the word was on the contrary a living thing with essential powers of signification; its root meanings were remembered because they were still in use, its wealth of force was vividly present to the mind of the speaker. We say "wolf" and think only of the animal, any other sound would have served our purpose as well, given the convention of its usage; the ancients said "tearer" and had that significance present to them. We say "agni" and think of fire, the word is of no other use to us; to the ancients "agni" means other things besides and only because of one or more of its root meanings was applied to the physical object—fire. Our words are carefully limited to one or two senses, theirs were capable of a great number and it was quite easy for them if they so chose, to use a word like Agni, Varuna or Vayu as a sound-index of a great number of connected and complex ideas, a key-word. It cannot be doubted that the Vedic Rishis did take advantage of this greater potentiality of their language,—note their dealings with such words as *gau* and *chandra*. The *Nirukta* bears evidence to this capacity and in the *Brahmanas* and *Upanishads* we find the memory of this free and symbolic use of words still subsisting.

Certainly, Dayananda had not the advantage that a comparative study of languages gives to the European scholar. There are defects in the ancient Nirukta which the new learning, though itself sadly defective, still helps us to fill in and in future we shall have to use both sources of light for the elucidation of the Veda. Still this only affects matters of detail and does not touch the fundamental principles of Dayananda's interpretation. Interpretation in detail is a work of intelligence and scholarship and in matter of intelligent opinion and scholarship men seem likely to differ to the end of the chapter, but in all the basic principles, in those great and fundamental decisions where the eye of intuition has to aid the workings of the intellect, Dayananda stands justified by the substance of the Veda itself, by logic and reason and by our growing knowledge of the past of mankind. The Veda does hymn the one Deity of many names and powers; it does celebrate the divine Law and man's aspiration to fulfil it; it does purport to give us the law of the cosmos.

On the question of revelation I have left myself no space to write. Suffice it to say that here too Dayananda was perfectly logical and it is quite grotesque to charge him with insincerity because he held to and proclaimed the doctrine. There are always three fundamental entities which we have to admit and whose relations we have to know if we would understand existence at all, God, Nature and the Soul. If, as Dayananda held on strong enough grounds, the Veda reveals to us God, reveals to us the law of Nature, reveals to us the relations of the soul to God and Nature, what is it but a revelation of divine Truth? And if, as Dayananda held, it reveals them to us with a perfect truth, flawlessly, he might well hold it for an infallible Scripture. The rest is a question of the method of revelation, of the divine dealings with our race, of man's psychology and possibilities. Modern thought, affirming Nature and Law but denying God, denied also the possibility of revelation; but so also has it denied many things which a more modern thought is very busy reaffirming. We cannot demand of a great mind that it shall make itself a slave to vulgarly received opinion or the transient dogmas of the hour; the very essence of its greatness is this, that it looks beyond, that it sees deeper.

In the matter of Vedic interpretation, I am convinced that whatever may be that final complete interpretation, Dayananda will be honoured as the first discoverer of the right clues. Amidst the chaos and obscurity of old ignorance and agelong misunderstanding his was the eye of direct vision that pierced to the truth and fastened on that which was essential. He has found the keys of the doors that time had closed and kept as under the seals of the imprisoned fountains.

AUROBINDO GHOSH

Chapter VI

RELIGIOUS TEACHINGS

I know the all-pervading Supreme Being who is exalted above all, glorious like unto the suns and aloof from darkness. By knowing Him alone is death conquered. Except this, there is no other road leading to Salvation.

Yajur, xxxi, 18

1. The Ten Principles

In previous chapters we have described the genesis of the Arya Samaj. It was originally founded at Bombay in 1875, but its Principles were revised at Lahore in 1877 when they were given their final shape. Its constitution was also finally settled at the same time. The Ten Principles to which every Arya is required to subscribe when he applies for membership constitute the only authoritative exposition of its beliefs and its doctrines:

1. God is the primary cause of all true knowledge and of everything known by its means.

2. God is All-truth, All-knowledge, All-beatitude, Incorporeal, Almighty, Just, Merciful, Unbegotten, Infinite, Unchangeable, Without A Beginning, Incomparable, the Support and the Lord of All, All-pervading, Omniscient, Imperishable, Immortal, Exempt From Fear, Eternal, Holy and the Cause of the Universe. To Him alone worship is due.

3. The *Vedas* are the Books of true knowledge, and it is the paramount duty of every Arya to read or hear them read, to teach and read them to others.

4. An Arya should always be ready to accept truth and to renounce untruth.

5. All actions must conform to virtue, i.e. should be performed after a thorough consideration of right and wrong.

6. The primary object of the Samaj is to benefit the whole world, viz. by improving the physical, spiritual, and social condition of mankind.

7. All ought to be treated with love, justice and with due regard to their merits.

8. Ignorance must be dispelled and knowledge diffused.

9. No one should remain content with his own good alone, but every one should regard his or her prosperity as included in that of others.

10. In matters which affect the general social well-being of all, no one should allow his or her individuality to interfere with the general good, but in strictly personal affairs everyone may act with freedom.[1]

Nothing beyond these Ten Principles has any binding force. The only doctrinal teaching included therein is that embodied in the first three Principles, which sum up the belief of the Arya Samaj in God, its conception of the Godhead, and its teaching about the *Vedas*. This, assuredly, is the simplest of creeds, to which no Hindu, at any rate, should have any difficulty in subscribing. A comparison of these Principles with those enacted originally at Bombay, in 1875, lends weight to the suggestion that their revision was devised to keep all dogma in the background and to free the Principles from all controversial issues. It is stated, in fact, that the object was to make the Arya Samaj as catholic as possible without sacrificing its Hindu character.

We have already mentioned that on the occasion of the Swami's visit to Calcutta in 1869 the leaders of the Brahmo Samaj conferred with him with a view to winning him over to their society and securing his powerful support for their propaganda. It took but little time, however, to make it evident that such an agreement was well-nigh impossible. The Brahmo Samaj would not accept the infallibility of the *Vedas* or the doctrine of the transmigration of souls: it was pledged to the negation of both. Swami Dayanand, on the other hand, could not be a party to any propaganda which would militate against or ignore either. In the words of Max Muller, "he considered the *Vedas* not only as divinely inspired, but as prehistoric or prehuman." To him everything contained in the *Vedas* was perfect truth. In this he was in

---

[1] The translation of these Principles must be regarded as approximate only. Some of the original words, such as Dharma and Adharma, have no exact equivalents in English. The Tenth Principle is intended to make personal freedom subordinate to the general welfare.

full accord with the ancient theologians of India, who all, without exception, regarded the *Vedas* as divine, or superhuman. To him a Church that ignored this basic principle of faith was unthinkable—all the more a Church that should be Aryan or Hindu in its origin and conception. He based his stand on the *Vedas*. These holy writings were his great weapon against the stronghold of the latter-day and corrupt Hinduism. Whatever was contained in the *Vedas* was, in his opinion, beyond all controversy, and in this he had the unanimous support of all that was sacred to the Hindus. Every branch of the sacred literature of the Hindus from the earliest times, down to the most modern compositions of the different forms of Hindu faith, was unanimous on that point, and unhesitatingly accepted the authority of the *Vedas* as final and conclusive.

From the *Upanishads*, to which Schopenhauer has paid the highest compliment possible for any human composition,[2] down to the latest manual of Puranic Hinduism, all branches of Hindu literature are in agreement on that point. Even the philosophers and freethinkers would not reject the *Vedas*: the great founders of the six schools of Hindu philosophy, each in his own way, accept the authority of the *Vedas* as conclusive. So does Shankaracharya; and so do the great lawgivers, viz. Manu, Yajnyavalka, Parasara, Apasthamba, and others. Even the Tantrikas profess to base their propaganda on their reading of the *Vedas*. The *Puranas*, of course, with one voice, accept them as divine and infallible. In fact, in the whole range of Indian thought and Indian culture, the only dissentients on the point are the Buddhists, the Jains, and the Charvakas (atheists), who were originally considered to be beyond the pale of Hinduism. Even the Brahmo Samaj had started out with faith in the revealed character and divine origin of the *Vedas*.[3] The *Vedas* were the

---

[2] "Oh! how thoroughly is the mind here washed clean of all early engrafted Jewish superstition and of all philosophy that cringes before that superstition! In the whole world there is no study except that of the original so elevating as that of the *Upanishads*. It has been the solace of my life, and it shall be the solace of my death."

[3] Max Muller, in his *Biographical Essays*, says: "Ram Mohan Roy also and his followers held for a time to the revealed character of the *Vedas*, and in all their early controversies with Christian missionaries they maintained that there was no argument in favour of the divine inspiration of the *Bible* which did not apply with the same or even greater force to the *Vedas*." (Page 168). Speaking of Ram Mohan Roy, Prof. Max Muller says: "He never became a Mahomedan, he never became

sheet-anchor of Dayanand's propaganda and his scheme of reform. In the words of Max Muller, the idea had taken "such complete possession of his mind that no argument could ever touch it." It was impossible to oust him from that position, as the leaders of the Brahmo Samaj soon discovered. So the attempt to win him over to the Brahmo Samaj failed as early as 1869.

In 1877, again, when most of India's eminent men were assembled at Delhi at the great Darbar which Lord Lytton, the Viceroy and Governor-General of India, had convened to announce the assumption of the title of "Empress of India" by Queen Victoria, an attempt was made to propagate doctrines which would be acceptable to Indians of all communities—Hindus, Musulmans, Christians, and Parsis alike. Dayanand, Syed Ahmad, and Keshab Chunder Sen were among those who participated in this conference, but they soon realized that the attempted reconciliation was out of the question. In our opinion it was even preposterous, however patriotic the attempt might have proved from a social and political point of view. Even on that occasion Swami Dayanand would not subscribe to any religion that ignored the *Vedas*.

We have reason to think that soon afterwards, when he visited Lahore, some persons tried to induce him to omit from the Principles of the Arya Samaj the article relating to the *Vedas*; but this was a proposition which he would not heed, and with good reason. His aim was the revival of the Vedic religion and the reform of the abuses that had crept into Hindu society, not the establishment of a new creed. All that he would assent to, was a change in the wording of the disputed Principle so that it would include all the varying opinions expressed about the *Vedas* by the renowned thinkers and writers of the various schools of Hindu thought prior to the birth of the Buddha.[4] It was not his wish to impose his own

a Christian, but he remained to the end a Brahman, a believer in the *Veda* and in the one God, Who, as he maintained, had been revealed in the *Veda*." (Page 33).

[4] "One more common element presupposed by Indian philosophy might be pointed out in the recognition of the supreme authority and the revealed character ascribed to the *Veda*... The Sankhya philosophy (Agnostic school) is supposed to have been originally without a belief in the revealed character of the *Vedas*, but it certainly speaks of *Sruti* (Sutras, 1.5). As long as we know the Sankhya, it recognizes the authority of the *Veda*, calling it Sabd (Word), and appeals to it even in matters of minor importance." *The Six Systems of Indian Philosophy*, Max Muller, 1903, p. 111. For a fuller discussion of the subject see page 206.

faith on all who could join the Arya Samaj. He wanted them to follow and abide by the unanimous opinion of the great sages, divines and scholars. When, therefore, it was mooted to him that in wording the Principles of the Arya Samaj he should adopt the language of the Rishis, he received the suggestion gladly and put it into effect.

Thus is explained the obvious difference between the language of the Principles as enunciated at Bombay in 1875, and as finally settled at Lahore in 1877.

2. *The Split in the Arya Samaj*

A great controversy has raged in the Arya Samaj for the last twenty-five years as to how far the opinions expressed by Swami Dayanand are binding on the Arya Samaj in toto. In 1892 the Arya Samaj split into two sections, ostensibly because of a difference of opinion (a) as to the righteousness of a meat diet, and (b) as to the lines on which the Dayanand Anglo-Vedic College at Lahore, founded in memory of Swami Dayanand in 1886, was to be conducted. The principle that underlay this difference concerned the authority of Dayanand. The party that was opposed to a meat diet and considered it unrighteous maintained that, as Swami Dayanand had expressed that opinion, it should be binding on the Arya Samaj, and no one who held a different opinion could be or remain a member of that body. Some members of this party—and their number was not inconsiderable then—went to the extent of maintaining that the Swami was infallible; others held that, so long as a greater authority on the *Vedas* did not emerge the Arya Samaj was bound by the teachings of Dayanand and by his interpretation of the *Vedas*. The opposite party would not accept that verdict. They averred that the teachings of Swami Dayanand were not binding on the Arya Samaj, and that a member was at liberty to believe in the Ten Principles only, and in nothing more, that although it was true that Swami Dayanand had expressed an opinion unfavourable to a meat diet, which the Samaj had tacitly accepted, yet the Samaj had no right to question the individual's right of private judgment in matters not strictly covered by the Principles. They conceded the right of the majority to determine what should be preached from the pulpit of the Samaj, but they would not consent to the majority sitting in judgment on individuals and dictating what they must believe beyond what was contained in the Principles of the Arya Samaj.

When the schism actually took place, it presented the unusual spectacle of large numbers of vegetarians, who were so both by conviction and by caste rules, uniting with those who upheld freedom of thought and conscience for the individual, and of some who actually indulged in a meat diet remaining with the opposing party. The position of the former party may be summed up in the language of one of its foremost exponents (namely, Mulraj, M.A., the first President of the Arya Samaj, when it was established at Lahore in 1877) in the following extracts from a lecture delivered at Lahore in 1892:

"It is known to all that he founded the Arya Samaj on the Ten *Niyams* (Principles, or Articles of Faith). He required that to become a member of the Arya Samaj one should believe in the Ten *Niyams*. If a man believed in the Ten *Niyams*, the Swami thought that he could become a member of the Arya Samaj whatever his opinion on other subjects might be. He did not make it an essential condition for membership of the Samaj that a man should believe his translation of the *Vedas* to be correct, or the opinions expressed by him in his works to be sound. He was not questioned as to his belief or disbelief in the many excellent theories and philosophical opinions with which the works of Swami Dayanand abound. He was never asked what he thought of the works of Swami Dayanand and of the translation he was making of the *Vedas*. He was never required to believe Swami Dayanand's translation of the *Vedas* to be infallible, or to state that he regarded the works of Swami Dayanand to be free from mistakes. He was never required to sacrifice his freedom of thought and speech."

Again:

"I believe the religion which the Arya Samaj preaches is the only religion which can become the common religion of the Hindus. It suits the masses and also the advanced section of the people. It can satisfy the orthodox Hindus as well as those who have received an English education. It can be accepted by people who are in different stages of intellectual development.

It is simple and so can extend over a large tract, if it cannot become universal. It requires belief in one true God and in the *Vedas* only. There are no theoretical questions or doctrines included in the Principles of the Arya Samaj. If Swami Dayanand had made it an essential condition for entering the Arya Samaj that a man should believe in particular doctrines, I do not think he could have succeeded so well in the achievement of his great object—the revival of the study of *Vedas* and the worship of one true God. Belief in particular doctrines presupposes a certain amount and line of education and a particular bent of mind. Only those who have a certain kind of education and the required mood of mind and training can accept a particular doctrine or philosophical theory. Those whose minds are not prepared for the understanding or reception of a theory can neither understand it nor believe it to be correct. The greater the number of the theories which a religion requires its followers to believe in, the smaller will be the number of men who can embrace that religion. If, then, Swami Dayanand had introduced philosophical questions, doctrines and theories into the Articles of Faith of the Arya Samaj, he would have limited the number of men who could have entered it. He would have thus curtailed the usefulness of the Arya Samaj by limiting the sphere of its action, and defeated his own object. For, the greater the number of men who can join together to revive the study of the *Vedas* and the worship of the unincarnate God, the greater will be the good they can do to themselves and to humanity. The greater the number of men who can enter the Arya Samaj, the greater will be the good they can do by spreading pure religion, truth, and godliness.

"We must be thankful that the Arya Samaj has been placed upon a very broad and catholic basis: the basis of belief in one eternal God and in the *Vedas*. We must be thankful that doctrines, philosophical matters and theoretical questions have not been included in the Articles of Faith of the Arya Samaj. The Hindus must be thankful that Swami Dayanand has turned their attention to the one religion which is pure and grand. He has not given them any new religion. He has drawn their attention to what was old and latent in the Hindu mind. He told them that the Aryas who were the ancestors of the modern Hindus, believed in one true God and in the *Vedas*, and he asked them to believe in the *Vedas* and to worship the Almighty God sung in them. On the broad and common platform of this religion, which is simple and free from philosophical theories, men whose minds are in different stages of development and who have different modes of thinking can come together to revive the study of the *Vedas* and to worship and glorify the Omnipresent Being Who was adored by our ancestors.

"I cannot help admiring the greatness and moderation of Swami Dayanand Saraswati. He was a great Sanskrit scholar...... He placed before the public his translation of the *Vedas* and the views he had on philosophical questions, and left the public to believe what was good in his interpretation and exposition... He admitted that the Rishis who had gone before him, the Rishis who had composed the *Brahmanas*, the Sutras, the Angas, Upangas, and the Upvedas were greater men than himself, and much better and abler scholars, and that his translations and expositions must be read in the light of the old commentators. He did not claim to be infallible......

"Swami Dayanand purposely abstained from entering in the *Niyams* any doctrinal points and philosophical questions. He believed in all he wrote, but he had toleration for the views of others. He knew that it is almost impossible to make all men have the same and identical views on doctrinal points and philosophical questions. He therefore wisely excluded from the *Niyams* all doctrinal points and pihlosophical questions, though he was not afraid of expressing his opinions on those matters frankly and boldly in his works. It would be indeed absurd to make a belief one way or the other in philosophical questions to be an essential condition for entering a religious society...... Is it not absurd that a man should be told that he cannot become a member of the Arya Samaj unless he believes in the doctrine of Niyog or the theory that vegetables have souls? Swami Dayanand was a wise man and saw this, and so purposely excluded doctrinal points and philosophical matters from the Principles of the Arya Samaj."

We have given this quotation from the lecture of Mulraj, because the lecturer had a certain right to say what were the intentions of those who co-operated with Swami Dayanand in reforming the Samaj in 1877, and in giving final shape to its

Principles. He was the first President of the reconstituted Samaj, and was in the confidence of the founder up to the latter's death, as evidenced by the fact that in 1882, when he made his will, he assigned Mulraj a high position (that of Vice-President) in the body which he nominated therein to act as his executors, with Maharana Sajjan Singh, the ruling chief of Udaipur, as its President. It is clear from this quotation that the founder and those associated with him in reorganizing the Samaj in 1877 did not intend to impose a creed on the members thereof beyond what was contained in the first three Principles, but it was soon manifest that it was impossible to carry on propaganda on those lines. The beliefs of Swami Dayanand were tacitly accepted as the doctrines of the Arya Samaj and formed its propaganda. No one raised any question for fully fifteen years, when the vexed question of meat diet was unfortunately pushed to the foreground on reasons more or less personal in their origin. Those who supported this practice argued that without a definite creed it was impossible to carry on any religious propaganda. They saw the perils of eclecticism, which had retarded the progress of the Brahmo Samaj, and did not wish the same fate to overtake the Arya Samaj.

In discussing the position of Christianity vis-à-vis "its relations to Hinduism," Mr. Blunt, I.C.S., makes the following observations in his Census Report for 1911:[5]

"The position of Christianity in India is very similar to the position it occupied in the early centuries of its era, in a Pagan Europe......It is that of a definite, clear-cut religion in opposition to an enormous and unwieldy congerie of divergent beliefs, both high and low. Its strength lies in its definiteness; the weakness of its opponent in its lack of cohesion." The "Christian always possesses the same creed, whilst a Hindu possesses no creed." Whilst we question the correctness of the view that the Christian "always possesses the same creed," we accept the general accuracy of the statement about Hinduism. The founder of the Arya Samaj saw through the difficulty and aimed at defining Hinduism. His definition has the merit of comprehensiveness and was made as little credal as was possible under the circumstances; but its vagueness and

[5] Page 144.

indefiniteness exposed it to the same danger from which it aimed to extricate Hinduism. The early leaders of the Arya Samaj, quite unconsciously, felt this indefiniteness, and, without devoting any further thought to the matter, made good what was lacking by adopting the beliefs of Swami Dayanand as the creed of the Arya Samaj, and on the strength of that creed gave battle to all who opposed them. When, therefore, in the early nineties, the question was raised by the so-called "meat-eaters" how far the Arya Samaj was bound by the doctrines of Dayanand, some of the vegetarians began to say that Dayanand was infallible, but the bulk of them wished to keep the authority of Dayanand unimpaired on the grounds stated above. They thought that there could be no propaganda without a definite creed; that the Arya Samaj had virtually and unambiguously accepted the creed of Dayanand. The "meat-eaters" acquiesced in so far as propaganda was concerned, but they would not interfere with the liberty of the individual in the matter of beliefs outside the Principles which had conceded to every individual the right to go his own way so far as his personal affairs were concerned.

There are obstacles to either view, which both parties recognize. They are prepared to permit a certain latitude to individual opinion on matters religious, but they are not prepared to be deprived of a creed. They feel that the moment they decided to do so, they would lose what so far has proved to be an invaluable element of force and weight in the general progress of their movement.

In his *Expansion of England*, Sir John Seeley passes a rather adverse judgment on the "facile comprehensiveness of Hinduism", which, in his opinion, "has enfeebled it as a uniting principle and rendered it incapable of generating true national feeling."

In the opinion of Sir Herbert Risley, "it may be admitted that the flame of patriotic enthusiasm will not readily arise from the cold grey ashes of philosophic compromise, and that before Hinduism can inspire an active sentiment of nationality, it will have to undergo a good deal of stiffening and consolidation.[6]

"The Arya Samaj," he adds, "seems to be striking out a

---

[6] *The Peoples of India*, by Sir Herbert Risley, 1904, p. 280.

path which may lead in this direction, but the tangled jungle of Hinduism bristles with obstacles and the way is long." In another place he gives the Aryas the credit of "a definite creed resting upon scriptures of great antiquity and high reputation," and characterises their teaching as 'bold and masculine" and "free from the limp eclecticism which has proved fatal to the Brahmo Samaj."[7]

A similar opinion has also been expressed by Mr. Blunt, I.C.S., in his Census Report for the United Provinces, 1911.[8] In his opinion, an element of strength in the Arya Samaj is its freedom from "the formlessness and indefiniteness of Hindu polytheism on one side and the weak eclecticism of such reformed sects as the Brahmo Samaj on the other."[9]

To sum up, we are quite secure in saying that the teachings of Dayanand, though not embodied in the Principles of the Arya Samaj, constitute its creed for all practical purposes. The teachings of Dayanand are, in their turn, the teachings of the ancient Indian sages based on the *Vedas*.

3. Creed of the Arya Samaj

A detailed statement of the teachings to which we have referred has been made in a previous chapter. Here we propose to discuss the meaning of the most important of them as accepted by the Arya Samaj.

The first and by far the most important is the Aryan conception of the Godhead. It is contained in the second of the Ten Principles of its official creed. In brief, the Arya Samaj believes in God and enjoins that He alone is worthy of our adoration. There is no longer any doubt in the minds of all competent and impartial students of Hindu scriptures and Hindu literature that the monotheism of Hinduism is of the most exclusive and most exalted kind,[10] as the following citations from the *Vedas* amply demonstrate:

[7] Ibid. p. 244.
[8] P. 133.
[9] "The Arya Samaj alone has provided a manly and straightforward creed which is in all essentials thoroughly Hindu."—*Census Report for U.P. for 1911*, p.143.
[10] Schlegel says: "It cannot be denied that the early Indians possessed a knowledge of the true God. All their writings are replete with sentiments and expressions, noble, clear, lovely, grand, as deeply conceived as in any human language in which men have spoken of their God."

From the "Rig-Veda"

1. They call Him Indra, Mitra, Varuna, Agni, and he is heavenly noble-winged Garutman.[11] He is one, sages call Him by many names, viz. Agni, Yama, Matarisvan.

R. i, 164, 46

2. Many are Thy names, O Agni, Immortal, God, Divine, Jatavedas, and many Charms of Charmers,[12] All-inspirer! have they laid in Thee,[13] Lord of True Attendants!

R. iii, 20, 3

3. Agni! men seek Thee as a Father with their prayers. They win Thee, O source of light, to brotherhood by holy actions. Thou art a Son to him who duly worships Thee. Thou guardest him from injury as a trusty Friend.

R. ii, 1, 9

4. What God shall we adore with our oblation?
The Great One who is the sole Ruler of all the moving world that breathes and slumbers, and is the Lord of bipeds and quadrupeds.

R. x, 121, 3

The Rev. J. Bryce admits that "there is every reason to believe that there existed a period in the Hindu history when the Brahma was the sole object of religious adoration."

The Rev. Mr. Ward says: "it is true, indeed, that the Hindus believe in the Unity of God. 'One Brahma without a Second' is a phrase very commonly used by them when conversing on subjects which relate to the nature of God. They believe also that God is Almighty, All-wise, Omnipotent, Omniscient."

Mr. Charles Coleman says: "The Almighty, Infinite, Eternal, Incomprehensible, Self-existent Being, He who sees everything though never seen, He who is not to be compassed by description and who is beyond the limits of human conception, is Brahma, the one unknown true Being, the Creator, the Preserver and Destroyer of the Universe. Under such and innumerable other definitions is the Deity acknowledged in the *Vedas* or the sacred writings of the Hindus."

Colonel Kennedy says: "Every Hindu who is in the least acquainted with the principles of his religion must in reality acknowledge and worship God in Unity."

Count Bjornstjerna, after giving a quotation from the *Vedas*, says: "These truly sublime ideas cannot fail to convince us that the *Vedas* recognize only one God, who is Almighty, Infinite, Eternal, Self-existent, the Light and the Lord of the Universe."

Maurice is assured "that the Brahman is seeking after one Divine, Unseen Object, nay, that his aim in his whole life and discipline is to purify himself from outward, sensible things that he may approach better to this one Source of Illumination."

Mr. Colebrook says: "The ancient Hindu religion, as founded on the Hindu scriptures, recognized but one God."

[11] Garutman: Sun.
[12] Charms of Charmers: attractive features and winning virtues.
[13] They have laid in Thee means the wise and pious sages have seen in Thee and realized them.

5. From Thee as branches from a tree, O Agni, from Thee, Auspicious God! spring all our blessings. Wealth (bestowed by Thee) swiftly, strength in battle with our foemen, the rain besought of heaven, the flow of waters.

R. vi, 31, i

6. With might hath Indra spread out heaven and earth. By His power hath the sun been lighted up. In Him are contained all the creatures and in Him the purified Somas.

R. viii, 3, 6

7. This Purusha (Being) is (in) all that hath been and all that is to be; the Lord of immortality, transcending all that grows by food.

R. x, 90, 2

8. Agni is Lord of Amrita in abundance, Lord of the gift of wealth and heroic valour. O victorious God, let us not sit about Thee like men devoid of strength, beauty and worship.

R. vii, 4, 6

9. What God shall we adore with our oblation?

The great One Whose are these snow-clad mountains as well as the terrestrial and celestial seas, and Whose arms are these heavenly regions.

R. x, 121, 4

From the "Yajur Veda"

1. There is no measure of Him Whose glory' verily, is great,

Y. xxxii, 3

2. O Agni, be our nearest Friend: be Thou a kind Deliverer and gracious Friend. Excellent Agni, come Thou nigh to us and give us wealth most splendidly renowned.

Y. iii, 25

3. Of sin against the gods Thou art atonement. Of sin against mankind Thou art atonement. For sin against the fathers Thou atonest. Of sin against oneself Thou art atonement. Of every sort of sin Thou art atonement. The sin that I have committed unconsciously, of all that wickedness Thou art atonement.

Y. viii, 13

4. Him we invoke for aid who reigns supreme, the Lord of all that stands or moves, Inspirer of the soul, that He may promote the increase of our wealth. He, our infallible Keeper and Guard and Well-wisher.

Y. xxv, 18

5. This very God pervadeth all the regions. Yea, existent from the beginning, He abides in the centre of all. He has been and ever will be. Facing all directions He stands before you, O men.

Y. xxxii, 4

6. Indra the Rescuer, Indra the Helper, Hero who listens at each invocation. I call upon the mighty Indra invoked of many. May Indra, Bounteous Lord, prosper and bless us.

Y. xx, 50

7. Even He is Agni, He is Aditya, He is Vayu, He is Chandramas, He is Sukra, He is Brahma, He is Apa, He is Prajapati.

Y. xxxii, I

8. May every mortal elect the friendship of the guiding God. Each one solicits Him for wealth. Let him seek fame to prosper him.

Y. iv, 8

9. Thou Agni art the guardian God of sacred vows among mankind. Thou meet for praise at holy rites. Grant this much, Soma! bring yet more. Savitar who giveth wealth, hath given treasure unto us.

Y. iv, 16

10. I sing my song of praise to Him, Savitar, pervading earth and heaven, strong with the wisdom of the wise, and the giver of virtuous impulses, bestower of wealth, the well-beloved thoughtful Sage To Him I sing, at whose impulse the splendid light shone in heaven. Most wise, the golden-handed, hath measured the sky with skilled design.

Y. iv, 25

11. He is our kin, our Father and begetter, He knows all beings and all ordinances. Obtaining eternal life in Him, the gods have risen upward to the third high stage.

Y. xxxii, 10

12. He who is our Father and the Progenitor of all things, who rewards every one according to his deserts, who knows all the heavenly bodies and habitable globes, who gives

names to the wise as well as to the worlds He creates, Who is One without a second, in Whom all things are comprehended: Him let all strive to understand by means of friendly discussions. *Y.* xvii, 27

13. He is whom the souls (or the vital air) are clad in the eternal, expansive, subtle material cause of the universe, whom the yogis, with purified souls, immost recesses of the eternal souls and the primordial atom, who is sustained by His own power, in whom all the worlds are established:—Him do ye realize. *Y.* xvii, 31

14. He who extends beyond (or is exalted above) the luminous bodies, who extends beyond the earth, who extends beyond (i.e. is above the reach of) even the wise, who extends beyond the ignorant, in whom the vital airs sustain desirable objects, whom the sages, rich in knowledge and wisdom, can alone realize:—Him do ye try to know.
Y. xvii, 29

From the "Atharva Veda"

1. (1) To Him who rules the Past, the Present and the Future, who presides over the entire universe, who is the Sovereign Lord of all, above the reach of Time and Death (self-effulgent), immutable and absolute bliss—even to Him, the most exalted Brahm, be our homage! *A.* x, 23, 4

(2) To Him, who makes the Sun and Moon, the eyes of the universe, at the commencement of every creation, who has made Fire like unto a mouth—even to Him, the most exalted Brahm, be our homage! *A.* x, 10, 13, 4, 32

(3) To Him who has, in the universe, made the Earth and other habitable globes in place of the feet, who has made space in place of the womb, who has made the luminous bodies in place of the head—even to Him, the most exalted Brahm, be our homage! *A.* x, 10, 13, 4, 33

(4) To Him who has made the atmosphere as the life of the creation, who has made the rays of light as its eyes, who has made the directions of space as the organs of hearing —even to Him, the most exalted Brahm, be our homage!
A. x, 10, 13, 4, 34

2. Renown and glory, force and happiness, the Brahman's

splendour and food and nourishment to him who knoweth this God as one without a second. Neither second nor third, nor yet fourth is He called. He is called neither fifth, nor sixth, nor yet seventh. He is called neither eighth, nor ninth, nor yet tenth.

He watcheth over creatures, all that breatheth and breatheth not. This conquering might is possessed by Him. He is the sole, the simple one, the One alone. In Him all gods become simple and One. *A*, xiii, 4, 16 17, 18 and 21

3. Wide as the space which heaven and earth encompass, far as the flow of waters, far as Agni, vast as the quarters of the sky and regions that lie between them spread in all directions, vast as celestial tracts and views of heaven, stronger than these art Thou and great for ever, yea, stronger than aught that stands or twinkles, stronger art thou than ocean, O Kama, O Manyu. To Thee, to Thee I offer worship.
A. ix, 2, 20, 21 and 23

4. All this the royal Varuna beholdeth, all between heaven and earth and all beyond them. He has counted even the twinklings of men's eyes. As one who plays, throws dice, He settles all things.

A. iv, 16, 5

5. Indra art Thou, Mahendra art Thou, Thou art the world, the Lord of Life. To Thee is sacrifice performed: worshippers offer gifts to Thee.

A. xvii, i. 18

6. (1) He is Aryaman, He is Varuna, He is Rudra, He is Mahadeva.

(2) He is Agni, He is Surya, He verily is Mahayam.

A. xiii, 3, 4, 5

(2) The Arya Samaj believes that some persons (of either sex) may have more of the divine in them, in proportion to the degree of exaltation to which their spirits have risen, but that they never can be the same as God, and therefore must remain imperfect. Such persons deserve all honour from ordinary men as prophets, teachers, leaders, or great men; but they can never be mediators, in the sense in which that term is used in orthodox Christianity. The Arya Samaj believes that these exalted persons are the great benefactors

and uplifters of the human race; that they deserve the respect of every man, regardless of nationality, colour or creed; that human souls receive the greatest possible support and enlightenment by coming in contact with them and their thought, but that the salvation of each human soul must eventually depend upon his or her own exertions, and that faith in no other human soul can, *ipso facto*, save him or her. This teaching of the Arya Samaj is in direct conflict with popular Hinduism, as well as with popular Christianity.

(3) The Arya Samaj does not believe in the infallibility, or immunity from mistake or sin, of any human being, however exalted he may be in the spiritual sense. "To err is human" is thus accepted in its literal and widest sense.

(4) The only approved forms of worship are: Contemplation, Communion, and Prayer (Stuti, Prasathna and Upasana) coupled with purity of thought, word and deed. The only approved form of expiation is repentance as shown by determination not to sin again, in addition to such sacrifices as may help in the purification and uplifting of the soul from the effects of the sin committed.

(5) The Arya Samaj believes in the doctrine of Karma,[14] that "acts must be followed by their consequences, that the results of actions cannot be warded off or atoned for by any means." Says an authority: "An act cannot wear away without bearing fruit, even in millions of years; a man must necessarily eat the fruit of his good and evil deeds." This leads to the doctrine of the transmigration of souls which forms a part of the propaganda of the Samaj.

(6) The Samaj does not believe in Fate, unless it be confounded with the doctrine of Karma stated in (5). Every one can make and unmake his or her own destiny, subject to the eternal laws of God, including the law of Karma. Action, right earnest action, with confidence and faith, is the only way to undo Karma, in the sense that the fruits of fresh energetic action may over-ride and supersede previous Karma. Surrender to inaction or Fate means death.

(7) Swami Dayanand did not recommend ancestor-worship, in the sense in which it is followed by the Hindus in popular

---

[14] For Vedic authorities see *Satyarath Prakash*, by Dayanand, and *Punjab Census Report for 1911*, footnote on p. 108.

belief. In his opinion, such only of the dead ancestors deserve our loving remembrance, respect and homage as have been virtuous in their lives, or good and great and learned benefactors and leaders of the community, the nation, or the race. He enjoins, however, respect to and service to living parents and grandparents.

(8) The Samaj accepts the *Vedas* as infallible and expects every man and woman to know them and to expound them for the benefit of others. As explained before, it leaves every individual free to interpret them for himself or herself, subject to certain well-known laws of interpretation. The idea of progressive interpretation finds favour with some leaders of the Arya Samaj.

These constitute the principal religious teachings of the Samaj.

4. Religious Observances and Practices

Of these the Arya Samaj retains and enjoins the following:

I. The five daily Mahayajnas, i.e. the five principal religious practices to be observed every day:

(*a*) Brahma Yajna, which is two-fold, Sandhya and Swadhya. The former is worship of God, morning and evening, by contemplation, communion and prayer; and the latter is the regular reading of some portion of the scriptures once a day.

(*b*) Deva Yajna. This is the well-known *Homa*, i.e. burning of Ghee (clarified butter) and other articles in the fire, and is one of the most ancient practices of the Hindus. No Hindu ceremony is complete without *Homa* in some form or other. The Vedic texts which are repeated in this ceremony are among the most elevating and uplifting pages in the *Vedas*. The Hindu's day must begin with *Homa*, which purifies the household both physically and spiritually. No period of Hindu history is known in which it was discarded. With the degeneration of Hinduism its daily performance by every householder has fallen into disuse, as have also the other daily yajnas.[15]

(*c*) Pitri yajna (lit., the worship of parents) Some daily

[15] For an explanation of yajna, see Max Muller's *Physical Religion*. (Collected Works), 1898, pp. 107-10.

act of service towards one's parents, lest in the care of self and family, duty towards parents be forgotten. In the absence of a system of State Pensions for old age, this system ensures the care of the aged.

(d) Athithi yajna. The feeding of some learned man or ascetic who has not been invited beforehand, but who must be sought out every day. Hindu law recognizes no regular organization for the help of the student and the learned. The householders are supposed to look after and support them. To guard against personal idiosyncrasies or negligence, it is incumbent that every householder must feed one or more students or scholars, or others who may be engaged in the work of religion. It was considered an act of religious duty that such persons should be fed and looked after before the householder's family is fed, in recognition of their services to the cause of learning and religion. The ancient Hindu system did not recognize regularly-organized and well-endowed religious institutions; yet it enjoined on every one to devote the first part of life, up to 25 years, to study and the last years of life to religion and the service of mankind. The question of these persons' maintenance and living was solved by making it incumbent on every householder to entertain one or more of them every day. This voluntary provision was in lieu of some such compulsory provision as the rates levied on modern British householders to pay for the education and feeding of school children. It was further enjoined that the householder should seek them out, bring them to his house and feed them, so that they might not feel humiliated as being the objects of charity.

(e) The fifth and the last daily duty was in recognition of human dependence on domestic animals, and also in recognition of one's duty towards the poor, the helpless, the crippled, and the orphaned. It is called Bali Vaishwadeva yajna. It consists in giving food to as many of them as one can afford, according to one's means.

2. The sixteen Sanskars, i.e. sacraments or sacred ceremonies, beginning with conception and ending with cremation after death. The ritual is generally very simple and inspiring. There is nothing new in it. It is as old as the Aryas and follows the lines laid down by ancient lawgivers. All the later addi-

tions, accretions, and modifications have been dispensed with. Only as much is retained as is common to all schools of Hindu thought and is free from any kind of image-worship. All superstitious rites have been disallowed. These sixteen ceremonies are, so to say, sixteen mile-stones in each individual human life, and are therefore of some importance, to be celebrated with a certain amount of formality and display, according to the means of the householder who performs them.

Such is the only ritual recognized by the Arya Samaj, and is contained in a book compiled by Swami Dayanand from ancient authorities on the subject. This book is named *Sanskar Vidhi*.[16]

---

[16] "Orthodox Hinduism is too apt to lead to irreligion; a religion which gives ritual in place of a creed and unintelligible mantras in place of religious instruction, is bound to have such a result. And a thoughtful man will often be driven to turn to other creeds. Amid all the religions such a man has the choice of four. Brahmoism is nothing but a limp eclecticism; it has discarded the *Vedas* and put nothing in their place; it has adopted a belief here and a doctrine there, and when doubt arises leaves the individual to decide the doubt for himself. Such a religion has little vitality....Christianity and Islam are utterly irreconcilable with Hinduism in any shape or form...But Aryaism is different....It offers... which he most specially dislikes; it bases the order and its whole teaching on ...a bold, straightforward monotheism; it bids him discard all those superstitions in the *Vedas* which he reverences deeply though he probably reverences nothing else; it gives him a creed that he can believe, ceremonies that he can himself carry out, and a hope of salvation, if his deeds are good. At the same time, he need not break completely with the Hindu social system..."—*United Provinces Census Report for 1911*, p. 138.

Sanskar Vidhi has been translated into English by Pandit Ganga Prashad.

CHAPTER VII

RELIGIOUS IDEALS AND AIMS

Let what you drink, your share of food be common, together with one common bond I bind you. Serve Agni, gathered round Him like the spokes about the Chariot's nave.

With binding charm I make you all united, obeying one sole leader, and one-minded.

Ath. iii, 30, 6 and 7

1. The Christianizing of India

At the birth of Dayanand, in 1824, British rule in India was in its preliminary stages. Large tracts of country of what came to be known as British India were still under Indian governments. The whole of the Punjab, Sindh, and the Central Provinces took about a quarter of a century to be brought under British sway. Even in parts in the immediate occupancy of "John Company," British rule was more or less in a fluid state, and British institutions yet in their infancy. Facilities for education were few and far between. "The very scanty encouragement originally given to education by the East India Company was confined to promoting the study of Sanskrit and Persian still in use in the Indian courts of law in order to qualify young Indians for government employment and chiefly in the subordinate posts of the judicial service."[1] Missionary propaganda, however, seems to have been in full swing, at least in the Presidency towns of Calcutta, Bombay, and Madras. By an easy effort of imagination we can see Raja Ram Mohan Roy discussing the merits of Christian religion with Mr. Arnot or Mr. Adam, in his garden house at Calcutta in the summer of 1818, about six years before Dayanand was born. The missionaries had also opened some schools. We are told by Sir Valentine Chirol that "it was in direct opposition to Carey and other earlier missionaries" that Dr. Alexander Duff made up his mind to

[1] *Indian Unrest*, by V. Chirol, p. 208.

establish "the supremacy of the English language over the vernacular" as a preliminary to the Christianization of India, and that it was Dr. Duff's influence, as much as that of Macaulay, which enabled Lord William Bentinck's government to decide that "the great object of the British Government ought to be the promotion of English literature and science."[2]

A study of Raja Ram Mohan Roy's life, and of the tracts published by him between 1820 and 1830, gives an inkling of the fierce controversy then raging between the Christian missionaries and the champions of the Hindu religion under the leadership of the Raja. It appears that no effort was spared to convert the Raja to Christianity. We have it on the authority of Professor Max Muller, who quotes a certain Mr. Adam, an American missionary, a contemporary and a friend of Raja Ram Mohan Roy, that "Dr. Middleton, the first Bishop of Calcutta, thought it his duty to endeavour to convert Ram Mohan Roy to Christianity, and, in doing so, he dwelt not only on the truth and excellence of his own religion, but spoke of the honour and repute, the influence and usefulness he would acquire by becoming the Apostle of India," and that Raja Ram Mohan Roy expressed his bitter indignation that he should have been deemed capable of being influenced by any consideration but the love of truth and goodness, and he never afterwards visited the Bishop again."[3]

It is well known in historical circles that the Christian missionaries wielded vast political influence on the East India Company's administration. Sir Valentine Chirol tells us that it was Dr. Alexander Duff "who inspired the probibition of Suttee and other measures which marked the withdrawal of the countenance originally given by the East India Company to religious practices incompatible, in the opinion of earnest Christians, with the sovereignty of a Christian Power," and who influenced the decision of the Government in favour of English education.[4] It is asserted

---

[2] Ibid. p. 209.
[3] *Biographical Essays*, by Max Muller, 1884, p. 24.
[4] *Indian Unrest*, p. 209. It would be more accurate to say; "who inspired the policy of the East India Company to interfere with such religious practices of the Hindus as in the opinion of earnest Christians were incompatible with the sovereignty of a Christian Power."

that Dr. Duff's authority was "great both at home and in India, and was reflected equally in Lord Hardinge's Educational Order of 1844, which threw open a large number of posts in the public services to English-speaking Indians."

It is thus clear that between 1824, the year of Swami Dayanand's birth, and 1845, the year of his flight from home, Christian missionaries exercised a predominant influence on Government policy. Dr. Duff himself opened an English school in 1830, and succeeded in converting some of his most brilliant pupils to Christianity.

By the time Swami Dayanand embarked on his public life, Christianity had made great strides in India. The country was dotted with Christian schools and colleges and covered with a network of Christian agencies. The voice of the Brahmo Samaj was a mere wail in the wilderness. The Brahmo leaders' chief weapon was rationalism, which could appeal to but a few. Even in the case of these, the Brahmo Samaj at that time was considered to be a sort of reformed or refined Christianity, resembling more the Unitarian Church than the monotheism of the *Vedas* or the Vedicism of Ram Mohan Roy. Whatever little of Hinduism it contained in its original form gradually dropped out, as the leadership passed into hands grown vigorous on English food and English thought. This phase of Brahmo teaching reached its zenith in the Christian rhapsodies of Babu Keshub Chunder Sen, whose teachings on Christ and Christianity left only a thin partition between orthodox Christianity and Brahmoism. Max Muller, in one of his letters to *The Times* (24th November, 1880), puts it into the mouth of one of Keshub's critics, the Rev. Charles Voysey, to say that "Believers in Keshub Chunder Sen have forfeited the name of Theists because this leader has more and more inclined to the doctrines of Christianity."[5] Keshub Babu's "earliest profession of faith in Christ" was made as far back as 1866. In a letter addressed to Professor Max Muller by Babu W. N. Gupta, on behalf of the Brahmo Missionary Conference in 1880, the writer added that "one of the main causes of irritation" was "the Minister's (i.e. Keshub's) allegiance to Christ."[6]

[5] *Biographical Essays*, p. 89.
[6] Ibid. p. 98.

Another Christian writer, Mr. Frank Lillington, in his book entitled *The Brahmo Samaj and Arya Samaj, in their Bearing on Christianity*, published in 1901, refers to "the Christianity of the Brahmo Samaj of India". It is true that the Brahmo Samaj never accepted the divinity of the historical Christ in the same sense in which orthodox Christianity accepts it, but it cannot be denied that it went perilously near doing so, and the Sadharan Brahmo Samaj was a protest against Keshub's interpretation of Christianity and his exposition of the New Dispensation started by him. Torn by internal dissensions of this character, the Brahmo Samaj had ceased to be an effective shield for the protection of Hindu theism from the assaults of Christians when Swami Dayanand completed his education with Virjananda about 1860.

Raja Ram Mohan Roy's teaching was a denial of the superiority of the West in matters spiritual. He maintained that Hindu theism was as good as, if not better than, Christian theism even at its best. Maharishi Debendranath Tagore was also firm on that point to the last, although he had repudiated the infallibility of the *Vedas* on the testimony of four young men sent to Banaras to study and to pronounce upon their teaching. But Babu Keshub Chunder Sen's development was in a way a confession of Hindu inferiority, which once more strengthened the hands of the Christian missionary who at that moment was engaged in a most bitter campaign against Hinduism based on the opinions of Western scholars of Sanskrit.

The movement inaugurated by Sir William Jones and his colleagues had affected India in two ways. On the one hand, it brought to light the immensity and variety of Indian literature and made known to the European world the fact that Indians had produced immortal works on religion, philosophy, poetry, mathematics, etc., and were not quite the unlettered barbarians which the early English settlers had thought them to be. On the other hand, it placed a powerful weapon in the hands of the Christian missionary to use against Hinduism and what it stood for. Thus, by the time Swami Dayanand entered the field, "India had witnessed a change," the like of which had never been known before, viz. "the intellectual and moral conquest of the people by Englishmen." The picture has been so well drawn by an acknowledged leader of the Arya Samaj, Lala Hansraj, that I cannot do better than quote his words. Speaking at the Anniversary of the Lahore Arya Samaj, he said:

"...During the palmiest days of Mahomedan rule, the Hindus had never acknowledged themselves beaten by their masters in intellectual and moral progress. A Mahomedan Babar might defeat a Hindu Sanga and dispossess him of a portion of his territory, but even he had to bend before a Hindu Nanak. Akbar, Faizi, Jehangir, and Dara Shikoh had to bear testimony to the learning and saintliness of Hindu devotees. But with the advent of the English the case has become different. Hardly a day passes when we are not reminded of our inferiority. The railway, the telegraph and the factory speak in unmistakable terms both to the educated and the uneducated that Englishmen are far superior to them in the knowledge of natural laws and their application to the conveniences of human life. The wonderfully complex machine of administration which regulates our affairs displays to us high powers of organization in the nation that bears rule over us. The dramas of Shakespeare, the poems of Milton, and the writings of Bacon attest the intellectual eminence of the ruling people. The perseverance, truthfulness, courage, patriotism, and self-sacrifice of Englishmen excite feelings of respect and admiration in our minds. What wonder is it then that in their company we feel ourselves conquered and humiliated?

"Just at this moment of weakness, the missionary comes to us and whispers that the superiority of the European over the Indian is the gift of the Son of God whom he has acknowledged as his King and Saviour, and that Indians can really become great if they come under His banner. The idea thus insinuated is daily fed and strengthened by the education that he imparts to us through a large number of Mission Schools and Colleges that cover the country with their network. The missionary criticizes the evils that have of late corrupted our society, and proudly points to his own community as entirely free from those curses. He compares our sacred books with Christian scriptures, and proves to the satisfaction of many misguided people that the latter are infinitely superior to the former. He is also encouraged in his proselytizing work by the apathy of the Hindus towards religious instruction. They send their children to schools for secular education without making any provision for religious training at home or at school, with the result that our boys grow up utterly ignorant of the religious principles of their *Shastras*. No Christian father will ever entrust his sons to the care of one whom he believes to be inimical to his faith, but we do it daily, only to bewail the result of our folly when some mishap befalls us. The godless education of Government Schools and Colleges has increased our indifference to religion, and we have been so completely won over to the world that we are ready to sacrifice our highest religious interests for the slightest worldly advantage to ourselves.

"The labours of the Sanskrit scholars of Europe have also facilitated, though unconsciously, the path of the missionary. Accustomed to receive secular truths from the West without the slightest hesitation, our young men, unacquainted with the sublime truths of their own scriptures, are led to put implicit faith in the opinions of Western scholars on the subject of Hindu religion....I do not mean to blame such distinguished savants as Professors Max Muller and Monier Williams, or cast a slur on the world-wide reputation which they have deservedly won after years of toil in the sacred field of Sanskrit literature. European savants...have been misled by the commentaries of Indian Sanskrit scholars whom they have closely followed, and it is no fault of theirs if they have failed in fields where men more favourably situated than themselves had shared the same fate...

"The godless education of our Schools and Colleges has sapped the foundations of faith in God and His revealed will; our boys are taught to despise their own religious books and prize those of the foreigner; above all, the conviction has been brought home to us by the writings of European savants that, although we possess some philosophical works of inestimable value, our religious books contain a great deal of rubbish and nonsense interspersed with a few gems of truth that lie embedded in it. We are told that the *Vedas*, which are the basis of our religion and science, embody the childlike utterances of primeval man, that they teach the worship of the elements, and enjoin the practice of foolish rites that could attract children but are disgusting to civilized man."

2. *The Forces against Dayanand*

The forces, then, that Dayanand had to face, may briefly be summed up as follows:

1. The host of Brahmins, learned and unlearned, who had created for themselves a position of Supreme authority in the Hindu hierarchy and whose interests were vitally involved in the proposed reform movement. Their impregnable citadel was the established caste system, and they were backed by all the forces of ignorance, superstition, prejudice, custom and conservatism.

2. The organized forces of Christianity, supported on the one side by all the resources of civilization, moral, intellectual and political; on the other by an inexhaustible supply of men and money—men who had consecrated their lives to the cause of their religion and had made it their sacred duty to defend and to disseminate it at all costs; and money which could establish a network of philanthropic activity, many-sided and hydraheaded, ungrudging in sympathy and unstinted in flow.

3. The analytic tendencies of modern science, which denied God, revelation and religion, and established secularism and materialism on the throne formerly occupied by God.

4. The collapse of the prevailing Hindu system of thought, religion and life before 2 and 3.

5. The pessimism and inertia which had been engendered by centuries of political and intellectual decline; the apathy and indifference of the Hindus and their conviction that they had been hopelessly crushed perhaps never to rise again; and shame and fatalism born of intellectual and moral subjugation and stagnation.

6. The ever-active propaganda of Islam, which registered its victories in every nook and corner of the country, almost daily throughout the year, without the Hindus realizing the extent to which it was gaining ground.

3. His Fitness for his Task

All his life, Dayanand had studied the Hindu religion. All its forms and manifestations were thoroughly well known to him. Of Christianity and Islam, however, he was totally ignorant when he embarked on his work in 1860, excepting what he might have observed during his long travels, of the practices of his Muslim and Christian countrymen. But, as soon as he took up the idea of engendering a radical reform in Hindu thought, Hindu religion and Hindu life, he found that Hinduism had formidable rivals in Christianity and Islam, both of which threatened its very existence, if left unchecked and unresisted in their systematic efforts to displace Hinduism from the position it occupied in India. He concluded that a movement directed against current Hinduism alone might reform it away altogether unless at the same time he could dislodge its opponents from the vantage positions they held against it. He therefore devoted himself to a critical study of both these alien religions, with the assistance of friends who knew English and Arabic, and with the help of such literature as was available to him in the vernacular of the country. By this study he attained the reasoned conviction that Vedic theism was in many respects superior to even the theism of Islam, and very much superior to dogmatic Christianity. Having reached this conclusion, it did not take him long to decide that his movement must aim not only at a defence of Vedic Hinduism, but must go further and establish a new era of propaganda and conversion; or, in other words, that he must take the offensive also. What he aimed at was nothing short of a complete revolution in the mental and spiritual outlook of the Hindus. He believed that, although other religions contained some truth, the religion of the *Vedas* was the only absolutely true religion; that it was for all mankind; and that it was their duty to present it to mankind, irrespective of caste, colour, or country.

Dayanand had thus at the outset the idea of a universal mission, but at the same time he never forgot the prior claim of the religion in which he was born and to which he had the honour to belong. He aimed at world-conquest in the spiritual domain but he knew that this colossal task must be initiated at home, and that his first converts must be won from among his own people, who stood in greater need of his light than any other: therefore he decided that he must not only first expound his Hinduism to the Hindus, but that he must also teach them to defend it against all aggressors. He also decided that the best interests of an effective defence required that the defender should be prepared at every opening to take the offensive against his assailants, throwing upon them, in turn, the onus of defence; in plainer language, that he should be ready not only to meet criticism at all points, but also, in turn to criticize his critics and compel them to see the beams in their own eyes.

He wanted the Hindu mind to turn from passiveness to activity, to exchange the standard of weakness for the standard of strength; "in place of a steadily yielding defence" to take "the ringing cheer of the invading host."

Islam and Christianity, the rivals of Hinduism in India, were both proselytizing religions; it was therefore necessary to give the same character to Hinduism. Hinduism had made conversions in the past; it was quietly and unconsciously making conversions every day;[7] all that was needed was to create a conscious by active proselytizing spirit, which would take pride in its work. This in brief was the Swami's attitude towards other religions. If one comes across some mistakes in his statements concerning other religions they may be the mistakes of his informants, or of those on whose authority they have been taken and criticized. Mr. Blunt, in his *Census Report for the United Provinces*,[8] complains that the Aryas study a religion only in the works of its opponents. If this charge is true—which we do not admit—we have only to reply that in that respect the Arya is perhaps too apt a disciple of the Christian missionary; and, if evidence be required of this, such evidence will be forthcoming in abundance in the tracts against Hinduism, the Arya Samaj and Islam issued by the Christian Literary Society of Madras. We do not admire this spirit, but it is impossible to isolate it altogether from proselytizing zeal. It should not be forgotten that the Christian missionary was the first in the

---

[7] *Foreign Elements in the Hindu Population*, D. R. Bhandarkar and *Conversion and Reconversion to Hinduism During the Muslim Rule* by Sri Ram Sharma in his *Studies in Medieval Indian History*.

[8] See Census Reports; also Sir H. Risley's learned work on *The Peoples of India*.

field of controversy: he declared war upon Hinduism, and in doing so used the strongest possible language branding the greatest of Hindu heroes, like Krishna, adulterers, fornicators, and what not.

Dayanand's attitude towards other religions was a necessity of the times in which he lived, and partly due also to his ignorance of the languages in which the best literature of these religions was to be found. But, in our opinion, there is no justification for his followers to continue to hold that attitude, and the sooner the Arya Samajists come to this conclusion, the better for them and for their cause. The other religions of the world, including those of India, must be studied in the writings of their best exponents, and always spoken of in terms of respect and consideration, even if one is unable to accept them as true in their entirety.

4. *The Arya Samaj as the Parent of Unrest*

The Lieutenant-Governor of the Punjab, in replying to a deputation of the leading Arya Samajists, who in 1907 waited upon him to assure him that the Samaj, as such, had no hand in the political or agrarian disturbances of the year, is reported to have said that his officers informed him that wherever there was an Arya Samaj, it was the centre of unrest. We wonder if he realized that this verdict paid the greatest tribute to the work and to the spirit of the Arya Samaj greater even than what its illustrious founder could have ever wished. Mental unrest is holy. There can be no progress without unrest. But, to be quite just, the Arya Samaj is not the only source of unrest in India. The Government itself, with its educational policy and its Western methods of administration, has contributed materially towards that same unrest. The Arya Samaj may quite logically be pronounced an outcome of the conditions imported into India from the West, and as such it has absolutely no reason to repent or be ashamed of its share in adding to the volume or modifying the character of the unrest that was the inevitable consequence of modern conditions of life in India. That the Arya Samaj is one of the most potent nationalizing forces, no one can or need deny. <u>The Arya Samaj aims at radical changes in the thought and life of the people.</u> It aims at the formation of a new national character, on the fundamental basis of Vedic thought and Vedic life. It was essential for it to arouse dissatisfaction with the existing conditions in Hindu society; to create an urge for better thought and better life, an urge that was bound to bring about unrest. The Arya Samaj began its work by recalling the greatness of ancient India, and impressed upon the Hindus that the land of *Vedas* and Shastras had no right "to sink into the role of mere critic or imitator of European letters" or European life. Yet that was at best the condition of the Indian mind at the beginning of Dayanand's apostolic career. The Hindu mind which, till then, could not emerge from the vicious circle of mere forms or mere habits—and to some extent is even now in bondage—had to be broadened. So it has to be told that habit was only a factor in the evolution of character and not character itself; that mere personal refinement could not take the place of active ends and ideals, which are the elixir of life of all social organisms as of individuals; that mere "quietness, docility, resignation, and obedience" could not form a national character and that it was necessary to foster also "strength, initiative, sense of responsibility, and power of rebellion". The whole idea is expressed so beautifully by the late Sister Nivedita (Miss Noble), who had so completely identified herself with the Hindus' cause and than whom no truer friend of Hinduism was born in the British Isles, that no apology is necessary for appending a long quotation from one of her essays on Aggressive Hinduism. Looking on Hinduism "no longer as the preserver of Hindu custom, but as the creator of Hindu character", she observes:

"It is surprising to think how radical a change is entailed in many directions by this conception. We are no longer oppressed with jealousy or fear when we contemplate encroachments on our social and religious consciousness. Indeed, the idea of encroachment has ceased because OUR WORK IS NOT NOW TO PROTECT OURSELVES BUT TO CONVERT OTHERS. Point by point, we are determined, not merely to keep what we had, but to win what we never had before. The question is no longer of other people's attitude to us, but, rather, of what we think of them. It is not, how much have we left? but, how much have we annexed? We cannot afford, now, to lose, because we are sworn to carry the battle far beyond our remotest frontiers. We no longer dream of submission, because struggle itself has become only the first step towards a distant victory to be won.

"No other religion in the world is so capable of dynamic transformation as Hinduism. To Nagarjuna and Buddhaghosh the many was real, and the Ego unreal. To Shankaracharya, the one was real and the many and the one were the same, reality perceived differently and at different times by the human consciousness. Do we realize what this means? It means that CHARACTER IS SPIRITUALITY. It means that laziness and defeat are not renunciation. It means that to protect another is infinitely greater than to attain salvation. It means that Mukti lies in overcoming the thirst for Mukti (salvation). It means that conquest may be the highest form of Sannyas (renunciation). It means, in short, that Hinduism is become aggressive, that the trumpet of Kalki is sounded already in our midst, and that it calls all that is noble, all that is lovely, all that is strenuous and heroic amongst us to a battlefield on which the bugle of retreat shall never more be heard."[9]

In our judgement this represents the spirit of Dayanand's ideas, and it is his spirit which is working in the Arya Samaj.

5. *Dayanand's Claims for the Vedas*

It is often said by way of reproach that Dayanand made an extravagant and absurd claim on behalf of the *Vedas* in striving to show that in them was to be found every scientific truth. This is not the proper place for examining this claim in detail, but it may be said here that:

1. Dayanand does claim, and rightly, that in matters of religion and in the domain of spirit the Western mind has *not* attained either the depths or the heights commanded by the ancient Indian mind; and in such matters it still has much to learn from the ancient Indian sages.

2. In matters social, Indian solutions arrived at in ancient times are as good, as sound and as effective, at least, as are those arrived at in the West by the best modern thought.

3. In the domain of philosophy India has nothing to learn

[9] *Aggressive Hinduism*, by Sister Nivedita, pp. 10, 11, 12; Nateson & Co., Madras.

from the West. The cream of European thought does not yet come up to the level of the cream of Hindu thought. The most modern Western thought is apparently still groping in the dark and endeavouring to scale the heights reached by Indians centuries ago.

4. In the realm of physical science, the Europeans are far in advance of the ancient Indians, though it may fairly and justly be claimed that most of the fundamental truths on which the superstructure of European science is raised, were known to the Indians. For example, it was known to them that the earth was round and that the earth, the sun, the moon and the stars were in motion; they had made great progress in military science; they were the inventors of algebra, of decimals, and so on. For centuries the Hindus have believed that plants were in essence as much to be regarded as living creatures as were animals; and it redounds to their credit that the latest discovery in the same line of research—that every particle of matter has life—has been discovered and demonstrated by one of their descendants, namely, Professor J. C. Bose, of Calcutta. The fact that Hindus were well acquainted with anatomy and surgery, and were also chemists of no mean ability, has been amply proved and ungrudgingly admitted by European scholars.

Dayanand's claims, therefore, rest upon a substantial foundation. His object was not to give the Hindus matter and occasion for boasting, but to lift them from that slough of despondence into which they had fallen, and to provide leverage for the removal of the great burden that lay on their minds. He wanted to inspire them with justifiable pride, and with confidence in the enormous value of their heritage so that they might consider it well worth the sacrifices which they might be called upon to make for the preservation of that heritage and for becoming worthy to possess it. Dayanand dreamed of a regenerated India, as spiritual, as wise, as noble, as learned, as chivalrous, and as great in every way as in its most glorious past, if not more so, and he wanted his countrymen to proceed to the realization of that ideal with confidence and fervour. He had no objection to their learning from the West whatever the West might be able to teach them, but with the desire only of rendering it again to the West with double interest, if possible. He wanted them to aspire to a role of honour in the comity of nations; to become once more the teachers of Humanity and the upholders of towering and magnificent ideals before mankind. He wanted them to achieve all this in the spirit of their past, in a spirit of devotion to truth for its own sake, of altruism, and of humility. This ambitious programme he thought could not be realized by mere imitation, by mere dependence on the West, by despising their ancestors and by aping exotic manners and habits. Not on such shifting foundations, but on the primal rock of self-respect and self-help did he desire them to build up their future nationalism, and to rear it thereon in the true spirit of Swajati and Swadharma. Yet, in spite of the greatness of the end, he countenanced no unworthy means for its attainment. He wanted the Hindus to win the whole world—but by righteousness and Dharma only. He warned them against the indulgences, the Bhoga doctrines of the West, and he protested vigorously against their drifting with the current as being unworthy of the blood of their virile and enterprising ancestors.

Time will show whether Dayanand was right or wrong in his ideas, but indications are not lacking to indicate that his countrymen are appreciating and imbibing his spirit. His followers do not, nor did he, care very much for the verdict of the foreigner. It is not in his nature to nurse spite or hatred. The difficulty with him, in fact, is not that he is too adamant, too dour, or too inflexible, but that he is, on the contrary rather too soft, too pliable, and at times too kind and selfless, even to the degree of sacrificing the best interests of his nation and his country on the altar of chivalrous generosity.

The ideals and aims of Dayanand are the ideals and aims of the Arya Samaj, and in view of what we have said above about the former nothing more need be added.

Chapter VIII

SOCIAL IDEALS AND AIMS

May life succeed through sacrifice, may life breath thrive by sacrifice. May the eye thrive by sacrifice. May the ear thrive by sacrifice. May the back thrive by sacrifice. May sacrifice thrive by sacrifice. We have become the children of Prajapati. Gods, we have gone to heaven! We have become immortal. Thou (sacrifice) art the ladder by which the gods ascended.

Yajur, ix, 12

1. Its Social Basis

The social ideals of the Arya Samaj are the ideals of the ancient Rishis of India. They are based on:
  (*a*) The fatherhood of God and the brotherhood of man.
  (*b*) The equality of the sexes.
  (*c*) Absolute justice and fair play between men and men and nations and nations. Equal opportunities for all according to their nature, karma, and merit.
  (*d*) Love and charity towards all.

2. The Caste System

The caste system of the Hindus has been their curse as well as their salvation. While it has been the principal cause of their social and political downfall, it has as a social and national organism averted complete disruption and total annihilation. It has saved them from absorption into other religio-social systems that attained more or less ascendancy in India, in different periods of her history.

For the last two thousand years it has been more or less a defensive bastion in the citadel of Hinduism. The Arya Samaj repudiates caste by birth; it condemns the numerous subdivisions into which Hindu society has been split up by reason of castes and subcastes; it considers the artificial barriers which caste in India has created to segregate men from their fellow-men as a system of apartheid; in its opinion, it is unnatural to divide society into, as it were, watertight compartments, or to exclude the possibility of people belonging to one caste having social relations with the other. Yet it cannot shut its eyes to the facts of life and has to recognize that by birth men are not equal; that they differ from one another in physical powers, in intellectual and mental faculties, in moral dispositions, and also in spiritual development; that they are born in different environments and that their position and status in life must, from the very nature of things, be affected by their environment; that heredity also plays its part in making them what they are at birth or in life.

Nevertheless, the Arya Samaj would give equal opportunities to all persons, men and women, to acquire knowledge and to qualify themselves for whatever niche in life they would like to fill. It admits the right of every person to choose his or her environment, fight it out, and rise as high as possible in the scale of humanity. The Arya Samaj believes that in Vedic times there was no caste by birth in India; though the *Vedas* recognized the division of humanity into four classes by virtue of their qualifications and occupations.

"Nor birth, nor sacraments, nor study, nor ancestry, can decide whether a person is twice-born (and to which of the three types of the twice-born he belongs). Character and conduct only can decide."[1] So declares the *Mahabharata*.

And Manu also says:

"Persons born into one caste may change into a higher or, by the opposite of self-denial, by self-indulgence and selfishness, may descend into a lower....The pure, the upward-aspiring, the gentle-speaking, the free from pride, who live like the Brahmanas and the other twice-born castes continually—even such Shudras shall attain those higher castes."[2]

Those who trace the caste system in the *Vedas* rely on *Rig-Veda*, x. 90, II, which, literally translated, means:

"Brahmans are the head of mankind (personified), Ksha-

[1] *The Mahabharata*, Vanaparva, cccxiii, 108.
[2] Manu, x. 42 and ix. 335.

triyas are made his arms, Vaishyas are what are his thighs, and Shudras are made his feet." That this alone is the correct meaning of the Mantra is evident also from the context. In Mantra 9 of this hymn, mankind is spoken of as a person. Mantra, 10 asks:

" What is his head, what are his arms, and what are said to be his thighs and feet?" The Mantra under consideration (No. 2) is a reply to this question...

The Mantra does not in any way countenance the caste system, but describes the constitution of human society by means of an analogy between mankind and the human body.

The Brahmans, or those who possess learning and direct other men to discharge their duties, are properly called the head or brain of humanity. The Kshatriyas, or those who possess strength and protect mankind, are aptly termed the arms of mankind. The Vaishyas, or those who move from place to place for the purpose of trade and commerce, are spoken of as the thighs of human society. And the Shudras, or those who are illiterate or otherwise unfit for the higher duties of life, are represented as the feet of human society. This is a division of mankind on the principle of 'Division of Labour'. It is based not on birth but on merits.

We need not multiply quotations, as even European scholars now unanimously hold that the hereditary castes did not exist in Vedic times. We shall quote the opinions of only two celebrated Sanskritists:

Professor Max Muller says:

"If, then, with all the documents before us, we ask the question, 'Does Caste, as we find it in Manu, and at the present day, form part of the most ancient religious teaching of the *Vedas*?' We can answer with a decided 'No'."[3]

Weber thus remarks about the Vedic age:

"There are no castes as yet; the people are still one united whole, and bear but one name, that of Visas."[4]

Mr. R. C. Dutt also says that in the entire range of the *Vedas* "we have not one single passage to show that the community was cut up into hereditary castes."

As instances of non-Brahmins by birth having been raised

[3] *Chips from a German Workshop*, II, 807.
[4] *Indian Literature*, 38.

to the dignity and status of Brahmanhood in ancient India, we may refer to those of:

(a) Satya Kama Jabala, son of a low-caste helot, mentioned in the *Chhandogya Upanishad*.

(b) Kavasha, mentioned in the *Aitareya Brahamana*.

(c) Aitareya, son of a Shudra woman, the author of the *Brahmana* and the *Upanishad* of that name.

(d) Viyasa, founder of Vedanta philosophy and reputed author of the *Mahabharata*, who was the son of a seafaring woman.

(e) Parashara, the author of a code of laws bearing his name, who was the son of a Chandal woman (one of the lowest possible castes, even lower than the Shudras).

(f) Vasishta, a Vedic Rishi of great renown, the son of a prostitute.[5]

(g) Vishvamitra, a Kshatriya by birth.

(h) Arishta Shena, Sindhudwipa, Devapi, and Kapi, all Kshatriyas by birth.[6]

(i) Two sons of Nabhga, a Vaishya by birth.[7]

One of the greatest services rendered by the Arya Samaj to the cause of social reform among Hindus is its championship of the right of the depressed and untouchable classes of Hindus to be admitted into the Arya Samaj on an equal footing with persons of the highest caste. But of this we will speak in the next chapter.

3. *The Relations of the Sexes*

It must be frankly admitted that when the Arya Samaj came into being the lot of Hindu women was deplorable. In certain respects it was even worse than that of men. A proportion of the men (though comprising only a very small percentage of the population) had received some sort of education, in the schools and colleges opened by the Government, the Christian missionaries and other private agencies, but very little had been done to further the education of

---
[5] Mentioned in the *Mahabharata*.
[6] Mentioned in the *Mahabharata*.
[7] Mentioned in *Harivansha Purana*, Chap. xi.

Indian women. The system of Government introduced by the British, necessitated the education of Indian men for administrative reasons.[8] Among the agencies that have worked for improvement in this respect, the Arya Samaj occupies a high position in the Punjab and the United Provinces of Agra and Oude. It can be safely said that there has occurred a metamorphosis in the outlook of men towards women.

English education and Western ideas have played an important part in engendering this change, but an equally great, if not even greater, part has been played by <u>an appeal to the ancient Hindu ideals of womanhood and to the teachings of the ancient Hindu religion in the matter of the relations of the sexes.</u> A study of ancient Hindu literature made it abundantly clear that the present unenviable lot of Indian women was due to a deterioration of their old ideal. In Ancient India, both in theory and practice, women were placed on a pedestal in society—equal to that of men, if not higher. As regards education and marriage they held an equal position. The girls were equally entitled to receive education, and no limitations at all were set on their ambition in this direction. Study was equally enjoined for the girls as well as the boys. The only difference was that, in the case of girls, their period of education expired sooner than in that of boys. The minimum age of marriage for girls was sixteen, as compared with twenty-five for boys. This was based on Hindu ideas of the physiological differences between the sexes. It is presumed that as regards the choice of a mate, both parties enjoyed equal freedom and equal opportunities. The ideal marriage was monogamic, and one contracted with the mutual consent of the parties. Yet, so many varieties of legal marriage are known to Hindu law as to leave no doubt as to the sensitiveness of the Hindus to the extreme difficulty, and indeed unnaturalness, of attempting to impose a single law upon both sexes. Some forms of marriage suggest that courtship was not altogether unknown in Hindu society, and furthermore, it was not regarded with any grave dis-

---

[8] The figures of literacy, according to the Census Report of 1911, stood as follows:
Males: 100 per 1000; Females: 10 per 1000; an average of 58 per 1000 of the total population.

approbation. Though as a rule subject to control by parents, husbands and even sons, Hindu mothers, wives, sisters and daughters occupied a higher position than their counterparts ever had in Christian Europe before the nineteenth century. In the family the position of the mother was higher than that of the father. According to Manu[9] she is entitled to a thousand times greater respect and reverence than the father. She was in supreme control of the house and at the helm of household affairs, including finances.

Hindu law recognizes the rights of the mother, of the widow, of the daughter, and of the sister to possess property in their own right, with exclusive control over it, even when a member of a joint family. A mother has an equal right with the father to the guardianship of her children. On the death of the father her right is absolute. An ideal Hindu wife is never expected to earn her livelihood. She has been exempted from this burden by virtue of the superiority of her mother-function. Male members have been made responsible even for the maintenance, etc. of unmarried girls and widows, though the latter are not debarred from acquiring property by inheritance, by gift, or by their own skill. In no case have males any legal control over the property of females.

The Hindu marriage is a sacrament, and as such, in theory, indissoluble. Says Manu:

"The whole duty, in brief, of husband and wife towards each other is that they cross not and wander not apart from each other in thought, word and deed until death. And the promise is that they who righteously discharge this duty here shall not be parted hereafter, by the death of the body, but shall be together in the worlds beyond also."[10]

Swami Dayanand interprets the ancient Rishis as disapproving of second or third marriages on the death of husbands and wives (Manu is supposed to lay this injunction on widows only).[11] In any case, Dayanand does not lay down any rule for women which he does not apply to men also, and in so doing he is merely following the spirit of the ancient lawgivers. There are certain conditions in which men are

[9] Manu, ii. 145.
[10] Manu, ix. 101; v. 165. See *The Science of Social Organization*, by Bhagavan Das, p. 211.
[11] Ibid. p. 212.

SOCIAL IDEALS AND AIMS

permitted to remarry even in the lifetime of the lawful spouse; for example, if she be barren,[12] or addicted to strong drink or guilty of immorality, or even when there is complete incompatibility of temperament. In similar conditions the wife, too, has the option of remarrying in the lifetime of her husband; for example, if he be impotent,[13] or deserts his wife, or falls into dissolute habits, or disappears without trace for a number of years, and so forth.

In special cases, Hindu law sanctions polygamy also, though only under very exceptional circumstances.

It follows from what we have stated above that the Arya Samaj is strongly opposed to child marriage. It has conducted a fiery crusade against this unnatural custom, and may be congratulated on its success in rallying public opinion to favour its view. It fixes sixteen as the minimum marriageable age for girls and twenty-five for boys, and it encourages celibacy up to the age of forty-eight.[14]

---

[12] Manu, ix. 80; Yajnavalkya, p. 418, v. 73.
[13] Manu, ix.
[14] It was an Arya Samajist member of the Indian Legislative Assembly who secured the passage of a Bill (Sarda Act in popular language) banning the marriage of boys under fourteen.—Editor.

Chapter IX

SHUDDHI WORK OF THE ARYA SAMAJ

If we have sinned against the man who loves us, have ever wronged a brother, friend or comrade, have ever done an injury to the neighbour who ever dwelt with us, or even to a stranger, O Lord! free us from the guilt of this trespass.

—*R.* v, 85, 7

1. Reclamation and Conversion

Literally, *Shuddhi*[1] means purification, but when used by Arya Samajists it also includes reclamation and conversion. The Arya Samaj, being a Vedic church, and as such a Hindu organization, engages itself in reclaiming the wandering sheep who have strayed from the Hindu fold, and converts any one prepared to accept its religious teachings. In this undertaking it comes into direct conflict with the proselytizing work of the Musulman mullah and the Christian missionary. The Musulman fanatic and the Christian zealot abhor it, and even the sober-minded moulvie and the broad-minded Christian have no liking for it. Yet the Samaj has achieved a considerable measure of success in reclaiming Hindus converted to other faiths, and in stemming the tide of conversion. But its greatest success consists in raising the social status of the depressed classes among the Hindus and preventing them from forsaking Hinduism for other religious denominations. In regard to the reconversions, the Census Commissioner of the United Provinces of Agra and Oudh remarks:

"Special efforts are directed to the reconversion of converts from Hinduism to Christianity or Islam, while persons who are Christian or Mahomedan by birth are also occasionally converted."

---

[1] *Shuddhi* is a Sanskrit word which means purification. In religious terminology it is now applied to (1) Conversion to Hinduism of persons belonging to foreign religions (2) Reconversion of those who have recently, or at a remote period adopted one of the foreign religions, and (3) Reclamation, i.e. raising the status of the depressed classes. (*Punjab Census Report for* 1911, p. 148).

"......of such Mahomedan converts I have myself known at least one case, and others have occurred. There is a society affiliated to the Arya Samaj which is known as the Rajput Shuddhi Sabha, which has as its chief object the reconversion of Mahomedan Rajputs to Hinduism via the Arya Samaj. On a single day 370 such Rajputs were converted to Aryaism. In three years, between 1907 and 1910, this society claims to have converted 1,052 Musulman Rajputs."[2]

2. Ceremony of Conversion

Another Census Commissioner of the same province (Mr. Burn, I.C.S.) states that the ceremony of conversion is simple. The would-be Arya lives on milk alone for a period of fifteen days,[3] this being known as the Chandrain birth. Admission into the Samaj is made an occasion for a public meeting, at which the convert declares his adherence to the Ten Principles of the Samaj, a great *homa* sacrifice is performed, passages from the Vedas are recited, and the convert distributes sweetmeats to those present."[4] In some instances a certificate of *Shuddhi* is issued, which facilitates social intercourse with Hindus.

3. Depressed Classes

But the greatest interest is being taken in the social uplift of the lower castes; this reclamation is on two distinct lines: (a) the raising of the status of castes not entitled to wear the sacred thread, by permitting them that privilege; and (b) raising untouchables to the rank of touchables, and educating them to higher social ideals, with a view to eventually putting them on a footing of social equality with other Hindus. This is effected by the Arya Samajes as such, and also by special organizations supported by the Arya Samaj and affiliated, directly or indirectly to the latter.[5]

---

[2] *Census Report for U.P. for* 1911, p. 134. Mr Udey Vir Singh, Barrister-at-Law, Aligarh, is the Secretary to this Sabha.
In 1923-1924, the Arya Samaj was responsible for taking back into the Hindu fold a very large number of Malikana Rajputs who, though formally accounted Muslims, had kept alive all their Hindu traditions—Editor.

[3] It has now been reduced to three days.

[4] *Census Report for 1901,* page 87.

[5] The best known of these organizations is the Dayanand Dalituddhar Mandal, Hoshiarpur—Editor.

Two years ago, the author, as the President of a large conference, delivered a speech on this subject on the anniversary of the Gurukula at Hardwar, and discussed the question from three standpoints: from the point of view of the Hindu community; as a question of all-India importance; and in its humanitarian bearing. Discussing it from the all-India point of view he said: "It is to be remembered that national decline has its origin in the oppression of others, and if we Indians desire to achieve national self-respect and dignity, we should open our arms to our unfortunate brothers and sisters of the depressed classes and help to build up in them the vital spirit of human dignity. So long as we have these large classes of the untouchables in this country we can make no real progress in our national affairs. Such progress requires a high moral standard; and this is unthinkable where the weaker classes are unfairly treated."

As recently as last December the author again discussed the subject, as the President of another large conference of the same nature at Karachi (Sindh). In the course of this speech he remarked: "The cause of the depressed classes combines in it the best of religion, the best of humanity, and the best of nationalism. It is a cause worthy of the best energies and the most strenuous efforts of a large number of India's daughters and sons, such as believe that 'Life is a mission and duty its highest Law'. The best fulfilment of that duty lies in the service and uplifting of those whom human tyranny and prejudices have put out of the pale of humanity, and who are unfortunately the victims of the idea that they deserve no better fate"

"In my opinion," continued the speaker, "no greater wrong can be done to a human being than to put him into circumstances which make him believe that he is eternally doomed to a life of ignorance, servitude, and misery, and that in him any sort of ambition for his betterment is a sin.

"No slavery is more harmful than that of mind, and no sin is greater than to keep human beings in perpetual bondage. It is bad enough to enslave people, but to create and perpetuate circumstances which prevent them from breaking their chains and becoming free, is infamous. No man or number of men have a right to do this, and those who attempt it deserve the severest condemnation of all who have a conscience. It is my firm conviction that injustice and oppression of fellow-men, the attempt to stifle legitimate human ambition, the desire to keep people down in order to profit by their misfortune, is sure to react on the authors and agents thereof, and that nothing can save them from a similar fate sooner or later except a timely consciousness of the gravity of their sin and a vigorous attempt to atone for it by undoing the mischief wrought.

"I am a Hindu and a firm believer in the doctrine of Karma. I also believe that every man makes his own Karma, and is thus the arbiter of his own destiny. I therefore look at the question thus: the ancestors of the Hindus in the insolence of wealth and power maltreated people whom God had placed under them to protect and bless. The degradation of the latter reacted upon them and reduced them to the subordinate position which has been their lot for so many centuries. This double degradation has resulted in the loss of the manly instincts of the race; and we find that, despite a strong and sincere desire to improve, we feel as if the wheels of progress are kept back by forces beyond our control. The highest interests of the nation therefore require that the best among us should devote themselves to the undoing of the mischief wrought by us or by our ancestors. We owe a heavy debt to those depressed classes; that debt must be paid, and paid as soon as possible. Living in the midst of large masses of people not conscious of their manhood, we cannot hope to progress towards a better type; a man living in an atmosphere of an infectious disease has to keep up constant war lest the germs of disease get admittance into his body and destroy it. We have, therefore, to realize that the best and highest sacrifices we may put forth for our national advancement cannot come to much as long as the depressed classes remain what they are. The question then, is one of national importance, and one which deserves to be placed almost at the head of the list of reforms needed to bring about our social efficiency. It is not a question of charity or goodwill but one of self-preservation. There is another aspect of the question which Hindus cannot ignore. The depressed classes are Hindus; they worship Hindu gods, observe Hindu customs, and follow the Hindu law. A great many of them worship the cow and obey their Brahman priests. They have no desire to go out of Hinduism unless it be impossible for them otherwise to better their position religiously, socially, and economically. Nay, they cling to Hinduism in spite of the knowledge that by giving it up and adopting other faiths they have an immediate prospect of rising both socially and economically. There are agencies prepared to receive them with open arms if they would give up their ancestral faith. Indications are not wanting that many of them have already become conscious of the wretched position they hold in Hindu society. Some have begun to resent it, and it will be no wonder if large numbers of them leave Hindu society. It is of paramount importance to Hindu society, that all those who call themselves Hindus should not only be properly educated, but should also be made to feel that there is no position in society to which they cannot aspire if they are otherwise fitted for it by personal qualifications.

"There cannot be much hope for a society which keeps a fourth of its total strength in perpetual bondage, doomed to dirty work, insanitary life, and intellectual starvation, and denies them opportunities of association with other members of the community. I am not prepared to admit that such a state of things forms an essential feature of Hinduism; it is enough to shame us that it should be associated with present-day Hinduism. Happily there is some awakening among the leaders of orthodox Hinduism also. The famous Gait Circular proved a good tonic for the apathy of orthodox Kashi. One fine morning the learned pandits of Kashi rose to learn that their orthodoxy stood the chance of losing the allegiance of six crores of human beings who, the Government and its advisers were told, were not Hindus, in so far as other Hindus would not acknowledge them as such, and would not even touch them. The ways of Providence are strange and inscrutable. The Gait Circular had a quite unexpected effect and galvanized the dying body of orthodox Hinduism into sympathy with its untouchable population. The possibility of losing the untouchables has shaken the intelligent section of the Hindu community to its very depths, and were it not for long-established prejudices and deep-rooted habits, untouchability would soon be a thing of the past. From the Hindu point of view too, then, the matter is of first-rate importance and cannot be ignored without serious loss to the body and soul of Hinduism. I would, therefore, appeal to every Hindu to be serious about it; this is no time for trifling. The Christian missionary is gathering the harvest and no blame can attach to him for doing so. He is in this country with the message of his God, and if the Hindus forsake their own people, he in any case, will not fail them. The depressed classes have no desire to leave Hinduism, if the latter make it possible for them to progress on humane lines; but if in its stupidity it hesitates and hesitates, they may not follow in its train much longer."[6]

The following extract gives an account of what has so far been done by the Arya Samaj in this connection:

"....In the Punjab and the United Provinces substantial work is being done by the Arya Samaj. The chief merit of this work lies in forcing or persuading Hindu society to assimilate these classes and raising them to a respectable position in the social scale. From that point of view the methods of the Arya Samaj are much more effective than those adopted in other parts of India. The Arya Samajists occupy an admittedly sound position in Hindu society. Hinduism in Northern India cannot be thought of without the Arya Samaj. It is not only a source of strength to Hinduism and Hindus, but is the principal effective agency, always and everywhere present, to defend them, to save them, and to serve them. The orthodox are furious with the Arya Samaj because of their audacity in admitting some of the depressed classes and untouchables into Hindu society. They threaten to excommunicate and in some cases they do fulfil their threats, but eventually find it is useless to break their heads against rocks. In their despair, they pour out vials of wrath upon the untouchables and persecute them, but at this stage the law intervenes and they have perforce to submit to the inevitable.

"The Arya Samajists reclaim these depressed classes by admitting them to the privileges of the Dwijas. They ad-

---

[6] Dr. Ambedkar succeeded in converting—at least nominally—a very large number of them to Buddhism recently—Editor.

minister Gayatri to a select number, invest them with the sacred thread, confer on them the privilege of performing Homa, and start inter-dining and in a few cases even inter-marriage with them. This startles the Hindus. The whole country where such a thing is done for the first time is thrown into convulsions. People begin to think and talk. Occasionally they resort to violence which in some cases leads to litigation, but eventually truth, justice and perseverance triumph. In the territories of the Maharaja of Jammu and Kashmere the whole strength of one of these castes (in one pargana), about 10,000 souls, has been admitted into the Arya Samaj. This is the result of about three years' work. The agitation is now subsiding and things are resuming their normal condition. In another district (Sialkote) over 36,000 of another caste have been similarly raised. A special organization has been formed to look after their education, etc., called the Megh Údhar Sabha (a Society for the uplift of Meghs), which maintains a Central School and several primary schools. The Central School has a splendid building of its own on which they have spent some forty thousand rupees.

"In another district (Gurdaspur) Pandit Ram Bhaj Dat has reclaimed several thousands within the last two years. The orthodox party is still agitated there, and no organization has yet been formed to look after those reclaimed. In another district (Hoshiarpur) thousands have been reclaimed and there is a regular organization looking after their educational and other needs.[7] In Lahore itself excellent work is being done among Hindu sweepers and Chamars. In July, I purchased a large plot of land at Lahore on the other side of the Ravi, at a cost of Rs. 21,000 to build a Central Home and a Central School for the Depressed Classes Mission.[8] We have used a portion of the balance of the famine fund, raised by me in 1908, towards the uplift of the depressed classes, and are maintaining some Primary Schools scattered over the province for the benefit of these classes. Some of these are receiving Government grants and others will soon earn them. The funds thus released will then be available

[7] As said above, the most active organisation at present in the field is the Dayanand Dalituddhar Mandal, an All-India organisation with its headquarters at Hoshiarpur—Editor.

[8] The land was sold and a Trust was founded out of the proceeds.

for other schools. There is hardly a district in the province where some work in connection with the uplift of the depressed classes is not being done, though in most cases it only forms part of the general programme of the Arya Samaj. But the best and most cheering part of this work is that in some places the orthodox party have become conscious of their duty towards the depressed classes and are in full sympathy with the Arya Samaj. At the last session of the Punjab Hindu Conference, at the suggestion of a Hindu Sadhu of the orthodox party, a resolution was unanimously passed to invite the depressed classes to send representatives to the Conference in future. In Lahore and some other places we find that high caste Hindus have no scruples in sending their children to the schools which we maintain mainly for the depressed classes. The children mix quite freely and on equal terms. In the U.P., the home of Hindu orthodoxy, the work is more difficult; but last year I succeeded in making a big hole in the orthodox fortress by reclaiming a number of *Domes* (one of the lowest untouchable castes in the U.P.) and admitting them into the Arya Samaj.

"I went to their houses in the interior of the hills and along with a number of high-caste Arya Samajists ate food cooked by them and drank water brought by them. Last year I went to Banaras and in that very centre of Hindu orthodoxy addressed a huge meeting on this question, and challenged the Pandits to outcaste me and others working with me. I did the same only lately at Muradabad and Bareilly. The Arya Samajists in these districts are maintaining a number of schools for the Chamar boys, who alone number 60 lacs in the United Provinces. The untouchables in the U.P. number about a crore and a quarter in a total Hindu population of about four crores, and the problem there is gigantic."

These extracts afford a fair idea of the influence of the Arya Samaj in the sphere of social uplift. It is a magnificent work, of which any single Indian organization may well be proud. But no one feels more than we do how little has yet been achieved in this line. We are yet only on the fringe of the area to be conquered, and many a battle will have to be fought before the victory is achieved. The Arya Samaj as a body, is, however, conscious of the magnitude as well as of the importance of the work.[9] Their feeling may well be expressed in the words of the poet:

It may be that the gulfs will wash us down:
It may be we shall touch the Happy Isles,
...but something ere the end,
Some work of nobel note, may yet be done.

Tennyson, *Ulysses*

---

[9] Now that the Constitution has outlawed untouchability and discrimination against members of these classes has become a penal offence, it may be said that much has been done in the matter. Unfortunately, the Constitution in safeguarding the interests of these classes seems to have perpetuated their isolation. Many thoughtful workers in the field feel that their integration in the Hindu society may have to be brought about on the lines chalked out by the Arya Samaj. The law may succeed in removing impediments but it can seldom bring about harmony—Editor.

Chapter X

PHILANTHROPIC ACTIVITIES

No friend is he who offers nothing to his friend and comrade who comes imploring food.

R. x, 117, 4

1. Philanthropic Work

Outside Christian circles the Arya Samaj was the first purely Indian association to organize Orphanages and Widows' Homes. The first Hindu orphanage was established at Ferozepur, in the Punjab, in the lifetime of the Founder of the Samaj; it still retains its position as the premier Hindu orphanage in India, has splendid commodious buildings, all erected by private charity, and maintains schools and workshops for training boys and girls. There are several other orphanages run on similar lines in northern India, controlled and managed by the Arya Samaj; and, besides these, many Hindu institutions and orphanages spread all over India bear the impress and influence of the Arya Samaj, and are indebted for their birth and efficiency to Arya Samajists.

2. Famine Relief in 1897-98 and 1899-1900

India was wont to be described as a land of famines. Between 1877 and 1910 there were about ten famines, of which no fewer than five were both intense and widespread. Famines in India are due ostensibly to the failure of the rains, but are in reality due to the inability of the Indian ryot and labourer to purchase food at enhanced prices. In normal years India produces foodstuffs in such quantities that, were there no export, a year's produce would suffice to feed her population for two years. But in undivided India, foodstuffs were largely exported every year, not only in normal years, but even in famine years. In 1899-1900 when the country was suffering from one of the severest famines of the century, millions of hundredweights of wheat were exported to foreign countries; in 1877-78, when 5,220,000 persons died of starvation, 16,000,000 cwt. of rice were exported from Calcutta port alone. The bulk of the population existed in chronic poverty. A single year's failure of seasonal rainfall results in an abnormal rise of prices and throws millions out of employment. This general poverty of the people was the real cause of famine in India and explained the frequency of famine conditions.

The Arya Samaj was the first non-Christian private agency which started a non-official movement for the relief of distress caused by famine. The writer of this book was among the first organizers of such relief. In the first two famines dealt with by the Arya Samaj, the movement was confined to orphan relief, and was called the Hindu Orphan Relief Movement. This was started in February, 1897, for the relief of Hindu children left destitute by the famine of 1896-97. Appeals for help, issued under the auspices of the Arya Samaj, were generously responded to by the Hindu community in general, and by the members and sympathizers of the Arya Samaj in particular. About 250 Hindu children were rescued by agents deputed by the movement and were diverted into the Punjab, where four new orphanages were founded to accommodate them, in addition to the one already existing at Ferozepur.

The failure of the rains in 1899 generated another famine, which as was evident from the very outset bid fair to be more disastrous than its predecessor. Moreover, the people hardly had respite to recover from the effects of the scarcity of 1897. By October, 1899, the pinch began to be felt severely in Rajputana, the Central Provinces, Bombay, Kathiawar, and parts of the Punjab. It was, therefore, resolved to revive the orphan relief movement and to push it on vigorously so as to be able to render help to as large a number of children as it might be possible to rescue. The Lahore Arya Samaj lost no time in putting words into deeds, and deputed one of its younger members (a senior student of the Dayanand Anglo-Vedic College, and Secretary of the local Young Men's Arya Samaj) to proceed to Rajputana and ascertain on the spot in what way and to what extent they could render help, and whether it was possible to enlist local sympathy in their cause in the famine-stricken areas themselves. On this mission Lala Dewan Chand Chaddha travelled to Jodhpur, and stayed at many places (amongst them Kishangarh, Ajmere, Beawar, Pali, etc.) to inspect the famine relief camps. He spent altogether a month in Rajputana, and on his return gave a graphic and touching account of his experiences which brought tears to many eyes and stirred almost the whole of Lahore to take immediate and vigorous action for the succour of the unfortunate Hindu waifs and orphans of Rajputana.

In several Native States Arya Samajic workers waited upon high officials, and tried to impress upon them their duty towards the orphans and other destitute children in their territories, explaining how necessary it was, in the interests of the States, to keep the children on their own soil and to save them in that distressing period, not only from perishing by starvation, but also from being carried off to distant places to be converted to alien faiths.

The missionaries were waging a noble battle, and it was not for us to stir up agitation against them in Rajputana. To save even a few hundreds, we found it necessary to convey them to the Punjab, where they were sure to be given sufficient food and clothing for survival till the end of the famine. But the Punjab itself was at this time in crying need of help, as some parts were seriously affected by the famine. Notwithstanding the efforts of the Government, there were still some who required external aid to avert starvation or conversion.

Valuable work was done by the Hissar Arya Samaj and the Bhiwani Hindu Orphanage. Under the leadership of the late Lala Chandu Lal, the President, and Lal Churamani, their Secretary, they relieved hundreds of children and fought a noble battle against death and misery. For Rajput children the Relief Committee submitted representations and memorials to the Commissioner of Ajmere, Merwara, who was also the Agent to the Governor-General in Rajputana, and to the Deputy Commissioner of Beawar; but elicited no response. Arya Samajic workers applied in person to the local officers in charge of the famine relief camps, but in vain, although there was reason to believe that large numbers of Hindu children were periodically made over to Christian missionaries and sent by them to distant places in India. In Bombay, workers travelled as far as Surat and Baroda, and strove to arouse the Hindu public to a sense of duty towards the little ones of their own community, who in dire distress, needed their help and sympathy. These visits and the readiness of the Arya Samaj to take charge of as many children as could be entrusted to its care, had due effect. The reasons for our failure to get children from Government famine relief works need not be set forth in detail, the most important being that the missionaries were everywhere too powerful for us.

Similarly, we launched a successful campaign in Kathiawar, the Central Provinces, and parts of Bombay, and succeeded in rescuing all told about 1,700 children. To safeguard and train them we opened several new orphanages in the Punjab, some being mere temporary shelters. All classes of the Hindu community, without regard for caste or creed, helped us in this undertaking, and the movement proved a blessing in more ways than one. It engendered unity in the ranks of the Hindus. It brought the educated classes into touch with the masses as never before, creating new bonds of sympathy between them. It posed fresh problems for solution by the community itself. It stimulated a healthy spirit of rivalry with powerful missionary organizations at work in the same field. It opened up virgin territory for the training of Hindu youths in methods of social service. And last, but not least, it enabled them to make several experiments in reviving indigenous industries through cheap time-saving machinery within the reach of modest means for providing the orphans with employment. All the girls rescued in 1897-98 and 1899-1900 were suitably wedded, almost invariably to men of castes higher than their own.

The movement finally received official recognition from the Government, some children were consigned to the different orphanages established under its auspices, and some small financial help was granted these institutions from the unused balance of the non-official famine relief fund.

During the famine relief work the young workers in the cause risked their lives in this noble enterprise, because it was no easy matter to travel in search of orphans in Rajputana and the Central Provinces, where not only was there dearth of food and water, but where cholera and fever were also raging. Their difficulties increased manifold because of their anxiety to keep expenses on their own comfort to the barest minimum, fully aware that the funds at their disposal and at the disposal of those who had deputed them were so meagre that economy was a stern necessity. Yet there never was any lack of volunteers willing enough to face these privations in their zeal to help the little ones of their community in time of dire calamity. Some of these workers did not expend even a pie of the public funds on their personal needs. An outstanding example of self-sacrifice in the cause of humanity was established to be emulated by other members of the rising generation. A tradition of humanitarian work was created to be followed in the future. This record of their work is a magnificent ray in the sunshine of Hindu revival, which we all look forward to with hope and pleasure."

3. Famine Relief in 1908

In 1908, however, the movement was expanded and general relief was the aim. The following extract from the *Census Report* of the United Provinces of Agra and Oude for 1911 will furnish some idea of the extensive scale on which work was done during the famine:

"The emissary of a well-known Arya leader came round distributing relief during the famine of 1907-8 and visited a certain village near which I had encamped. After his visit, the recipients of his bounty, being not quite sure whether they were doing right in accepting private charity when Government was looking after them, sent a deputation to ask me whether they might keep his gifts. I, of course, told them to take all they could get; and then their leader asked me who was the man (*the Arya leader*) who was distributing money in this wholesale way."[1]

4. Social Service

The philanthropic work of the Arya Samaj is not, however'

---

[1] He evidently referred to me as the head of the Arya relief movement. The italics are mine—L.R.

confined to famine relief, but includes various kinds of social service. In times of pestilence it organizes medical relief, nursing the sick, and helping in the disposal of the dead. At the time of the great earthquake in the Kangra Valley in 1904 it organized relief on a large scale for its victims, and earned the thanks of the people and the Government. In this calamity the Arya Samajists were the first to reach the afflicted area. This example has, within recent years, been largely followed by other organizations, and there is now a network of social-service agencies throughout India. The Arya Samaj was the pioneer in social service work in an organized form and on a large scale, at least in northern India.

Chapter XI

EDUCATIONAL WORK

DAYANAND ANGLO-VEDIC COLLEGE

By Tapa and Brahmacharya the holy saints drove away death (attained salvation).
By Brahmacharya did they receive heavenly light from God.

—*Ath.* xi, 5, 19

The eighth of the Ten Principles of the Arya Samaj points out to the Arya that he should endeavour "to diffuse knowledge and dispel ignorance." The Samaj as a body, and its members in their individual capacities, have accordingly been engaged in educational work of considerable importance. In the Punjab and the United Provinces its work, in extent and volume, is second to no other agency except the Government. Christian Missions maintain a large variety of schools, but no single mission can claim to have as many schools for boys and girls as the Arya Samaj.

On the side of boy's education it has two typical Colleges, one affiliated with the Government University, the other independent of official control.

1. Dayanand Anglo-Vedic College at Lahore

The educational aims of this institution may be gathered from its official reports. The first of these, is a valuable document for giving the genesis of this important institution in the language of one of its founders, and we append two extracts therefrom. A draft scheme was circulated in 1885 for public discussion before the institution was actually started. Its preamble declared in part:

"It will be conceded by all right-thinking minds that to secure the best advantages of education, it is necessary to make it national in tone and character. No doubt, speaking broadly, the primary aim of education is to develop the mental faculties, to invigorate them, and to practise them by proper and healthy exercise. As it is impracticable that every member of a nation should receive thorough education, it is peremptorily necessary, and absolutely desirable, that those who do receive education at the national cost, should receive it in a manner best suited to make them useful members of the community. In fact, the system of education should be so devised as to strengthen the ties which naturally bind individuals into a common nationality.

"The rush of foreign ideas, by the introduction of English literature into this country, has had, no doubt, the effect of enlightening and improving many thousand minds, of a few of whom the country may well feel proud. But foreign education has produced a schism in society which is truly deplorable. An educated class has been created—a class which moves by itself; a class incapable of materially influencing, or being influenced by, the uneducated masses; and a class without precedent in any country on earth. This result, sad in itself, is the inevitable consequence of the one-sided policy of education imparted through a foreign agency.

"But the mistake is not past remedy; there is still ample time to set matters right, did we but know how to use our opportunities. The reaction towards a national education is asserting itself everywhere, and the demand for the study of national literature is growing. This points out to us the remedy, namely, to make provision for the efficient study of the national language and literature, and carefully to initiate the youthful mind into habits and modes of life consistent with the national spirit and character.

"Besides no means exist at present in this country for imparting technical and practical education, which is so essential to its economic and material progress.

"Influenced by these important considerations we propose to establish an educational institution which will supply the shortcomings of the existing systems, and combine their advantages. The primary object will, therefore, be to weld together the educated and uneducated classes by encouraging the study of the national language and vernaculars; to spread a knowledge of moral and spiritual truths by insisting on the study of classical Sanskrit; to assist the formation of sound and energetic habits by a regulated mode of living;

to encourage sound acquaintance with English literature; and to afford a stimulus to the material progress of the country by spreading a knowledge of the physical and applied sciences."

We cite the following also from the first report:

"The institutions of a nation are the best indexes and emblems of its intellectual progress. They form so many stages along the path of a country's civilization. They are not the outcome of chance, but the deliberate consequences of intelligent causes incessantly moulding the destinies of a nation. Swami Dayanand Saraswati, in the course of a few years, revolutionized the intellectual and social thought of Hindu society. There is hardly a school of thought, hardly a social custom, which has not been affected by his preaching and writings.

"His was a power which has permeated Hindu life, and has created herein tendencies which have sprung up, and will spring up, into multitudinous institutions and movements that, in their turn, will continue to multiply, and influence the destiny of the nation for centuries onward. Important and prominent among these tendencies is the strong desire created by him in the public mind for an exploration of the treasures of classical Sanskrit. It needed the power and persuasion of a preacher of Swami Dayanand Saraswati's calibre of mind and learning to direct public attention to this long forgotten but most precious heritage. The effect produced by this awakening was at once vehement. Partial attempts were made here and there, under the auspices of the Arya Samaj, by opening classes for teaching Sanskrit; but these were obviously inadequate and too isolated to satisfy the growing passion.

"While the agitation was daily gaining ground in the public mind, and before any practical steps could be undertaken on a sufficiently large scale, the founder was suddenly taken away from this world. His death, in 1883, cast a deep gloom. But the interval of despair was temporary: despondency was soon dispelled by firm resolution, and his death instead of discouraging the movement, brought it redoubled vigour. It united with the movement a desire for expressing public gratitude by some permanent commemoration of the great benefactor. The necessity for giving practical shape to the movement for the study of the *Vedas* and classical Sanskrit could be no longer postponed. The result was that soon after Swamiji's death, the proposal to found the Dayanand Anglo-Vedic College Institution was simultaneously made in several places, notably at Ferozepur, Multan, and Lahore. It was publicly put forward at a meeting called by the Lahore Arya Samaj on November 9th, 1883." "On this occasion the spirit of grief had been replaced by gratitude, and the touch of enthusiasm seemed to reverberate through every nerve and heart. There was one united purpose that the glorious life of the departed Swami should be immortalized, and the proposal to found an Anglo-Vedic College in honour of his memory, was unanimously adopted. The sight that followed was worth observing. Though the meeting was composed mostly of middle-class men, from 7,000 to 8,000 rupees were subscribed on the spot. Women and children and even poor menials zealously came forward with their mite."[1] The movement which was thus auspiciously and enthusiastically inaugurated at Lahore, soon spread itself throughout the Province, and identical resolutions were immediately adopted by other Samajes.

The objects of the Dayanand Anglo-Vedic College Institution, as recorded in the registered Memorandum of Association, are the following:

"1. To establish in the Punjab an Anglo-Vedic College Institution, which shall include a school, a College, and Boarding-house, as a memorial in honour of Swami Dayanand Saraswati, with the following joint purposes, viz.:

(a) To encourage, improve, and enforce the study of Hindu literature.
(b) To encourage and enforce the study of classical Sanskrit and of the *Vedas*.
(c) To encourage and enforce the study of English literature, and sciences, both theoretical and applied.

"2. To provide means for giving technical education in connection with the Dayanand Anglo-Vedic College Institution as far as is not inconsistent with the proper accomplishment of the first object."

The enterprise was of an entirely novel character in this

[1] *Arya Patrika* of 20th June, 1883.

Province. At first there was cause for discouragement, some thought the attempt impractical and destined to end in failure like other native enterprises. But it had been inaugurated to commemorate a man whose name and work could never die; and it was this auspicious connection and the national character of the movement, which supported it at critical moments and encouraged its promoters to tide over all difficulties.

These efforts and sacrifices might have ended in nothing but for the timely offer of a young man who agreed to give his time free. This young man, Lala Hansraj, had just graduated after a brilliant University career and had an equally bright future before him. The call of duty to religion and to the Motherland, however, proved too strong to be ignored, and he offered to serve the Institution as a teacher free of any remuneration, his elder brother agreeing to share his scanty salary of Rs. 80 with him. For the first two years he served as Honorary Headmaster, and then for twenty-four years as Honorary Principal.

This sacrifice made it possible for the promoters to open the first department of the College, i.e. the school, in 1886. Lala Hansraj became the guiding star and mainstay of this Institution. In the interests of the College he has not spared himself in any way. His personality is unique in the history of the modern Punjab, the only other of whom we could speak in the same breath being Lala Munshi Ram, the founder of the Gurukula at Kangri. It is impossible to think of the Arya Samaj without these two names next to that of the great founder, Dayanand, himself. It is equally impossible to think of the Dayanand Anglo-Vedic College without Lala Hansraj. There are other names worthy of remembrance like those who have by their devotion and service contributed to the success of the College, one of them being the late Rai Bahadur Lala Lal Chand, sometime judge of the Punjab Chief Court; but the one person among the founders, whose name will always take pride of place in respect of those who loved the College, and whose name and life-work stands or falls with this College, is Lala Hansraj. While others have had other interests in life, professional, social, political or industrial, his only concern has been the service of the

D.A.V. College and the Arya Samaj. There may have been some others who have perhaps given the best in their life to this Institution, but he stands alone as the one who has given his all for it. It was the one object of his devotion throughout his life. In his work he met with all kinds of opposition, criticism, and misfortune. He was misunderstood, misrepresented and maligned. His best friends sometimes differed from him, but he stood firm, leading a life of unique simplicity, of unostentatious poverty, of unassuming renunciation, and of singleminded devotion—a life irreproachable in private character and unique in public service.

The feeble seedling planted in 1886 by even more feeble hands, in the course of time, grew into a stately tree, and was in 1914 the biggest institution in Northern India, and probably the second in the whole of India, in point of numbers. The following extract from a speech delivered by the author in June, 1914, at the Founder's Day celebration in London, will further explain the principles on which the Institution has been conducted, and its success.[2]

"I have already spoken of the main objects of the College: I wish now to say a word about the principles on which it was understood that it would be conducted. Some are embodied in the constitution, others are assumed. It was provided in the rules that the management should be in the hands of elected representatives of such Arya Samajes as contributed to its funds, with the addition of a few Hindus representing the professions and the classes; and that rule has been acted upon without exception. No non-Hindu has been associated with the management of the College.

"The second principle, nowhere recorded but generally accepted, was that the teaching should be exclusively done by Indians, and there has been no exception on this point. The College teaches Sanskrit, Hindi, English, Persian, Philosophy both eastern and modern, History, Political Economy, Logic, Elementary Physics, Chemistry, Elementary Botany, Elementary Biology, and Higher Mathematics. The results have been excellent. Our students have often headed the lists of ordinary passes, as well as honours passes, in Sanskrit and Mathematics. They have several times headed the

[2] We have preferred this form because of its being more impressive.—Author

list in English, Political Economy, History, Philosophy, Chemistry, Persian, and other subjects. A considerable number of Government and University scholarships, granted on the results of University examinations, have every year been won by our students, and also medals and prizes. In the M.A. class we coach only in Sanskrit. All this has been achieved by the labours of Indian teachers, unaided by any foreign agency.

"The third principle (which is also an unwritten law) imposes on the managers <u>the moral obligation not to seek monetary assistance from the Government</u>. This principle has been acted upon, unless a petty grant of a few thousand rupees made by the University be considered an exception.

"The fourth principle was to aim at <u>giving free education. The paucity of funds, and Government and University regulations, have prevented us from giving effect to this</u>; but still our fees have generally been 50 per cent less than those of Government schools and colleges.

"Now one word about the reasons for these principles. They were not adopted in any spirit of hostility or antagonism to the British, or the Government, or any other community. The object was primarily to try an experiment in purely indigenous enterprise: secondly, to develop a spirit of self-help and self-reliance in a community in which those qualities had, by lapse of time and lack of opportunity, degenerated. Everyone who knows the Punjab, knows how well we have succeeded in this direction; probably no other province in India has developed private enterprise in education to the same extent and with the same success as we have in the Punjab. This spirit of self-help, called exclusiveness by our critics, has cost us dear, because on that account we have always been under the shadow of official mistrust. No bureaucracy loves people who can do big things without their help and guidance; much less a foreign bureaucracy. They wish to keep the strings of all public activities in their own hands, or in the hands of those who can be used as tools. We set a different standard, and so we were disliked. Yet, on the whole, the attitude of the Department and the University towards us has not been unfair. They have generally given us credit for our work, and praised our public spirit, but they have never been at ease with us. Once or twice when we sought their help to acquire land for a building site and playgrounds, they would not oblige. Lately they have compulsorily requisitioned a piece of land, which we had secured with great trouble and after protracted litigation, and refused to give us in lieu one of the Government plots lying under our own walls. But this is only *en passant*. The general attitude of the Department and the University has been fair, though both have often been influenced in framing new regulations by the fact that our School and College were formidable rivals to the Government and aided institutions of similar nature.

"The School department was opened in June, 1886, and at once became popular. The College department was opened in June, 1889, and began with less than a dozen students. The popularity of the institution can be judged from the fact that on 31st December, 1913, we had 1,737 students in our School, and 903 in the College, besides a number in the purely Vedic Department, in the faculty of Hindu medicine, in the engineering and tailoring classes.

"Yet we have managed to achieve all this with very scanty funds. The total funds of the College (including the cost value of its buildings property) amount to a little over a million rupees. The operations in 1886 commenced with less than forty thousand rupees, while no single donation has ever exceeded ten thousand rupees (about £700). Our success is mainly due to the spirit of self-sacrifice which has animated our workers. Until 1911, the Principal was an honorary worker. The present Principal is also practically honorary. He receives only £5 per month for his expenses, and so do some others.[3] The officers of the managing committee have always been honorary, and the investment of funds judicious. The University has, under the new regulations, compelled us to sink a large amount of our funds in buildings, which, as they stand, are splendid, stately, and adequate. For a number of years in the beginning we depended very largely on monthly subscriptions and other seasonal

---

[3] Lal Sain Dass, M.A. (Calcutta), B.SC. (Cantab), is the Principal. The others, are Lal Diwan Chand, M.A. (Eng. and Philosophy), B. Ram Rattan, B.A., B.T., and Lala Mehar Chand, M.A.

collections, etc., and we had to lodge ourselves in poor buildings.

"Yet I cannot help remarking that if Lord Curzon's educational policy had been in force when this College was proposed, it could not have come into existence at all. Thus we have every reason to congratulate ourselves on having started rather early and having succeeded so well. Let me add that we are not quite satisfied with what we have achieved. It is true we have popularized University education and turned out hundreds of graduates and thousands of other scholars, so much so that there is hardly any department of public and private activity in Upper India in which old D.A.V's are not to be found doing their part creditably and honourably. It is also true that we have given a great impetus to the study of Hindi and Sanskrit which stood very low in the Province when we started, and it is equally true that we have created an atmosphere of nationalism and developed a spirit of self-help and self-reliance among them; but when all has been said, we cannot say that we are very near the ideals that we set before us. Among the old D.A.V's, and men connected with the College, the Province has some of its best and most reliable public men; some of them have also done literary and journalistic work; others have been, and are, pioneering trades and industries; some hold high appointments under Government; others hold distinguished positions in the professions; yet we cannot say we have produced any high-class writers or scholars, nor have we so far been able to make any provision for original research.

"In the D.A.V. College we have a large number of resident students—697 in the College Department and an equally considerable number in the School Department; but the discipline enforced and the life lived in the Gurukula at Kangri is more in accordance with genuine Hindu ideals than those in the College."

2. *The Gurukula*

Another College was established and is being managed by the vegetarian section of the Samaj. Its origin is due to the same spirit of revolt which compelled Dayanand to forsake his parental home and become a wanderer in quest of truth. The founders had originally taken part in the starting of the D.A.V. College, but within a few years they found that the system of education followed was not after their heart; that it did not come up to their ideal of Vedic education; that the managers cared more for University results than for sound national education; that the fact of its affiliation with the official University prevented them from making radical changes in the curriculum of studies, and materially interfered with their independence.

For a time they carried on an agitation aiming at radical changes in the Institution, but finding that the majority of those entrusted with the management were determined not to make such changes, they resolved to secede and go their own way. At first they thought of concentrating their entire energies on propaganda work, but soon found that the effective success of that work also required an educational seminary, embodying their ideals of education. The dominating idea was to give a good trial to the system of education propounded by Dayanand in his works. High proficiency in Vedic Sanskrit, and character building on Vedic lines were the objectives of the scheme.

The following account of the aims of the Institution is in the words of the founder himself:

"The Gurukula is an educational institution founded with the avowed aim of reviving the ancient institution of Brahmacharya (continence), of rejuvenating and resuscitating ancient Indian philosophy and literature, conducting researches into the antiquities of India, of building up a Hindu literature incorporating into itself all that is best and assimilable in Occidental thought, of producing preachers of the Vedic religion and good citizens possessed of a culture compounded of the loftiest elements of the two civilizations which have made their home in this ancient land of sages and seers."

I give an account of its history, progress, and success in the language of an American visitor, Mr. Myron Phelps of America, whose letters on the subject were published in the *Pioneer*, the most influential Anglo-Indian daily of North India, and have been republished in pamphlet form by the founder himself as containing a true account of the institution.

EDUCATIONAL WORK

About the history of the Institution, Mr. Phelps says:
"The Gurukula was established in 1902, chiefly through the efforts of the present Principal and Governor, Mr. Munshi Ram, formerly a successful pleader of Jullundher. Mr. Munshi Ram was by nature an earnest and devout man. He became a member of the Arya Samaj in 1885. How the Gurukula came to be started will be best stated in his own words:

" 'Our object was a school where strong religious character could be built up on the basis of pure Vedic instruction. We recognized two great wants of the people—men of character and religious unity—and we set out to do what we could to supply these wants.

" 'Our primary aim is simply to give our boys the best moral and ethical training it is possible to give—to make of them good citizens and religious men, and to teach them to love learning for learning's sake. Our model is the great universities of ancient India, such as that of Taxilla, near Rawalpindi, where thousands of students congregated, and which were supported, as were also the students who attended them, by the munificence of the State and wealthy citizens.

" 'The managing committee of the Samaj soon after took up our scheme. They authorized the starting of a Gurukula when Rs. 30,000 should be subscribed and Rs. 8,000 paid in. The project hung fire for some months, then I went out myself to raise the money. I was not satisfied with Rs. 8,000, and secured Rs. 30,000 in cash in a short time. Then we started it.

" 'I was not at that time engaged in active business, having retired a short time before from the practice of law, finding it uncongenial, and not having yet taken to any other avocation. I, therefore, had some leisure to give to the Gurukula, and found myself insensibly drawn into its permanent management.

" 'While I was searching for a suitable spot we were offered the gift of a large tract of land (900 acres), chiefly jungle, three miles below Hardwar. We examined it, and found its location and character satisfactory.' "

About its work and strength Mr. Phelps says:
"There are now in the Institution 274[4] boys, of whom

---
[4] There are now over 300.

fourteen are in the college, and 260 in the ten classes of the school. The boys when entering are usually of the age o seven or eight years. They are taken with the understanding that they are to remain sixteen years. On entering, the boys take a vow of poverty, chastity, and obedience for sixteen years, and this vow they renew at the end of the tenth year. The pupils are not allowed to visit their homes during this long period of training, except under exceptional and urgent circumstances, nor can their relations come to the school oftener than once a month. Usually they come about twice a year.

"The discipline is strict, though at the same time parental, personal, and even tender in its mode of application. The boys are under constant supervision both during and outside school hours. There are, besides the teachers, thirteen superintendents who are with the boys at all times when the latter are not actually in the schoolrooms. The boys forming classes or sections of a class live together in large rooms, in each of which also lives a superintendent.

"The whole school is pervaded by an atmosphere of affectionate familiarity and mutual confidence, which characterizes the relations of the pupils with each other, and with the teachers and the superintendents. This feeling finds its strongest expression towards the Governor, Mr. Munshi Ram. All teachers, officials, and pupils alike feel for him the sentiments of a son for a father.

"When I first came to the Gurukula, Mr. Munshi Ram outlined to me the aim of the management as regards the relations which they have sought to establish among those in the community. 'The feeling is cultivated,' he said, 'that all are members of the same family—brethren. The boys are taught to share all their pleasures with their comrades, and to seek no enjoyment that cannot be so shared. Even when their parents come here the boys will not accept individual presents from them. They are ready to make great sacrifices for each other. If one of their members is sick, they nurse him by turns at night.

"The Governor receives no pay, and has given all his property, between Rs. 30,000 and Rs. 40,000 to the school. Some of the best of the teachers have promised their services for life at a salary which is no more than a living allowance.

"The rising gong is sounded at 4 a.m. for all except several of the youngest classes, which are given an hour's longer sleep. Half an hour is then given to dumbbell exercises and other calisthenics. The next half hour, from 5 to 5.30 is allowed for bathing and completing the toilet. Next follows the morning worship. This consists of Sandhya, a prayer, silently and individually offered, and the agnihotra, a fire oblation made by the boys in groups.

"All the boys next assemble to listen to a conversation with the Governor on some moral or ethical subject. This occupies a half or three-quarters of an hour.

"A little light food, usually milk or nuts, is then distributed. Two hours of study follow. At 8.45 the morning meal is taken. The school boys assemble in two dining-halls, the college boys and the Governor mess by themselves. The food is plain but substantial and well prepared. Half an hour's rest follows the meal.

"From 9.45 to 4.15 are the school hours of the day—that is during the colder half of the year. An intermission of half an hour occurs soon after midday, during which the pupils are given milk or other light refreshment. From 4.15 to 4.45 the boys are left to themselves. From 4.45 to 5.30 is the play hour. Regular participation in games is required of all students.

"From 6.00 to 6.30 Sandhya and agnihotra are again performed as in the morning. Then follows the evening meal, which is substantially a repetition of that in the morning. A little later comes an hour's study. All retire to rest at 9, with this exception, that the college boys are allowed lights until 10. Holidays occur four times in each lunar month. There are also about twenty other holidays during the year, and long vacation covering the months of August and September."

The following on moral and religious instruction is an extract from another letter:

"Moral and ethical instruction is regular, and extends over the whole ten years of the school course. In the earlier years a large number of helpful Sanskrit verses are memorized by the student. Then follow three text-books made up of selections from the *Manu Smriti*. Appropriate parts of Swami

Dayanand's works are also used. To these subjects three to seven periods per week are given.

"The moral and religious character of the student is further powerfully stimulated and developed by the study of the Sanskrit sacred literature, to which a large proportion of each of the sixteen years of the course is given."

About the scheme of studies, Mr. Phelps remarks:

"With all the attention the Gurukula gives to the Vedas and other sacred books it is the aim of the management to make it a first-class institution for the study of Western literature and modern science. The full development of this part of the scheme has, however, hitherto been impossible for want of adequate funds. But the effort has been made to keep the school up to the requirements of the pupils who are still for the most part in the lower classes. English is begun in the sixth year and is compulsory during the subsequent eight years. They have, therefore, the mental equipment for keeping in touch with the thought and activities of the world. They have had installations of the telephone and wireless telegraphy in the laboratory. The library is fairly large and well chosen, and the reading room is supplied with a number of Anglo-Indian and Indian dailies as well as magazines. On the private library shelves of college students I noticed such authors as Bacon, Locke, Goethe, Emerson, Martineau, Mallock, Sir Oliver Lodge, and in these volumes work was attested by abundant underscorings. Students in agriculture are each required to cultivate a plot of ground under the supervision of a graduate of an American Agricultural College. In Sanskrit they are far advanced. It is said that tenth year boys are well acquainted with Sanskrit. They read, write, and speak Sanskrit with ease. I have myself attended these club meetings, and heard Sanskrit spoken fluently by both school and college boys.

"Tenth year boys have also given much time to Indian philosophy and logic. The Gurukula students have far better knowledge of Hindi than those of other schools, since it is the only usual medium of instruction.

"So far as I can gather, the boy at the end of the tenth year of the Gurukula is at least on a par in intellectual equipment with the student who has reached the F.A. standard in other colleges.

"The advantage of a Gurukula student is due in a still greater degree to the fact that instruction is imparted to him in his own language and is therefore readily understood and assimilated. The use of Hindi as a medium of instruction is one of the features of the school which is regarded as exceedingly important."

Why the Gurukula does not invite Government aid and why it is held in suspicion is further explained:

"From what has been said in previous letters it will be readily seen why it is impossible for the Gurukula to invite Government co-operation, that is, to submit to Government supervision as an aided school. This would mean, in the first place, that Sanskrit must be displaced in favour of English, as the first language of the school. In the next place the use of Hindi as a medium of instruction is a feature of the school regarded as essential to sound education, but which Government rules for aided schools would not permit. Thirdly, the school to a large extent uses its own text-books, which the regular system would exclude in favour of standard text-books. Finally, were the school recognized, the courses of study in the work of the institution would necessarily be subject to the usual University examinations.

"It ought, therefore, to cause no surprise, and should be no ground for suspicion that the school does not seek recognition or aid from the government. <u>Its aims and methods are so radically different from those which govern the regular educational system that it cannot do otherwise than stand alone</u>.

"The complaint is also made that the Government is not open with the Gurukula. Reports constantly come to their ears that men high in authority speak of the institution as a breeder of anarchy and a source of danger to the State.

"It is believed that misrepresentations of the institution have been made to the Government both by Mahamedans and by Christian missionaries. The latter particularly, having ready access to those in authority, are credited with a good deal of responsibility for the false impression. I have myself known of Christian missionary statements being quoted as authority by a Government official against both the Gurukula and the Arya Samaj, which statements I am satisfied were outrageous slanders."

These suspicions were first articulated by Mr. (now Sir) Valentine Chirol in his articles on modern Indian unrest in the (London) *Times* in an article on "The Punjab and the Arya Samaj".

But the authorities put themselves into closer touch with the institution. When he visited the Gurukula for the first time, the Lieutenant-Governor of the Province, Sir James Meston, said on 6th March, 1913:

"The Gurukula is one of the most original and interesting experiments carried on in these provinces, in fact in the whole of India. One of the most wonderful, interesting, and stimulating institutions; we have a band of ascetics devoted to their duty, and working in the wilderness following the traditions of the ancient Rishis, combined with the most modern scientific methods, and working practically for nothing, and a set of students of strong physique, obedient, loyal, thoughtful, devoted, extraordinarily happy, and extraordinarily well fed."

In the course of his speech he explained that one of the reasons for his visit was that "he wanted to meet a community which had been described in official papers as a source of infinite, terrible, and unknown danger." The right answer to this, he added, "was to come myself." Sir James Meston repeated his visit to the Gurukula and laid the foundation stone of a sister institution at Mathura, where in the course of his speech he paid a high tribute to Lala Munshi Ram, the founder of the Kangri Gurukula, and affirmed that the Arya Samaj was not a political body.[5]

Besides these two colleges, the Arya Samaj have founded and are maintaining a large number of boys' schools, Primary and Secondary, Gurukulas and Patchalas. A good many of these are high-class educational institutions, and are being carried on at a great cost, and with a great deal of self-sacrifice.

For the education of girls the Arya Samaj maintains a

---

[5] The Gurukula, Hardwar has now been recognized as an autonomous college granting its own degrees and receiving grants from the University Grants Commission as if it were a University.—Ed.

college, and a large number of girls' schools, both Primary and Secondary. The college is at Jullundher (Punjab) and is called the Kanya Mahavidyala. It has a very large boarding-house attached to it where girls and lady students live under the charge and under supervision of Indian lady-teachers. It is a very successful institution and a monument to the public spirit and zeal of its founder, Lala Deva Raja of Jullundher. Among the subjects taught are Music, Domestic Economy, Cooking, Needlework, English, Sanskrit, Hindi History, Geography, Mathematics, Political Economy, etc. For the school department they have compiled their own series of readers. Hindi is the medium of instruction. The institution receives no aid from the Government.

APPENDIX

A RED-LETTER DAY

June 1 is a red-letter day in the history of modern Panjab. Seventy-nine years ago on 1st June, 1886, the first independent educational institution in India, the Dayanand Anglo-Vedic High School, Lahore opened its portals to students. It was the first educational institution in the country with an entirely Indian management. Though some of the members of the D.A.V. College Trust and Management Society were officials, they held office in the Society in their personal capacity as ardent Arya Samajists elected by fellow Arya Samajists. It was thus an entirely public— as distinct from an official, officially sponsored or one enjoying official patronage—venture in the field of education. More than that it was the first venture in community development—in the truest sense of the term—not only in the field of education but in the entire sphere of social services. If its funds owed nothing to government grants, they neither represented princely generosity nor aristocratic munificence. The entire sum of rupees thirty-two thousand that the society had when it established the D.A.V. High School in 1886 had come in the form of countless donations from the Arya Samajists of limited means in Panjab and elsewhere. A community had bestirred itself to provide a social service not for its members alone but for the entire neighbourhood. The continued maintenance of the institution was guaranteed by the *Atta* Fund and *Raddi* Fund collections, besides small monthly cash subscriptions and the annual donations collected at the time of anniversary celebrations. Though it could be dubbed a middle-class movement, the services it was to provide were not confined to the middle classes only. Its portals were open to all without distinction of caste, creed or class.

In another way as well, 1st June, 1886 became a red-letter day in the history of Panjab, nay of the whole of India. On that day young Hansraj assumed office as the *honorary* headmaster of the D.A.V. High School, Lahore. He was the first Indian thus to devote himself to the service of the community without receiving any recompense. His sacrifice was all the greater because he was not a member of a rich family which could easily afford to pension one of its members from the collective income of the joint family. His elder brother—the only other member of the family—was then employed at Rs. 80 a month in the Post Office. When Hansraj decided to make the dream of the Arya Samajists a reality by dedicating himself to the new cause, his brother shared his enthusiasm for its success and offered to make an allowance of forty rupees a month—one-half of his meagre salary—to his younger brother. This opened a new chapter in our social consciousness—a penance undertaken not for personal salvation but to serve a social end. Here was a modern Sagar dedicating not his sons but his all so that the Ganges of knowledge might quench the thirst for knowledge of Panjab.

It was an *Anglo-Vedic* High School that opened its portals to seekers after knowledge that day. Here English education was to be offered under the protective colouring of Indian cultural traditions. Its alumni were not hypocrites believing in one thing in the school and another at home. They were offered chances for integrated development under its early motto—learning, piety and patriotism. It was neither to turn out agnostic patriots nor fanatical guardians of a single community's interests. It offered an open challenge to Macaulay's hopes expressed in the Minute on English Education in India. It attempted to make Western education safe by harnessing both its scientific quest as well as liberal leanings to the service of the community.

If one swallow does not make a summer, it certainly heralds it. The high school of 1886, became a college in 1889. Soon, however, it gave birth to a great educational movement in Panjab. At first, schools and then colleges were opened up and down the country, by Hindus, Sikhs and Muslims. It survived the tremendous shock of the partition in 1947. Today the D.A.V. College Trust and Management Society with its headquarters at Delhi—which most Panjabis now consider to be a part of Panjab—has seventeen colleges, three polytechnics and more than 80 higher secondary and high schools under its management. It is the biggest educational trust in India today.

In another sphere as well, the D.A.V. School at Lahore began a movement. The example of Lala Hansraj was followed by Pandit Mehar Chand who joined the Sain Das Anglo-Sanskrit High School at Jullundur as its honorary headmaster. In the first decade of the twentieth century the order of Life Members was formally organized, a band of selfless workers devoted to the cause of education and the Arya Samaj and receiving a meagre pittance for their services.

A very substantial contribution of the D.A.V. College Trust and Management Society has been training in government by committees, supposed to be a peculiarly English institution. In a country where the personality cult prevails so largely, government by committee was hard to come by. Yet the D.A.V. College Trust and Management Society by its organisation and procedure brought both high and low together in its service. Here in its conclaves, the employees may challenge the employers, the unemployed may seek to teach wisdom to the most profitably employed, a non-lawyer member may openly seek to get the house to override the legal opinion of a member of the highest judiciary in the country. Its procedure for selection of its staff offers an example of how to secure the best talent available for specific services. The discussion on its "budgets' may sometimes give points to our legislators. Its office-bearers so seldom 'bear' an office that they have to be persuaded to accept the office through which the community seeks to get the best out of them.

But above all, the D.A.V. College Movement created a tradition of independent thought and action which earned for its members the proud title of rebels under the alien rule. Now that conformity threatens to become synonymous with democracy, independence of thought and action that its tradition keeps alive here and there may still prove to be the nerve-centre of creative thinking without which democracy can neither flourish nor survive.

Sri Ram Sharma

EDUCATIONAL INSTITUTIONS

of

Higher Learning under D.A.V. College Trust and Management Society

1. D. A V. College, Amritsar.
2. D. A. V. College, Jullundur.
3. Hans Raj Mahila Mahavidyalaya, Jullundur.
4. D. A. V. College, Ambala.
5. D. A. V. College for Women, Yamnna Nagar.
6. D. A. V. College, Chandigarh.
7. Dayanand College, Hissar.
8. D. A. V. College, Abohar.
9. Hans Raj College, Delhi.
10. Girdhari Lal D.A.V. College, New Delhi.
11. Dayanand Ayur-Vedic College, Jullundur.
12. Sohan Lal Training College, Ambala.
13. D. A. V. College, Sholapur.
14. Dayanand College of Education, Sholapur.
15. Dayanand College of Commerce, Sholapur.
16. D. A. V. College, for Women, Amritsar.
17. Mehr Chand Polytechnic, Jullundur.
18. Mehr Chand Technical Institute, Jullundur.
19. Dayanand Polytechnic, Amritsar.
20. Dayanand College of Law, Sholapur.
21. D. A. V. Girls College, Batala.
22. Dayanand College of Divinity, Hissar.

Chapter XII

ORGANIZATION OF THE ARYA SAMAJ

Intelligent, submissive, rest united, friendly and kind, sharing each other's labours. Come, speaking sweetly each one to the other. I make you one-intentioned and one-minded.

Ath. iii, 30, 5

1. *In General*

The most striking feature in connection with the Arya Samaj, which makes it at once the most powerful and the most influential of all reform movements in the country, is its complete and unique organization. Every Arya Samaj is a unit in itself. Generally, there is one in every city or village which has come under its influence, but in some cities there are more, either because of the distances separating the different parts of the same city, or of some slight variations in principle. The latter distinction is mostly confined to the Punjab.

2. *Membership*

Effective membership involves (a) the acceptance of the Ten Principles; (b) the payment of one per cent of one's income, either monthly or yearly, towards the revenues of the Samaj; (c) attendance at meetings; (d) upright conduct.

3. *Weekly Services*

The Samaj meets once a week for congregational service, which consists generally of (a) Homa; (b) singing of hymns; (c) prayer and sermon; (d) lecture. The service can be conducted by any member, regardless of caste, whom the officers of the Samaj select for the purpose. The Samaj does not ordain ministers or priests. Any layman can officiate at the services or at ceremonies and be asked to lecture.

The weekly service meetings are open to the public, and no distinction is made between members and non-members, or between Hindus and non-Hindus. Anybody can come into the Church of God and occupy whatever seat he likes.

4. *Executive Committee*

The affairs of each Arya Samaj are controlled by an executive committee comprising elected officers and as many members as may be elected in proportion to the size of the Samaj. Only effective members can vote in the election of officers and the committee. The officers are: (a) President; (b) one or more Vice-Presidents; (c) one or more Secretaries; (d) Accountant; (e) Librarian. They must be effective members themselves. They are elected for the year at an annual meeting convened for the purpose, where the voting is by ballot. At this annual meeting the outgoing officers and the committee render to the general body an account of the income and expenditure of the Samaj during the year together with a report of the year's working: after which the meeting proceeds to elect officers and committee for the coming year. The outgoing officers and committee are eligible for re-election. In the larger Samajes, the general body of members is divided into groups of ten, for electing representatives on the committee. This is in addition to a few members, not exceeding five, who are elected by the whole body of members. The Samaj may meet for the transaction of such business as may be referred to it by the committee, or by the officers, or on the requisition of a certain number of members, for the consideration of such proposals as they wish to bring under purview by the general body.

Failure to pay the stipulated one per cent of income, or any other misconduct, may lead to suspension of a member by the Samaj, or may remove his name altogether from the register of effective members. This is no bar to readmission at the discretion of the committee, from whose decisions in all matters there is, moreover, the right of appeal to the general body. Neither the committee nor the general body is empowered to make changes in the creed, or the constitution, of the Samaj.

5. Provincial Assembly

In each province there is a provincial assembly consisting of representatives of the Arya Samajes in the province, the number of representatives which each is entitled to return being determined by the size of the Samaj. Every Arya Samaj contributes 10 per cent of its gross income to the funds of this assembly, but the assembly has the right to raise, and does raise, funds for general or special purposes as its governing body may determine. This assembly arranges for the dissemination of the Vedic religion by honorary and also paid preachers; sometimes publishes newspapers and controls the publication of official literature and does all that is necessary in the interests of the movement. It may manage the educational institutions if there is no separate organization for the purpose. This assembly can amend the rules of management by a general referendum of all the effective members in the province, but even so is powerless to alter the principles or the creed. The general assembly is elected every three years, but the officers and the committee of the provincial assembly are elected every year.

6. The All-India Assembly

Foremost is the All-India body, which is constituted by the representatives of the different provincial assemblies and forms the connecting link between the different provinces.

7. Young Men's Arya Samajes

Connected with the Samajes in different cities are young men's Arya Samajes, which serve as recruiting centres for the main body. The parent Samaj admits adults only. The young men's Samaj admits all, and insists on nothing more than a belief in God and the payment of a trifling monthly subscription.

8. Meeting Places

Every Arya Samaj has its meeting-place. In the principal cities all over India, it owns palatial buildings, containing

ORGANIZATION OF THE ARYA SAMAJ

lecture-halls, committee-rooms, etc. In smaller places it hires rooms for meetings. The young men's Arya Samajes generally use the premises of the main body, but occasionally have separate rooms of their own. In some places the premises are utilized for daily prayers and for club amenities as well. Every Arya Samaj is supposed to arrange for the teaching of Hindi and Sanskrit to such members as are unacquainted with those languages.

Chapter XIII

THE ARYA SAMAJ AND POLITICS

As heaven and earth are not afraid and never suffer loss or harm, even so my spirit fear not Thee.

As day and night are not afraid, nor ever suffer loss or harm, even so my spirit fear not Thee.

As sun and moon are not afraid, nor ever suffer loss or harm, even so my spirit fear not Thee.

As Brahmanhood and princely power are not afraid, nor ever suffer loss or harm, even so my spirit fear not Thee.

As what hath been and what shall be fear not, nor ever suffer loss or harm, even so my spirit fear not Thee.

Ath. ii, 15, 1-5

1. Not a Political or Anti-British Movement

The foreign rulers of India were never quite easy in mind about the Arya Samaj. They always disliked its independent attitude and its propaganda of self-confidence, self-help, and self-reliance. The national side of its activities aroused their antagonism. They could not look with favour on an indigenous movement which, to their way of thinking, could succeed in big projects without enlisting outside help and guidance, and thereby established a species of government, within the Government. The progress it made, the impressive hold which it acquired on the minds of the people, the popuarity which it won in spite of its heterodoxy and its iconoclasm among the Hindus, the influence which it possessed, the immense "go" which characterized it in all its doings, the national spirit which it aroused and developed among the Hindus, the ready self-sacrifice of its members, the independence of their tone and the rapidity with which the movement was diffused throughout India, and last, but not least, the spirit of criticism which it generated, gained for it the suspicion of the ruling bureaucracy. This suspicion more than once brought the wrath of the authorities on its members which took the shape of deportations, prosecutions, dismissals, etc.

In order to provide the reader with a fair picture of both sides of the question, we propose to quote somewhat copious extracts from the writings of those who have tried to discredit the Arya Samaj as a political and anti-British movement. We will begin with the writings of one who is believed to be among its most virulent and bitter critics, occupying at the same time a high position among the English publicists of the day. Sir Valentine Chirol, as a special correspondent of the *London Times*, visited India in 1907-10, and contributed a series of articles on Indian unrest, which were widely read and applauded in the British Isles. It was shortly afterwards that their author was knighted. These articles have since been published in book form, with a dedication, by permission, to Lord Morley, the Secretary of State for India in those troublous times. One chapter deals almost exclusively with the Arya Samaj; but, before we come to his criticisms, we must inform the reader of the general conclusions formulated by Sir Valentine Chirol on the whole question of Indian unrest.

He is disposed to think "that the more dangerous forms of unrest are practically confined to the Hindu",[1] and that, instead of calling it Indian unrest, it would be "more accurate" to call it "Hindu unrest", and that "its main-spring is a deep-rooted antagonism to all the principles upon which Western society, especially in a democratic country like England, has been built up." That he was entirely wrong in both these propositions has been abundantly proved by the events that happened since he wrote.

Coming to the Arya Samaj, however, Sir Valentine Chirol thinks that "the whole drift of Dayanand's teachings is far less to reform Hinduism than to range it into active resistance to the alien influences which threatened, in his opinion, to denationalize it." In support of this assertion he relies upon a string of stray expressions, (without giving the references) alleged to be the translation into English of those used by the Swami in his writings; refers to the useful social work done by the Samaj, and concludes: "These and many other new departures conceived in the same liberal spirit at first provoked

[1] *Unrest in India*, p. 5.

the vehement hostility of the orthodox Hindus, who at one time stopped all social intercourse with the Arya reformer. But whereas, in other parts of India, the idea of social reform came to be associated with the bogie of Western ascendancy, and therefore weakened and gave way before the rising tide of reaction against that ascendancy, it has been associated in the Punjab with the cry of 'Arya (Vartī) for the Aryans', and the political activities of the Arya Samaj, or, at least, of a number of its most prominent members who have figured conspicuously in the anti-British agitation of the last few years, have assured for it from Hindu orthodoxy a measure of tolerance and even of goodwill which its social activities would certainly not otherwise have received. That the Arya Samaj, which shows the impress of Western influence in so much of its social work, should at the same time have associated itself so intimately with a political movement directed against British rule, is one of the many anomalies presented by the problem of Indian unrest."

2. Sir V. Chirol v. the Arya Samaj

The facts on which Sir Valentine Chirol has relied in respect of his conclusions may be thus enumerated:

1. That "in the Rawalpindi riots in the year 1907 the ringleaders were Aryas."

2. That "in the violent propaganda which for about two years preceded the actual outbreak of violence none figured more prominently than Lala Lajpat Rai and Ajit Singh, both prominent Aryas."

3. That in certain legal proceedings taken against another Arya, Bhai Parmananda, some letters were produced written by Lajpat Rai to Parmananda while the latter was in England in 1905, in which some political works had been asked for the use of students and certain opinions had been expressed about political conditions in the Punjab.

4. That this Bhai Parmananda "was found in possession of various formulae for the manufacture of bombs."

5. That, in Patiala, the Aryas "constituted the great majority of defendants, 76 in number......who were put on their trial...... for seditious practices"; and that "so seriously were the charges

felt to reflect upon the Arya Samaj as a whole that one of its leading members was briefed on its behalf for the defence."

6. That, though "it is impossible to say......how far the evidence outlined by Counsel" for the prosecution "would have borne out" the "charges, one may properly assume it to have been of a very formidable character, for after the case had been opened against them the defendants hastened to send in a petition invoking the clemency of the Maharaja" and "expressed therein their deep sorrow for any conduct open to misconstruction, tendered their unqualified apology for any indiscreet acts they might have committed, and testified their 'great abhorrence and absolute detestation' of anarchists and seditionists. Whereupon His Highness ordered the prosecution to be abandoned, but banished the defendants from his State and declared their posts to be forfeited by such as had been in his service, and only in a few cases were these punishments subsequently remitted."

7. That Shyamji Krishna Varma, whom the founder of the Arya Samaj appointed a member of the first governing body in his lifetime, and after his death a trustee of his will, has said that "of all movements in India for the political regeneration of the country, none is so potent as the Arya Samaj," and that "the ideal of that society, as proclaimed by its founder, is an absolutely free and independent form of national Government."

Now, it is a great pity that many of these so-called facts should be either false or mere half-truths; that a writer of Sir Valentine Chirol's status should have been guilty (a) of not giving chapter and verse for his quotations; (b) of suppressing important facts which must be within his knowledge and which throw quite a different light on the incidents relied on by him; (c) of having ignored evidence which undermined his case to its very foundations; and (d) generally of *suggestio falsi*.

3. *Reply to Sir V. Chirol's Charges*

The true facts are as follows:

1. The so-called Arya "ringleaders" in the Rawalpindi riots were all acquitted by a European judge, a senior member of the I.C.S., who presided over their trial and who found

that the evidence submitted by the prosecution against them was false and fabricated. This judgement was never contested by the Government, and these facts ought to have been known to Sir Valentine Chirol when he wrote his articles.

2. Sirdar Ajit Singh's connection with the Arya Samaj was openly repudiated by the leading Arya Samajists. He never claimed to be an Arya, and it was not known that he ever became a member. In fact, it is well known that for "two years immediately preceding the outbreak of violence in 1907" he was an atheist, and made no secret of his lack of belief. No evidence is forthcoming that before 1907 he carried on any propaganda at all, much less a violent propaganda. This is strongly corroborated by the further evidence that no notice whatever was taken of him by the Government except in 1907. He was not known to the press or to the police, and earned his living by teaching Indian languages to English officers, civil and military, and European ladies. The charge framed against him in 1910, after he had left the country, had no connection with the events of 1907 or before. These facts were all before the public at the time Sir Valentine Chirol was writing his book.

3. As far as Lajpat Rai is concerned, it is significant that:

(a) He was never put on his trial.

(b) That, in spite of his repeated demands to be apprised of the reasons for his deportation, these reasons have not been forthcoming.

(c) That even Sir Valentine Chirol, with the whole machinery of the Government of India at his back, has not been able to give any quotations from Lajpat Rai's speeches or writings to justify his statements about him.

(d) That even Lord Morley could not do so, and that, in his revised speeches, since published in book form, his lordship has considered it necessary to delete almost all accusations that he had made against Lajpat Rai in the House of Commons in justification of his policy of deportation in 1907.

(e) That Lajpat Rai has thoroughly vindicated his political character by obtaining judicial verdicts in his favour in the highest courts in India and in England, in suits which he launched against powerful journalists in these countries.

(f) That he has never concealed his political opinions, and even Sir Valentine Chirol has given him, in one place, a disposition for frankness.

(g) That Indians of the highest standing (some of them in the confidence of the Government), men of admitted veracity and unimpeachable character, have publicly associated with him both before and after his deportation, and have spoken and written in his favour in most unambiguous terms.

(h) That the stray expressions culled from his letters produced in the case against Bhai Parmananda were fully explained by him on oath in the course of Bhai Parmananda's trial, and no exception whatever was taken to his statement either by the court or by the government prosecutor.

4. Bhai Parmananda has always denied that he was ever in possession of any formulae for the manufacture of bombs, though his denial was not accepted by the court.

5. and (6) It is well known in the Punjab that the Patiala prosecution was due to the over-zeal of a retired British Police Official, and instituted by the State under the impression that the British Government would feel gratified. As soon, however, as it was found that there was practically no evidence in support of the serious charges brought forward—that even Sir Louis Dane, the Lieutenant-Governor of the Punjab, one of the greatest enemies the Arya Samaj had, had given a sort of certificate to the Samaj exonerating the latter as a body from any charge of sedition—His Highness became anxious to stop the proceedings. The petition referred to by Sir Valentine Chirol was the outcome of certain negotiations between the State and the defendants, and contains no admission of guilt or of any truth in the charges brought against the defendants. The order of banishment was in the nature of "saving face" of the prosecution. Several of the defendants belonged to British territory, and most of the others, if not all, were allowed to re-enter the State. Some of them are at present in the service of the State that nominally banished them. In fact, we are not aware of any native of the State against whom the order still subsists. But the most significant fact is that the principal accused in the case, the President of the Patiala Arya Samaj, who was a British-Indian Officer of high rank

(an Executive Engineer in the P.W.D.) lent to the State, is still in the sevice of the British Government, and in full enjoyment of his rank and emoluments. These details must be known to Sir Valentine Chirol, since they were public property at the time when he published his book. The officer in question, we may add, received his full pay for the period during which he was under suspension pending trial, and on the administrative side his case was decided by the Governor-General-in-Council.

7. In regard to Mr. Shyamji Krishna Varma, the facts are as follows:

In 1881 or 1882, when Swami Dayanand appointed him a trustee in his will as "one of the governing body" of his Press, Mr. S.K. Varma had not expressed any political opinions. Swami Dayanand's will created no trust of the Arya Samaj. It only created a trust of the property which belonged exclusively to him in his own right, and which he had accepted in gift for public purposes and which was under his sole control. Among these trustees were a number of persons who never belonged to the Arya Samaj, as for example, the late Mr. Justice Ranade, of the Bombay High Court. Mr. Varma was then holding a high position in a native State, and for several years afterwards enjoyed the confidence of high British officials (Political Agents of the native State where he served, Agent to the Governor- General, and others). Mr Varma denies that he ever was a regular member of the Samaj, and it is well known that, immediately before leaving India for good, he was on exceedingly bad terms with the Arya Samajes in general, and with the leading Arya Samajists in particular. The opinions of Mr. Varma about the Arya Samaj are not the opinions of the latter, yet there is nothing in the expressions quoted which in any way justifies the conclusions of Sir Valentine Chirol. One is in the nature of a prophecy and the other talks of an "ideal" which is as different from actualities as it is remote from practical politics.

Of far greater significance, however, than the opinions we have just criticized, are those expressed by eminent Anglo-Indian officers actually engaged in the work of administration and occupying positions of trust and responsibility in the Government of British India. Of these the most significant is the letter written by the Chief Secretary of the Punjab Government in 1910, on behalf of Sir Louis Dane, the Lieutenant-Governor of the Punjab, in which he stated that the Government was not convinced that the Arya Samaj as a body was seditious or even political.

The utterances of Sir James Meston, the Lieutenant-Governor of the United Provinces of Agra and Oude, are even more lucid and emphatic. They leave no doubt that the Government does not consider the Arya Samaj to be a political association.

4. *Official Testimony in favour of the Arya Samaj*

We proceed to give in their own words, and with references, a few opinions expressed by other responsible officials.

In his *Census Report* for the Punjab, for 1891, Sir Edward Maclagan (then Mr. Maclagan, I.C.S.) said: "The fact that the Aryas are mainly recruited from one class and that the Samaj possesses a very complete organization of its own has laid it open to the charge of supporting as a body the proclivities of a large section of its members: but the Samaj as such is not a political but a religious body."

Mr. Burn, I.C.S., of the United Provinces of Agra and Oude, said in his *Census Report* for those Provinces for the year 1901 "That the Aryas are would-be politicians is true, but that they are so because they are Aryas is a proposition in the highest degree doubtful."

The point has again been discussed at some length in the *Census Report* for 1911 by Mr. Blunt, I.C.S., of the same United Provinces, and we tender no apology for the following somewhat voluminous extracts therefrom (page 135 *et seq.*):

"Long ago the Samaj was charged with being a mere political society, with objects and opinions of a dubious character; and of late the charge has again been made, and with greater insistence. The heads of the charge seem to be three—firstly, that many prominent Aryas are politicians with opinions not above suspicion;[1] secondly, the Samaj strongly supports the Gaurakhshini movement; and thirdly, that the Samaj grossly attacks other religions. As regards the first

[1] In the opinion of Anglo-Indians, all nationalist politics are suspicious.

allegation, it is doubtless true. The Arya Samaj has many politicians of good and bad repute in its ranks...... There is of course, no doubt whatever that the Samaj doctrine has a patriotic side...... The Arya doctrine and the Arya education alike 'sing the glories of ancient India', and by so doing arouse the national pride of its disciples, who are made to feel that their country's history is not a tale of continuous humiliation. Patriotism and politics are not synonymous, but the arousing of an interest in national affairs is a natural result of arousing national pride. Moreover, the type of man to whom the Arya doctrine appeals is also the type of man to whom politics appeals, viz. the educated man who desires his country's progress, not ultra-conservative with the ultra-conservatism of the East, but, to a greater or less extent, *rerum novarum cupidus et capax*. It is not therefore surprising that there are politicians among the Arya Samaj. But it is impossible to deduce from this that the Arya Samaj, as a whole, is a political body. From the first the Samaj has consistently affirmed that it is not concerned with politics, has laid down this principle in various rules, has discouraged its members from taking part in them and disavowed their actions in express terms when they needed disavowal....The position indeed is that the tree has been judged by its fruit, the society by the action of its members....The judgment, whether right or wrong, is at all events natural, but it nevertheless seems to me to be absolutely necessary that a distinction should be drawn between the action of the Samaj as a whole and the action of its individual members—or, to go to the utmost length, of its individual sabhas (though the attitude of most sabhas, as of the central Sabha, has always been correct)."

Mr. Blunt then quotes the opinion of Mr. Burn, and adds: "Ten years later, there seems no need to alter this opinion, save that one may perhaps safely put it in even less undecisive terms, and also add the rider that 'Aryaism of its very nature appeals to men to whom politics will also appeal, and turns out a stamp of man who is likely to take some interest in national affairs.' But, having said so much no more can be said. The Samaj, as a whole, is not a political body, all Aryas are not politicians, and those Aryas that are politicians have not necessarily opinions that lead to or connote disloyalty."

As regards the second argument, Mr. Blunt begins by saying: "The connection of the Arya Samaj with the Gaurakhshini movement is a trifle obscure," discusses the position of the founder and the members in relation thereto, and then concludes:

"The sum of the matter is that, though the Gaurakhshin movement, in unscrupulous hands, is a political weapon, and too often is used as such, yet, with the majority of its Hindu adherents, it is still a religious matter pure and simple. With some Arya adherents it may be also a matter, almost unconsciously, of religion; but, whatever their reasons for supporting it, it is impossible to suppose that they are all insincere and unscrupulous in that support."

With reference to the third point, Mr. Blunt says: "That the attitude of the Arya Samaj to other religions is often objectionable cannot, unfortunately, be denied....The matter touches the question of politics, however, only at one point, and that is, how far the Arya Samaj, in attacking Christianity, can be said to attack the British Government. It seems certain that the Arya Samaj does fear the spread of Christianity. There is no question that Dayanand feared it...in part because he considered that the adoption or adaptation of any foreign creed would endanger the national feeling he wished to foster. But no more than this can be said. There seems no reason to hold that Dayanand, in attacking Christianity, had any thoughts of attacking the British Government and, if he and his followers attack Christianity, they attack Hinduism and Islam also."

5. *Position of the Leaders*

The position which the leaders of the Samaj take on this question of politics may be stated in several quotations from their speeches and writings, which we give. We take the first from a speech delivered by L. Munshi Ram, the acknowledged leader of the Gurukula section of the Samaj, at Lahore in November, 1907:

"The Arya Samaj is a society that promotes arts of peace......
I say...of all religions in the world the Vedic Religion alone is universal. Its doctrines are of universal applicability, without

reference to geographical or ethnological limits or to the 'colour Line'.......Revolutions, bloodshed, disorder, clannish malevolence and racial hatred are fatal to the spread of true Dharma and therefore the Arya Samaj has set its face against them."

Again: "The Arya Samaj is a self-respecting religious body whose activities are perfectly lawful. Politics forms a part of the duties of Grihasthas. The Arya Samaj in its collective capacity is a Sanyasi and, therefore, cannot have anything to do with politics—for that would be encroaching upon the work of Grihasthas."

Our second quotation is taken from a voluminous work published under the joint names of Lala Munshi Ram and Professor Ram Deva, of the Gurukula, Kangri, in 1910, and entitled, *The Arya Samaj and Its Detractors*:

"The Vedic church is undoubtedly a Universal Church. It preaches that the *Veda* was revealed in the beginning of creation for all races...When the Arya Samaj sings the glory of ancient India, forces of nationalism receive an impetus, and the aspirations of the young nationalist who had persistently dinned into his ear the mournful formula that Indian history recorded the lamentable tale of continuous and uninterrupted humiliation, feels that his dormant national pride is aroused and his aspirations stimulated.

"The Arya Samaj takes us back to a period of Indian history long anterior to the birth of Zoroastrianism, Buddhism, Christianity, and Mahomedanism. Rama and Sita, Krishna and Arjuna, are national heroes and heroines of whose magnificent deeds and righteous activities all Indians—without distinction of caste, creed, or race—might well feel proud. The *Upanishads* and the Darshanas are in a peculiar manner the common heritage of all Indians, no matter to what religion they belong now. So patriotism, which is the handmaiden of Vedicism, is unifying. Instead of fomenting discord, it promotes love and fosters harmony. The Vedic Church supports Indian nationalism, by inspiring nationalists with pride in the past and hope in the future. Though, as we have shown above, Vedicism fosters healthy patriotism, which statesmanship like that of Morley and Minto recognizes as a force to be encouraged and enlisted on the side of law.....

There is yet another fruitful cause of misunderstanding. The Vedic Dharma, like all great religious movements that have left their mark in the world, is not only a creed, but a way of looking at things, a point of view. The *Vedas* teach us all about the ideals of individual and social conduct, of social governance and political philosophy. If professors in Government Colleges who teach or recommend to their boys books like Mill's *Liberty* and *Representative Government*, Bentham's *Theory of Legislation*, Bagehot's *Physics and Politics*, Spencer's *Man Versus the State*, are not regarded as political agitators, there is no reason why the Arya Samaj, which preaches Vedic ideals of social reconstruction and modes of social governance, should be regarded as a political body...."

The third of our quotations is taken from an article in which the writer, believed to be a prominent member of the other section of the Samaj, reviewed a book[1] published in the form of a novel, in which it was insinuated that the Arya Samaj was a seditious body and its institutions the nurseries of seditious propaganda:

"Before we finish we want to state for the one hundredth time the position of the Arya Samaj in the clearest possible terms. It is its mission to unfasten the chains of intellectual, moral, religious, and social bondage. The Arya Samaj is for everything good in human nature, and if loving one's country and one's people is good, the Samaj stands for it and is not ashamed of it. The Arya Samaj stands for progress on solid foundations and is, therefore, engaged in building up the character of its people. Whatever the Samaj does, it does openly. Our schools are open, our meetings are open, our services are open, and we challenge anyone to give one single proof of the Arya Samaj having ever encouraged secrecy. In fact, the complaint sometimes is that it is too outspoken and too open. It discourages sycophancy and double dealing of all kinds. Well, if all this leads to a desire for political freedom, it has no reason to say, 'no', to it."[2]

It should be carefully noted that Dayanand's followers do not deny that he was a great patriot. His personal views

---

[1] *Sri Ram, the Revolutionist.*
[2] From an article entitled "Sri Ram, Revolutionist", published in *The Vedic Magazine* and *Gurukula Samachar*.

on politics are expounded in his book, *Satyarath Prakash*. He says, in the sixth chapter:

"Foreign Government—kind, beneficent and just though it may be—can never render the people perfectly happy."

Elsewhere in the same work he "praises the superior social efficiency, better social institutions, self-sacrifice, public spirit, enterprise, obedience to authority and patriotism" of the rulers of India, and tells his countrymen that:

" 'It is the possession of such sterling qualities and the doing of such noble deeds that have contributed to the advancement of Europeans'."

6. *A critical phase*

The Arya Samaj passed through a serious crisis in 1907-1910. For some time it was the object of singular and not very intelligent persecution on the part of officials who should have known better. Some Aryas in Government service were dismissed for the simple reason that they were members, or active members, of the Samaj. In the case of a regimental clerk so treated, it was admitted that "all his certificates" were "good" but that it was subsequently discovered that "he was a member of the Arya Samaj, and it was considered undesirable to have a member of that society in a Sikh regiment."

In other cases men were asked to resign the membership of the Samaj. Some complied with the order, but others refused and were consequently dismissed. At one place the officer commanding a brigade issued an order to the effect that "all ranks" were "forbidden to attend the meetings of the Arya Samaj or any other political body." In another place it was proclaimed by beat of drum that "all the books belonging to the religion of the Arya Samaj have been forfeited and confiscated to His Majesty." The Collector of the district where this happened, however, repudiated having authorized the proclamation.

In some districts a census of the Aryas was taken, and their names entered in Police Registers as suspects. Similarly, Departments of Administration caused special lists of Aryas in their employ to be prepared, with a view to their being

THE ARYA SAMAJ AND POLITICS

coerced into severing their connection with the movement. Some fathers were ordered to remove their boys from Arya schools, on pain of dismissal from their posts. The police kept a vigilant eye on every Arya and shadowed the prominent members' every movement. A vast system of espionage was introduced to ascertain the true sentiments of the community. One Government is known to have twice deputed special officers of outstanding detective ability to report on the Samaj.

Eventually it was discovered that there was no substantial reason to suspect the organization of any evil design against the Government; so it was decided to inaugurate a policy of conciliation towards them, the credit of which is due to Lord Hardinge and to Sir James Meston.

APPENDIX

(a)

The Hon'ble Mr. F. A. Robertson's confidential Memorandum on his conversations with a number of members of the advanced party among loyalists in the Punjab, dated 11 July, 1907.

"In the first place it is quite clear that the 'advanced party' is far from being one. <u>The orthodox Hindus are often at variance with the Arya Samaj and in the Arya Samaj itself there are two divisions</u>. The Aryas are possibly correct in stating themselves to have been at the inception a purely religious body, but that one section has been much mixed up with political agitators and has used its organization for its furtherance, hardly admits of doubt and this section has been to the fore in its dislike for Europeans and British rule and administration and has been marked by a strange animus against Christianity. On more than one occasion I asked various persons to tell me frankly what they thought of Lajpat Rai. Most seemed to think that he was not really disloyal. Several Aryas said that when <u>Lajpat Rai wanted the Arya Samaj to take part in political agitation, there was much opposition and discussion and that there was very nearly a serious split. The final result was that Lajpat Rai succeeded in capturing a number of the Aryas, getting them to assist him in his agitation, and in to some extent, making use of their organisation.</u> This was not really approved of except by very few. It was he and his influence certainly which dragged the Arya Samaj into the arena, in most cases against their will, <u>Lajpat Rai, they all said, was the heart and soul of the political side of the Arya Samaj</u>."

(b)

"The head and centre of the entire movement (of unrest in the Panjab) is Lala Lajpat Rai, a Khatri pleader. He is a revolutionary and a political enthusiast who is consumed with the most intense hatred for the British Government. His most prominent agent in disseminating sedition is Ajit Singh." (Minto's summary of the Punjab Minute asking for the issue of a warrant against Lala Lajpat Rai) in *India, Minto and Morley*, (pages 124 and 125.)

APPENDIX

(c)

"It is quite lately since the arrest of Lajpat Rai that we have become aware of the attempts to corrupt native officers and soldiers."

"We have had some curious information too of communication from Lajpat Rai and other agitators with the Amir. He probably puts all such letters in his wastepaper basket, if he has any." (Minto to Morley on August 29, quoted in *India, Minto and Morley* by Lady Minto, pages 151-52).

(d)

But when Minto had examined all the evidence that the Punjab Government could produce, he wrote:

"There is nothing whatever that I know of to justify his (Ibbetson's) assertion that one of Lajpat Rai's main objects is to tamper with the loyalty of the Indian Army. I have never seen any evidence in support of this. Lajpat is undoubtedly a man of high character and very much respected by his countrymen. If, when asked to arrest him, I had known what I know now, I should have required much more evidence before agreeing." (Minto to Morley, 5 November, 1907 in Morley Papers, VII, cited in *India Under Morley and Minto* by M.N. Das, page 135).

(e)

"When I was at Peshawar, I ventured to ask one in authority why a man of such high reputation should have been selected for attack. In defence of the Punjab Government, he said, 'You see it was just because he was so good that they fixed him. If he had been a rotter, they would have left him alone."

"It was because they hoped to strike at the Arya Samaj at the same time. The authorities in Northern India had long regarded the Samaj with special enmity. Much of the information (against the Arya Samaj) is based on false information. The editor of the *Hindustan* (Dina Nath), for example, was described as a graduate of the D.A.V. College, though he had hardly been there a month and owed the rest of his training to a Christian Mission School. Ajit Singh was described as a prominent Samajist, though he had never belonged to it."

(Nevinson in his *New Spirit in India*, pages 303 and 304).

"Lajpat Rai, a man of austere and generous life, one who had given up great worldly success for the service of the poor. By nature averse to politics, he devoted himself to the deep questions which lie beyond the touch of government." (Nevinson, ibid, 295, 296).

(f)

"10th May had been fixed by some Anglo-Indian journalists as the date for a probable rising against the British. Owing to their warnings, preparations were made for withdrawing the British residents, especially in Panjab towns, into the forts."
(Nevinson, ibid. 20).

Chapter XIV

CONCLUSION

Thine, Thine, O Lord is this Thy worshipper, he hath no other friends, O Mighty Lord! R. CXLII, 1.

Minds may doubt and hearts may fail when called to face new modes of thought or points of view; but the time must come when what is false in all things will fade, and what is true will no more seem strange.

Dr. Illingworth's *Reason and Revelation*

1. Will the Arya Samaj become Christian?

Friend and foe alike are in accord that the Arya Samaj is a great movement and wields great influence, at least in Northern India. Mr. Blunt, I.C.S., of the United Provinces of Agra and Oude, writing in 1912, dubbed it "the greatest religious movement in India of the past half century."[1] Sir Herbert Risley considers it to be the "most conspicuous movement" of the times.[2] Writing in 1902, Mr. Burn, I.C.S., of the United Provinces, thought it was "the most important of the Hindu movements in those Provinces,"[3] Sir Edward Maclagan (then Mr Maclagan), in writing his *Census Report* in 1891, described it as the "most important of the modern sects" in the Punjab. Sir Henry Cotton, in his book *New India*, characterizes the history of the movement as "one of the most important and interesting chapters of modern Hindu thought."[4]

In the opinion of Sir Herbert Risley, "it is a notable fact that the Hindu sectarian movement which appeals most strongly to the educated classes is bitterly opposed to Christianity and lays itself out not merely to counteract the efforts of missionaries but to reconvert to Hinduism high caste men who have become Christians." Further in his book,

---
[1] *Census Report for U.P. for 1911*, p. 129.
[2] *The Peoples of India*, p. 245.
[3] *Census Report for U.P. for 1901*, p. 82.
[4] *New India*, Sir H. Cotton, p. 278.

he adds: "....It (i.e. the Arya Samaj) offers to the educated Hindu a comprehensive body of doctrines purporting to be derived from Indian documents and traditions and embodying schemes of social and educational advancement, without which no real progress is possible."

"In this revival of Hinduism, touched by reforming zeal and animated by patriotic enthusiasm, Christianity is likely to find a formidable obstacle to its spread among the educated classes."[5]

It is not unnatural, then that the Arya Samaj should have encountered the most merciless criticism and the bitterest opposition from the Christian missionaries. In a paper read before the World Missionary Conference held at Edinburgh in 1910, it is described as "chief among the modern Neo-Hindu movements, both in point of activity and influence.... which hinder the spread of Christianity in India."[6] This explains the psychology of the minds that predicted an early dissolution of the movement. There were others, however, also missionaries, who thought that the movement was only paving the way for Christianity. One of them, Rev. Holland, of Allahabad, is reported to have said that "the ideas which the Arya Samaj raises without ability to satisfy them and the manifest contradictions of its system mean a not remote collapse into the arms of Christianity."[7] Another Christian writer, Mr. Frank Lillington M.A., says:

"The Arya Samaj has assumed a position which is becoming more and more clearly untenable. There seems good reason to believe that as Christianity is shown to be universal, the prejudices which have given birth to the Arya Samaj will die, and its antagonism to Christianity will cease." The slender foundations on which opinions like these are based may be gathered from the following references which Mr. Frank Lillington gives as footnotes on page 112 of his book. "They (i.e. the Arya Samajists) openly declare themselves to be enemies of ours, but they acknowledge, more frankly than most, the sinfulness of men and the need of strenuous efforts to obtain salvation."[8] "In—— a branch of the Arya

[5] *The Peoples of India*, pp. 244-5.
[6] *Report of the Conference*, Vol. I, p. 17.
[7] Ibid. p. 17.
[8] *Delhi Mission Report for 1895*, 37.

Samaj has been established which I cannot help looking upon as an indirect result of our work.... I believe that it is a real move forward and an attempt to accept Christianity without the 'offence of the Cross'."[9]

But the statements just quoted are valueless. They are figments of the imagination, and only represent the pious hopes of their authors. In his concluding chapter, Mr. Lillington prophesied that "In the Arya Samaj the Christian Missionary has an avowed enemy, but one who appears to be susceptible to courtesy and likely to become Christian when the increase of knowledge and a brotherly love of the Christians has warmed their hearts and enlightened their minds." Mr. Burn examined these statements and these hopes rather closely and says that "there is nothing improbable in the view that Christianity has had an effect on the doctrines of the Samaj. During the nineteenth century Christianity had advanced in India; its success may have had some influence as far as causing an inquiry into the reasons for belief and forms of dogma... is concerned, but I find no trace of any doctrine directly borrowed or imitated, such as has been noticed in other reforming movements...Their attitude towards it (Christianity) is far more iconoclastic than eclectic." Mr. Burn then compares the Arya Samaj with the Brahmo Samaj and concludes as follows: "I am, however, unable to see in its history or principles any warrant for the belief held by many missionaries that the Aryas will end by becoming Christian."[10]

2. *The Future of the Arya Samaj*

The conditions in India are so mutable and the influences at work so complex, varied and numerous, that it is impossible to see very far ahead. We have no qualifications for the role of a prophet. In our personal capacity as Indian, as Hindu and especially as Arya Samajist, we hope that the Hindus will be true to the faith of their forefathers, and will not change their national character so completely as would be involved by their becoming Christians. But we know that

---
[9] Ibid, pp. 38, 39.
[10] *Census Report for U.P. for 1901*, pp. 89-90.

powerful influences are at work in favour of Christianity. It would be futile to deny that Christianity is gaining ground. It is no satisfaction to be told that "the work of conversion to Christianity is now limited mainly to the depressed classes in the Punjab."[11]

The simple truth is: "they could get no other than low class converts."[12] It is further admitted that their greatest weapon is the ample provision they can afford to make for the *corpus sanum* of their converts. In a poverty-stricken country like India, with its recurring famines, earthquakes, floods and other visitations, that is the most effective argument any propagandist can advance in support of the superiority of his or her religion. This is all true, but what the Hindu reformer dreads most is the political argument.

We have already noticed that one of the reasons why the Arya Samaj is considered anti-British is that it is anti-Christian. In the *U.P. Census Report for 1901*, Mr. Burn conceded that the "future of Christianity was of some importance apart from its spiritual aspect."

We ourselves have heard Indians openly expressing themselves in favour of the wholesale conversion of India to Christianity for the sake of political unity and political progress. One may deplore the Machiavellian naïvete of the suggestion, but it is impossible to overlook its significance. Those who offer these suggestions, however, are very slightly acquainted with their country and their people. They quite forget that even Islam could not conquer Hinduism. Nor must the significance of the fact be ignored that no sooner had Christianity launched its work in India than Hinduism prepared to meet the challenge with its own weapons. The Brahmo Samaj was the first rampart of Hinduism against the Christian invasion. And, immediately the Brahmo Samaj displayed signs of weakness, the more formidable Arya Samaj sprang into being.

So critical an observer and scholar as Sir Herbert Risley said that, "The supremacy of Hinduism as the characteristic religion, of India, is not as yet seriously threatened. The Animistic hem of the garment may, indeed, be rent off, and

---

[11] *Punjab Census Report for 1911*, p. 191.
[12] Ibid.

its fragments be parted among rival faiths. But the garment itself, woven of many threads and glowing with various colours will remain intact and continue to satisfy the craving for spiritual raiment of a loose and elastic texture which possesses the Indian mind."

"It has often been said," proceeds Sir H. Risley, "that the advance of English, education, and more especially the teaching of physical science, will make short work of the Hindu religion, and that the rising generation of Hindus is doomed to wander without guidance in the wilderness of agnosticism.

"It may with justice be said, in justice to the adaptability of Hinduism, that a religion which has succeeded in absorbing Animism is not likely to strain at swallowing science. Nor is this the last refuge of Hinduism. If it appeals to the intellect by its metaphysical teaching, it also touches the emotions by the beatific vision which it offers to the heart and the imagination. But, whatever may have been its origin, the idea (doctrine of *bhakti*) has now taken its place among the characteristic teachings of Hinduism; it has been absorbed in the fullest sense of the word. And a religion which rests both on philosophy and on sentiment is likely to hold its ground until the Indian temperament itself undergoes some essential change."[13]

Mr. Burn also pointed out that the belief that the Aryas will end by becoming Christians "starts out with the assumption that Hinduism is a moribund faith, an assumption which was strongly contested by Sir A.C. Lyall. The faith of the Arya Samaj appeals strongly to the intellectual Hindu by its adherence to the philosophy and cosmogony which are familiar to him, and by its maintenance of the inspired nature of the *Vedas*, while even its position with regard to pantheism and image-worship is not unfamiliar. Further, while the attitude of the orthodox Hindu towards Christianity is for the most part one of indifference, the Arya Samaj has taken up an attitude of active hostility, and directs special efforts towards the conversion of persons who have embraced Christianity or Islam. For these reasons the Arya Samaj appears

[13] *The Peoples of India,* pp. 245-6.

to me to contain the elements of a certain success as a religious movement."[14]

All competent and impartial observers are thus agreed that in the immediate future there is no fear of Christianity dislodging Hinduism from its predominant position among the religions of India. On the other hand, the greater the activities of the Christian missionaries to convert India to Christianity, the greater the chance of the Arya Samaj to work, to struggle and to thrive. The Arya Samaj is not afraid of struggle.

In the words of Rev. C.F. Andrews, the Arya Samaj has been from the first "decidedly militant in spirit and policy"; for the simple reason that it has two militant Churches to counteract, viz. Islam and Christianity. Any increase in the activities of the latter is its chance and from its past history we may safely conclude that it is not likely to miss it.

It must be remembered that the militant spirit in the Arya Samaj does not aim at destruction.

"Today it is by far the most powerful indigenous reforming movement in the North of India."[15] Much of its vitality lies in active constructive propaganda. It has a complete social programme and is ever active. Here it should be noted, however, that every time the Arya Samaj has been in distress, it has emerged stronger. The greatest crisis in its history arose in 1907, when its very existence was endangered by the Government. This crisis continued till the end of 1910, but in the *Census of 1911*, it was found that its numbers had more than doubled within the preceding ten years.

The Arya Samaj is militant, not only externally, i.e. in its attitude towards other religions, but it is equally militant internally. Its members do not spare one another. It is not infrequently the case that the press and the platform are both vigorously embroiled in internal warfare. The less educated members do not always use refined language in their criticisms of the opposite party, or even in their inter-party criticism. We much prefer this spirit to the indifference and stagnation that characterized the Hinduism of pre-Arya Samaj days. The one gratifying and hopeful feature is that

---
[14] *Census Report for U.P. for 1901*, p. 90.
[15] Rev. C.F. Andrews, in *The Indian Renaissance*, p. 122.

its members know how to close their ranks whenever they are assailed from outside. Whenever a serious crisis had to be faced, the Arya Samaj has been ready to confront it. It was so in 1902, when the Christians proposed to deal them a crushing blow by prosecuting one of their presidents for kidnapping an orphan Hindu girl, of whom they had taken charge in the time of famine. The girl was married. In the period of scarcity their home had been broken, and they had strayed away from each other in search of food. The girl was taken charge of by a Christian agent and eventually transferred to the keeping of a lady hotel-keeper in Simla, who, the girl alleged, oppressed and ill-treated her. She fled and took refuge in the house of the president of the local Arya Samaj. The lady appealed to the police, who arrested the president, and kept him in custody for several days, refusing bail. After a costly trial, however, the case was decided in favour of the Arya Samaj. Both sections took a united stand. Again, in the troubles of 1907 and 1910, the same thing occurred.

The mutual recriminations in which the Arya Samajists indulge are not at all a pleasing feature of their activities.

3. The Future of Hinduism bound up with the Arya Samaj

In the opinion of many, the future of the Arya Samaj is practically the future of Hinduism. The Arya Samaj teaches the true and genuine Hinduism of the *Vedas*, it works in the interests of the Hindus, and it defends the Hindu community from the onslaught of alien religions. It does not aim at any future, outside and beyond the pale of Hinduism.

For a brief space of time in the history of the Arya Samaj there rose a tendency to break away from Hinduism altogether, but that was due principally to the dislike which the Aryas bear for the term "Hindu", which they consider to be foreign in origin and to mean "a slave".

On this point we have the incontestable testimony of the Census Commissioner of the Punjab. Referring to Mr. Maclagan's remark in the *Report of 1901* that "the stricter Aryas" had "a prejudice against being classed as Hindus", he observes: "But this objection was, and still is, based upon the contemptuous meaning which the foreign term, 'Hindu', acquired during the Mahomedan period." Yet when, "at the time of issuing instructions to enumerators, the chief authorities at the headquarters of the Arya Samaj were consulted as to whether they should be returned as professing a separate religion or not, although taking exception to the term 'Hindu', they did not wish to be treated as separate from the Hindu society, and consequently decided that the Aryas should return themselves as Hindu by religion and Arya or Vedic Dharm by sect. Of course the Aryas do not regard their faith as a sect... Considering that the term 'Hindu' has come to be universally accepted as representing the religious and social practices of people known as Hindus, no course was open but to treat the Arya Samaj, as a sect."

It is true, as Mr. Blunt says, that "the Brahmin priest hates and fears the Samaj", but it is not correct to add that "the educated among the orthodox abhor their teachings, the educated Hindu hates and fears and is seldom unready to speak evil of them."[16] He admits, however, that "a great majority of Arya converts belong to the educated classes," and that, on the whole, "Aryaism appeals rather to the educated and to the higher castes than to the illiterate and the lower castes."[17] The statement that "the stricter members of the orthodox Hinduism would never regard Aryas as true Hindus" and that "no one (among the orthodox?) would think of taking water from them"[18] are probably extravagant generalizations from his experience in the United Provinces. Even Mr. Blunt has to add that "there is some evidence that Aryas are beginning to gain a footing with the orthodox" and also that "the orthodox Hindus are willing enough to claim the Aryas as a Hindu sect when it happens to suit their political aspirations."[19]

Pandit Hari Keshan Kaul's description of the present situation is much more accurate in this respect. He says: "Owing to the lapse of time the opposition of the Sanatanists (the orthodox) to the Arya Samaj has become feeble, and, with the marked change in the ideas of the majority of educated Hindus, much of the Arya Samaj propaganda has been accept-

[16] *Census Report for U.P. for 1911*, pp. 137-38.
[17] Ibid. p. 139.
[18] Ibid.
[19] Ibid. p. 140.

ed by the Hindu community, while, on the other hand, the Arya Samaj have moderated their tone of criticism and begun to show more respect for some of the orthodox Hindu institutions. The result is that a greater harmony now prevails between the Arya Samajists and the orthodox Hindus... and the two communities work together in several lines, such as the revival of ancient festivals, the promotion of the study of Sanskrit and Hindi, the spread of female education and the introduction of social reforms."[20]

In the opinion of the present writer, the Arya Samaj can have no loftier or nobler ambition than that its entire teachings, or at least its spirit, may be adopted by Hinduism as its own.

In this increasing friendliness with orthodox Hinduism lies the strength of the Arya Samaj but therein also lurks the danger of a deterioration of standards of reform. We should not like the Arya Samaj to be lost in the vast sea of Hinduism. We should like it to exist for Hinduism first and for the rest of the world afterwards; but we should deplore its being merged in Hinduism or in any other *ism*. Its independence is the charter of its existence and of its usefulness. Its members have no hesitation, and will never have any, in staking their all on the defence of the Hindu community; but the strength of an advocate lies in his independence in spite of identifying himself with the cause of his client. There is another danger against which we would warn the Arya Samaj—the multiplication of institutions beyond its immediate resources. We have it on the testimony of Rev. C. F. Andrews that "its powers of expansion have not yet reached their limit," but the best interests of expansion on safe and sound lines demand a certain amount of concentration. Having "too many irons in the fire", might prove a grave source of weakness in a crisis. It might seriously hamper the singleness of purpose, the homogeneity of motive and the devotion to principle which have enabled the Samaj to maintain its powerful advance. Too great a diffusion of energy, with an easy-going conscience and a desire to reconcile all conflicting interests to which unrestricted expansion gives rise, has of yore brought ruin to empires, and, to compare small things with great, the same defective organization might, if not properly guarded against, wreck the yet tiny bark of the

[20] *Punjab Census Report for 1911*, p. 134.

Arya Samaj. The Arya Samaj should devote its utmost energies to putting its house in order. The enemies of the Arya Samaj are brilliant strategists, and instead of a frontal attack, they may aim at destroying or at least weakening the Samaj by flanking movements. Mutual confidence, mutal respect and regard, are the bed-rock upon which the edifice of the Samaj has been built. Compromise in details, in methods, in points of view, in procedure and even in measures, is the first principle of a regulated public life.

A certain amount of conservatism also is essential for orderly progress. What the Arya Samaj should aim at is mobility tempered with conservatism. In the confidence that we have a mission in life, that we have a task to fulfil which is at once noble, grand and high; in the faith that we have the will and the capacity to reach the goal; in the determination to reach that goal, in spite of difficulties, obstacles, and perchance persecution too; in the hope that we are always ready, in the future as in the past, to suffer for our convictions and to prove the strength of our faith by our sufferings, we should march on with a sure step, taking every unavoidable risk without sacrifice of principle, so far as individuals, are concerned, but jealously and zealously guarding the corporate life of the organisation.

The life of the Samaj is dearer to us than the life of any member or members thereof, but what is still more dear to us is the character of the Samaj—the character bestowed on it, the character bequeathed to it, by its founder. The founder of the Arya Samaj had many opportunities of acquiring large estates, of becoming rich as the head of great and wealthy religious institutions, or as leader of different religious orders existing in the country. But he spurned all. If he was indifferent to hate and malice he was also unaffected by love and sympathy. What he most avoided was the sympathy of his enemies. Let the Arya Samaj never forget that institutions are only means to ends. The Hindus were in error where they confounded the two. Up to a certain stage, means are no doubt ends in themselves, but not always, and not absolutely. Let not the Arya Samaj repeat the mistake of Hinduism.

Hinduism possessed vitality enough to survive that grievous mistake; Hinduism created the Arya Samaj; Hinduism has vitality enough to save itself by other means if the Arya Samaj would become an everlasting shame to those on whom the mantle of Dayanand has descended. He extorted admiration even from an enemy. It was of him that a broadminded missionary has stated:

"For Dayanand's personality and character there may well be almost unqualified admiration. He was a puritan to the backbone, and lived up to his creed. He was a fighter, strong virile, independent, if somewhat imperious in behaviour... His courage in facing his own countrymen through years of contumely and persecution was nothing less than heroic. He was a passionate lover of truth."

Dayanand stamped the Arya Samaj with his own character. Let the administrators of the Dayanand Anglo-Vedic College, which bears his hallowed name, and also the founders and managers of the Gurukula, whose object is to follow his footsteps more closely, recollect that and be true to their ideals.

It is useless gloating over our past unless we can chart out a future worthy of that past. The record of bygone glories may legitimately elate us: but, in order to be alive, we must live in the present.

CHAPTER XV

THE ARYA SAMAJ AND ITS IMPACT ON CONTEMPORARY INDIA

(In the Nineteenth Century)

IN order to understand the ideas and aims for which the Arya Samaj stands and their impact on contemporary life, it is necessary to have first a chronological outline of the life of its 'founder', his ministry and the development of the Arya Samaj after his death.

Swami Dayanand—Mul Shankar as he then was— was born in about 1824. After a thorough schooling of the orthodox type in a Brahman household, he left home when he was about 22 in 1846 and set about the task of searching for truth in the usual Indian tradition of a wanderer. About 1848 he became a Sanyasi but this did not prevent his sitting at the feet of another Sanyasi, Virjanand, from 1860 to 1863 at Mathura and relearning all that he had so far learnt about Indian culture. Three years' arduous studies here did for him what the earlier fourteen years had failed to do. He now acquired a sense of a mission. For twelve years more he went from place to place, delivering sermons, holding disputations, denouncing superstitions and trying to impart to others the truth as he saw it. Though he acquired some followers during these years, it was only on 10th April, 1875 that he founded the Arya Samaj at Bombay, defined his beliefs and set up an organisation to propagate them. 'The Principles of the Arya Samaj' were redefined at Lahore in 1877; organisational matters were separated from beliefs. His *Satyarath Prakash— Mirror of Truth*—was published in 1875, though a revised and expanded definitive edition appeared in 1884 after his death. He died on 30th October, 1883 when he was less than sixty. He was a voluminous writer. His Commentary on parts of the *Rig Veda*, and the *Yajur Veda* is a monumental work and was preceded by his *Introduction to the Commentary on the Vedas*. His works would cover some 15,000 pages of medium octavo size.

After the foundation of the Arya Samaj, Swami Dayanand lived for eight years. He had been speaking in Sanskrit till about 1874 when he delivered his first sermon in Hindi in Banaras. His is thus a very short ministry as compared with that of many other religious teachers. Even if some earlier years of his preaching be included, his period of active work for the truth as he finally saw it would not extend further back than 17th November, 1869 when he stormed the citadel of Hindu orthodoxy and held a disputation with the Pundits of Banaras. Fourteen years is a very short period for a religious mission, but Dayanand left voluminous works behind him with an active organisation to carry on his work. That explains, among other things, why his impact on his times and the years following has been much greater than his short ministry would otherwise warrant.

Dayanand did not know English and could not have, therefore, been influenced by the West or the Western tradition that was sweeping the country. He was very well read in Sanskrit and its traditional lore but even here we must remember that receiving his impulse from Virjanand, he rejected much that was passing at that time under the garb of traditional religious thought. He threw away the accretion of many centuries and claimed that he would accept nothing as truth which was not backed by the *Vedas* as he understood them. He parted company with the orthodox on the very term, the *Vedas*, and refused to include in it anything beyond the text of the *Rig*, *Sama*, *Yajur* and *Atharva*. Thus though claiming to be orthodox, his orthodoxy went centuries beyond what was then understood by the term. If he took up the cry, "Back to the *Vedas*," he made it mean the Vedic text, not the medieval commentaries thereon. He had no use for the vast bulk of literature that at that time was accepted as religious. Little wonder that orthodoxy rejected him, founded as it was on texts much nearer home.

Revolutionary though his concept of the foundation of Hindu religion was, his attitude to the world in which he lived was no less so. Like the orthodox Hindus, he accepted ultimate salvation as the objective towards which all men must strive. But he refused to confine these strivings to individual and personal ends alone. He declared service—the physical, moral and spiritual uplift of others—not only a cardinal principle, but the motivating rule of life.

Dayanand knew that devotion by itself soon ceases to be a social virtue. Whereas the doctrine of rebirth had been used to keep the unhappy, the miserable and the downtrodden content with their 'station' in life for centuries, he used it to further the cause of social justice by making it incumbent on those who were better off to assure themselves of a still better life after death by serving their less fortunate brethren. He denounced all claims based on custom and status alone. He accepted the division of society into four 'castes', but caste to him was synonymous with an occupational group, a professional corporation, thus rejecting the claims based on birth alone. He would not concede that women had a lower status in society, he hurled a string of women Vedic scholars at those who thought so. Neither custom nor tradition was to be accepted unless either could prove its worth in the service of society. Everything was subject to examination.

This led to his emphasis on the place of knowledge in human affairs, all the more so as he recognized no 'mysteries' in religion, much less any guardians of such sacred and secret lore. Propagation of knowledge he exalted into another cardinal principle, but his 'knowledge' was not confined to the studies of the medieval schoolmen nor was it limited to religious lore alone. To him the *Vedas* embodied all knowledge that humanity was capable of grasping; naturally all strivings after truth, in whatever direction it led one, were to be encouraged. He invited all men to seek the truth on their own and not to take their beliefs ready-made from a priestly class, ordained or unordained, based on birth or apostolic succession. He set up pathshalas and schools during his own life-time; the Arya Samaj, Lahore established an Academy for the study of Western science soon after his visit to the city.

His cry of 'Back to the Vedas' was accompanied by a restatement of India's hoary past. In rejecting the literature that was honoured among the orthodox, he cleared the way to a new vista of India's past, beyond the ages when this literature was produced. Against the current praises for autocracy and divinity claimed for the rulers—be they Ranas, Thakurs, Rajas, Governors. Viceroys or the reigning monarch—he unearthed the duties of the rulers as enunciated in Manu and supplemented them with the *Sabhas* and the Assemblies that he claimed to discover functioning in the good old days. Against the current belief about India's sordid past, he delved deep into literature and tradition and painted a golden age when woodcutters had corrected the mistakes in diction of the rulers or when a ruler could boldly assure a Sanyasi that there was no hunger, want, ignorance or immorality in his state. For the first time after the Western assault on India, he gave the educated Hindus some cause to be proud of their past and enabled them to look the followers of other religions in the face without feeling ashamed of themselves.

His was a practical programme. Though he was the first great Sanskrit scholar inviting the literate masses to share with him his knowledge of religious literature by expounding it in the language of the people, Hindi, he insisted on the superiority of practice over belief and devotion. He acknowledged the validity of mystic experience and had much to say both about *Yoga* and *Samadhi*. But he seemed to assert that one should busy oneself in doing right in a spirit of devotion and dependence on God, rather than ignore his humdrum obligations to society to enjoy pseudo-religious experiences.

Like the *Bhagavadgita* he seemed to assert that the place of a Bhakt or a Yogi in society depended upon what he did for it, not on his own alleged strivings towards personal salvation. It was the cult of the good or just man that he preached, rather than that of a great devotee or a great Yogi. His good man seemed to derive his inspiration for doing good because of his faith in God, belief in Whom, he asserted, could give a man strength enough to keep on discharging his duty towards his fellow beings in rain or sunshine. He did not expect God to move mountains in the service of His devotees; he believed that He would give men strength and wisdom enough to move mountains if they had to be moved. By expounding the Vedic religion as he understood it in Hindi, he also denied the necessity of a priestly class specially charged with the duty of guarding, preserving and propagating it. He recognised no priestly class by birth or occupation. He denied, like Buddha, the necessity of any intermediaries between man and God. As in Islam, he entrusted the task of propagating the newly rediscovered old gospel to laymen, but his scheme of things had no place even for specially qualified qazis or their equivalents.

The Arya Samaj that he created for carrying on his work is a body of laymen, held together by their belief in the 'Ten Principles of the Arya Samaj,' fired by his message of service and self-sacrifice, and sworn to a crusade against superstition and apathy towards the ills from which contemporary society suffered. The field of service of the Arya Samajists included all—women and untouchables among the Hindus, all afflicted people without distinction of caste or creed. His monotheism had rejected all belief in the influence for good or evil of what were currently regarded as lesser deities, the Sun and the Moon, the constellations of stars, the heavens and the earth, the spirits, alive or dead. His followers rejected image worship, scoffed at contemporary belief in astrology and refused to concede that heavenly bodies—whatever the term might imply—were either interested in human affairs or could be propitiated to work for a man's advantage.

Dayanand rejected contemporary monism as strongly as he did polytheism. Whatever the philosophic attraction of Sankara's Vedanta, in the hands of his followers it had ceased to affect human conduct and become reduced to an intellectual pastime. It was an irony of history that untouchability stalked unashamed in those very areas of the country where belief in monism was held most strongly—nay worse, untouchability therein had become unapproachability. He proclaimed his belief in the eternal nature of three verities, God, the individual soul and matter. His followers vehemently rejected the prevailing conception that the world was either an illusion or a myth. To them it was a battlefield where every individual had to work out his own salvation in the light of the eternal principles governing human conduct.

He had rejected the caste system as it had prevailed in the country, based on birth with infinite gradations and as many taboos based on them. But he accepted the four-fold functional division of society wherein the thinkers, the seers and the teachers occupied the highest place. The Arya Samaj thus succeeded in creating a new group of Pundits, truly scholars, drawn from different classes, high, low and middle-brow.

The propagation of the faith, in the early years of the Arya Samaj, was the work of these lay preachers, numbering among them teachers, lawyers, public servants, men of letters and even shopkeepers. They did not claim to act as the intermediaries between man and his God. Every man was left, with God's grace, to find out the truth for himself with such help as he could enlist. In performing his daily religious duties an Arya Samajist needs no help from outsiders; no priest hears his confession to grant him absolution, no one blesses his 'act of worship' by making him partake either what the worshippers had laid at the feet of God or what the priest had blessed by using it in worship.

In rejecting monism Dayanand also dealt a blow at the prevalent belief in predeterminism. Men had been content to look upon themselves as playthings of fate. The doctrine of rebirth had come to imply that men were no longer free to act; in some hoary past, their 'free deeds', had wound up a machinery which was supposed to be capable of keeping going for almost all time. Without laying down any precise boundaries, Dayanand reemphasized the place of free will in human life, asking every man to act on the assumption that he bore no shackles and could work unhindered for his own salvation.

Dayanand did not discard ritualism altogether, though he cut it down to size. The Arya Samaj did build 'temples' but they could as well be used as school rooms or as assembly halls as for the weekly religious gathering. They were of all sizes and built in all shapes. The weekly meeting was supposed to turn around the congregational performance of the daily duties: the recitation of Vedic hymns, a prayer in the language of the locality and songs and tends to reproduce in public what every individual is supposed to perform in the privacy of his home. Even the weekly sermon is only an elongation of the daily self-study which is enjoined upon every member. The sixteen sanskars' which span a man's life from conception to death are again not very elaborate affairs. Here services of 'professional' pundits may be required, but they can as well be performed with the help of well-read laymen and are actually so performed. The professionals are not ordained priests, they may not even be—they seldom are—persons entirely devoting themselves to this work. The ceremonies themselves are devoid of any 'mysteries', no gods are invited to bless the occasion, no vicious beings are propitiated. All ceremonies, except that at death, include prayers through Vedic hymns and performance of Havana. Some demand the making of vows, as the initiation into student life, marriage, entry upon the life of a householder or recluse or of renunciation of worldly ties in Sanyas. Dayanand himself wrote on the 'Five Daily Duties' and published *A Manual of Sixteen Religious Ceremonies*.

Though Dayanand travelled up and down the entire country and founded the first Arya Samaj at Bombay, his mission took strong roots in Panjab, U.P., parts of Bihar, Rajasthan and Hyderabad State. There are Arya Samajes in all parts of India, even outside India wherever educated Indians are found. Most of the States have their provincial synods. Some have more than one such body. There is even an 'International League of the Arya Samajists'. But these do not pretend to exercise any divine or semi-divine authority, they can employ no 'sanctions' against an individual or an institution, they are not even federal organizations aiming at creating unity in diversity. They are institutions where the Arya Samajists may think aloud, where they may seek common remedies for common ills. Many of them have one or more institutions of social service attached to them or managed through one or more separate organizations. In some areas of 'Indian India', as in Hyderabad, the Arya Samaj formed the only forum where people, otherwise denied this privilege, could meet to discuss all questions that concerned them. The programme of the Arya Samaj was wide enough to make the discussion of most of them a part of its religious programme so that banning such activities carried on under its banner would become an attack on religion.

The study of the impact of the Arya Samaj on contemporary life may best begin with some aspects of these bodies. Communal worship every week brought men together more frequently and more regularly than they had ever done before. In the governing councils of these bodies, men mostly elected by the entire community, met on equal terms and pondered on the problems facing them all. These bodies were action-minded service-motivated, sworn to positive action rather than performing the negative and preventive duties which Panchayats might have performed. Again, they were not elders of the community holding office on account of their status, they were elected by the entire community, including among them men of every status, high and low, belonging to different castes and communities. Here they met on a footing of equality, bandying words with one another, exchanging arguments. No outsiders were ever invited to 'guide' them, no patrons could pull strings from behind the curtain. Here that peculiarly English virtue of working through committees was cultivated as nowhere else.

<u>These bodies were action-minded. Men did not assemble here to discuss things, they met to decide their line of action—in fact to frame the necessary response to the challenge of their times.</u> Educational institutions were managed, famine relief organised, measures devised to help and rehabilitate victims of such calamities as earthquakes or floods, plans for medical relief for the ailing considered, campaigns for funds launched for these and various other activities. No calamity was accepted as ordained by God and therefore to be endured meekly. All this work was voluntarily undertaken and usually carried through by men who were paid nothing for the work they did. Hansraj, the honorary headmaster of the D.A.V. High School, Lahore was probably the first Indian to so devote himself to a cause in 1886. He did not receive a pie for his services. Service and sacrifice in the cause of their fellow beings which had so far been the monopoly of the Christian Missionaries became a badge of this new tribe. This was such a startling phenomenum in contemporary India that an Arya Samajist was prosecuted for 'abducting' a young girl from famine-stricken Rajputana to the shelter of an Arya Samaj and acquitted only in the Sessions Court. Another worker in plague-sticken Multan happened to meet a missionary doctor by the bedside of a victim of plague. Alas! bewailed the doctor, this was his morning visit and he had not brought his instrument case with him. The victim, however, could not hope to survive, the missionary declared, unless the eruptions were immediately lanced. Rala Ram bit into it, spat out and cleansed his mouth. The victim was saved; even Rala Ram survived his 'foolish' audacity. The work of community development—and that through

voluntary effort without much help from the state—was thus undertaken by the Arya Samaj long before the word had become current coin.

But all this needed funds. A third result of the impact of the Arya Samaj on contemporary India was the canalizing of funds for common organized efforts. Hindus were proverbially charitable no doubt, but their charity was haphazard and individual. Occasionally wells were dug for common use or temples built. The Arya Samaj diverted such scattered donations to various common causes, Even though it had no worldly returns to promise the donors, it almost always succeeded in raising enough money for whatever cause it espoused at the moment. The funds did not come from the Arya Samajists alone; the Arya Samaj was trusted to use its resources wisely and 'make one Rupee do the work of two, nay more' in the words of a Civilian Vice-Chancellor of Panjab University. Hindus and even non-Hindus responded to its appeal for funds. In its campaigns for alleviating human suffering it made no distinction of caste or creed and never sought converts.

The work done by the Arya Samaj in the educational field deserves special mention, as its impact on the direction and provision of educational facilities especially in Panjab, U.P. and Hyderabad was very great. The establishment of the D. A. V. High School, Lahore in 1886—it became a college in 1889—started an educational movement in Panjab and U. P. which was soon followed by other religious societies as well. The movement had a twofold impact on contemporary India. Now that it was proved that a knowledge of English and Western sciences could be safely imparted to Indians without either converting them to Christianity or making them hypocrites, Macaulay's fond dream of seeing India converted to Christianity through the impact of Western education faded away and the spread of both was assured. The D.A.V. College movement further implied that the task of diffusing English education was to be shouldered mainly by non-official organisations.

Another result of this movement was that the Arya Samaj acquired some control over the syllabus of school education to be imparted and a very big place in its direction. Young men educated in its institutions, even when they did not become Arya Samajists, acquired its bent of mind. This considerably widened its sphere of influence. These institutions put their indelible stamp on those who happened to pass through them so that in Panjab and Hyderabad, at least, public service of all kinds was mainly in the hands of the Arya Samajists. When the Arya Samaj came under official wrath, the students receiving education in its institutions had their share of it. I still remember the sensation caused at Taradevi railway station once when the police held up the train carrying passengers to Simla for over ten minutes because it took them that much time to get particulars of his movements from a student attending such a school.

Dayanand's presentation of India's past, made the Arya Samaj a revivalist body. The golden age that he pictured was certainly a thing of the past but he believed—and inspired millions to believe—that it could be recaptured. During the centuries when India was ruled by Muslim dynasties, big and small, Hindus had maintained an air of aloof superiority which even the rulers dared not question. With the advent of the Western onslaught, Hindus were found defenceless because Western scholarship delivered smashing blows not only on current religious thought and beliefs, it shook their very foundations by exhibiting them as built on sand. Dayanand provided a new incentive for a study of India's past which had hitherto been lacking. When the past had been mainly a story of our pitiful floundering down the ages, few educated Indians could be interested in its study. We took the current Western claim to its monopoly of 'civilised' inheritance for granted. But with Dayanand's shrugging off the accretion of centuries, an older past seemed to be faintly visible in which Indians could take pride. Dayanand's interpretation of the *Vedas*, whatever its shortcomings, was a mighty challenge to Western scholarship. It certainly tripped it up for its dependence on medieval schoolmen rather than on earlier commentaries. Now began an era of investigation where Indian scholars started by assuming that they could better unfold the mysteries of Indian culture. They began with a self-confidence which had hitherto been lacking.

Long before Campbell-Bannerman, Dayanand had declared that good government is no substitute for self-government. Dayanand raised his voice for 'swaraj' long before the Indian

National Congress adopted it as its goal—in fact even before it was born. The first generation of the Arya Samajist leaders included a large number of civil servants, besides a ruling prince or two. They were loyal to the government that they served but they were also inspired by a belief that in some distant future Indians could again be masters in their own country. For another, Dayanand had given them a vision of a government at work in the past with the active participation of its citizens. No wonder then that the D.A.V. High School, Lahore —and later some other similar institutions established elsewhere—adopted 'learning, piety and patriotism' as its motto. All Arya Samajists were avowedly and unashamedly patriots in action. They adopted 'Swadeshi' long before the boycott movement. Their programme also included a war on superstition and ignorance and a crusade against social maladjustment and resultant evils. When educated Hindus were attracted by government service and liberal professions only, the Arya Samaj helped to open the way to trade and industry in fields which had stood closed to Hindus of the 'higher' castes. The Arya Samajists were busy working in the service of their countrymen independently and in their own way. A regenerated India, they believed, could certainly stand on her own feet as she had done before. It is interesting to find today that some foreign as well as Indian students of present Indian economy and polity are asserting that no solid progress can be assured for the country unless a social reorganization of the type the Arya Samaj has been advocating takes place. Be that as it may, the religious and the social programme of the Arya Samaj, it was early discovered, made for a stronger and therefore more self-reliant India. As the material and moral progress of India was an avowed aim of the British in India—an annual report on the subject had to be presented to the British Parliament—it did not bother the British officials very much if the Arya Samaj was also working in the same direction. Occasionally the local officials welcomed its doing good in fields wherefrom they were themselves excluded or doing more briskly what they were themselves engaged in doing. It was only after the deportation of Lala Lajpat Rai in 1907 that Arya Samajic activities came to be looked upon with suspicion and under the lead of *The Times*, (London), not only did Arya Samajists come to be dubbed seditionists but the Arya Samaj itself came to be similarly misunderstood as being a political organisation rather than a group of religious reformers. It was easy to read into its self-reliance a challenge to the powers that be. It was easier still to present it as a danger to the British Raj because it set out to do certain things on its own—and do them better at that—which the Government was also trying to do. But that would bring the story well into the twentieth century with which we are not much concerned here.

It may be well to mention here a field of research where work done under its inspiration was successfully and fruitfully used in a vital political controversy, though in the twentieth century. When against the unanimous stand of the British civil servants in India, the British Government set about taking 'a substantial step' towards its newly declared goal of setting up responsible government in India, that eminent civilian historian of India, Vincent Smith, rushed into print to prove that the attempt to set up self-governing institutions in India was bound to fail as being alien to the Indian genius or Indian character. Sir Sankaran Nair, then a member of the Governor-General-in Council, based his Minute of Dissent to the despatch of the Government of India, whittling down the Montague-Chelmsford proposals on Kashi Prashad Jayaswal's *Hindu Polity* written to expand Dayanand's hints on the place of the Sabhas and similar bodies in the working of government in ancient India.

But we must get back to the nineteenth century. The impact of the Arya Samaj is to be seen again in the adoption of Hindi as a language of administration in Rajputana and U.P. Swami Dayanand, though a Gujrati by birth, used Hindi as the medium for conveying his thoughts to the masses. He wrote all his works in Hindi or in Sanskrit and Hindi when he came to his Commentary on the *Vedas*. Now Urdu had come to be adopted as the language of administration under the East India Company more for the convenience of the British administrators than for any intrinsic virtues of its own. Under the able lead of that ardent Arya Samajist, Sir Pratap Singh of Idar, several states in Rajputana were persuaded to adopt the Hindi script for official work. It came to be adopted as an alternative medium of administration in U.P. early in the twentieth century. The

Arya Samajic educational institutions in U.P. and Panjab tried to make its study popular and even use it as a medium of instruction in schools where this was permissible. They used Hindi exclusively as the medium of instruction so far as women's education was concerned. The Constitution may thus be said to bear the impress of the Arya Samaj in its Article making Hindi the official language of the country.

The present preoccupation of the Government with the welfare of the Harijans has its roots in the work that the Arya Samaj started for the betterment of the untouchables long long ago. If it refused to recognize a caste system based on birth, it also conceded the right of all within the Hindu pale—and even outside—to share to the full in all its privileges. As the untouchables were at that time considered practically outside the charmed circle of Hinduism, it admitted them within its fold after a 'purificatory' ceremony. But this done, they rose to the status of the Dwijas, the twice born. But even without this ceremony, the Arya Samaj took them under its wing, admitted them freely to all its institutions and adopted a comprehensive programme for their betterment. When the Government dared not do much for them for fear it would be considered interference in matters religious and 'political parties', mainly consisting of caste Hindus, were not much interested in their lot, the Arya Samajists made it a part of their religious duty to work for their welfare, because they claimed they were their co-religionists. It was when the educational and social services in Baroda had been entrusted to the Arya Samajists that Dr. Ambedkar was sent on a scholarship to England by the Government of the Gaikwad of Baroda. Again it was the Arya Samajists who threw all discretion to the winds at Kottayam in Travancore and challenged the well-entrenched tradition of unapproachability by leading a procession of the castes forbidden the roads on to the roads which had been closed to them for centuries. Again when separate hostels were being maintained for Christian converts from these classes at least in some of the missionary colleges in the south, students of the D. A. V. College, Lahore went on strike when the Brahman cooks refused to serve a student of the untouchable classes in the mess.

Another Arya Samajic breach in the orthodox tradition

raised some inconvenient questions. Where Dayanand refused to accept the caste system based on birth, against the entire Hindu tradition as it was then understood, the Arya Samaj opened wide its portals to all who cared to seek refuge in it. It not only welcomed back into the Hindu fold Christian and Muslim converts from Hinduism but admitted Christians and Muslims as well into its religious fold. No wonder this was resented both by the Christians and Muslims alike, though in different degrees. It even cost the Arya Samaj the lives of two of its leaders. Though sober history later on discovered that the theory of Hinduism being a closed circle embracing those born into it alone was a pure myth, the Hindu orthodoxy still kept shy of readmitting into the Hindu fold even those who had been forcibly converted to other faiths. In the days of the Hindu-Muslim entente in the twenties of the present century the Arya Samaj was sometimes accused by politicians, Hindu and Muslim alike, of endangering this understanding by its 'proselytizing' activities. It was curious that those who condemned the Arya Samaj for this never had a word to say against either the Christians or the Muslims whose right to make converts seemed to have been tacitly assumed whereas even to readmit Christian and Muslim converts to Hinduism was supposed to be a sin against 'genuine' Hindu traditions! When a reprint of articles published by the Calcutta University on the *Conversion and Reconversion to Hinduism During the Muslim Period* was brought to the notice of Mahatma Gandhi by a very close associate of his in the forties, he was reported to have been surprised at this 'discovery.' The friend had the reprint translated into Marathi and Gujarati and got at least the Marathi translation published. It is unjust to accuse the Arya Samaj of inventing in its 'Shuddhi' campaign a new method of disturbing the tranquil waters of Indian politics.

Closely allied to this charge was that of intolerance of which the Arya Samaj and the Arya Samajists were often accused by critics who should have been better informed. Once again it was probably a departure from what was believed to be a Hindu tradition that was sought to be condemned. Hinduism was catholic, it was asserted. It could mean anything to any man. When the Arya Samajists asserted that it meant what they said it did, it was asserted that they claimed a monopoly of truth. It was forgotten that was exactly what every reformist movement and every religious leader had done in India and outside India. It was then asserted that they used very harsh language against prevalent beliefs and customs. This ignores the history of every crusade, religious and political, where exaggeration, ridicule, satire and even downright abuse has figured as prominently, if not more so. But the Arya Samajist hurled arguments at their opponents not blows. They did not possess the power to condemn anyone with 'bell, book and candle'. They could not even wield the weapon of excommunication against any heretics, rather the reverse. It is surprising how well the Arya Samajists kept their temper when they were being violently attacked for suggesting a programme at which few would take offence today. Some of them lost their lives for daring to preach and practise what they did. It has never been even remotely suggested that their 'intolerance' ever went beyond their violent hatred of what they considered to be evil. That lay at the back of all their crusades, that was what made them activists rather than believers in determinism and prevented them from acquiescing in evil.

This charge sometimes appeared in a different and milder form. The Arya Samajists have often been accused of being 'difficult' to deal with. When this implies that try as one would, there was no way in which one could get the better of some of the Arya Samajists, it is a compliment rather than a slur. If it implies that they were apt to ask inconvenient questions when others were in a hurry to get on and would better ignore them, it represents an attitude of mind that is vital for the success of democatic government. Government by open challenge that democratic government is supposed to be, it is necessary for its success that inconvenient questions be not ignored but be properly raised and answered. There are some who believe that the present falling off in moral values is partly the result of most of us trying to avoid being 'difficult', ignoring difficult questions and making ourselves 'pleasant' to all those around us. Some of those who criticise the Arya Samaj for introducing this element in our life have had, occasionally, to call upon them to play this very part in the interests of their erstwhile critics. When Sir Fazl Hussain embarked upon his campaign of debasing administration by extending communal representation from the legislatures to services and admissions to educational institutions, the Congressmen in Panjab had to call upon an Arya Samajist—who was not even a Congressman himself—to present their case before the sub-committee of the All India Congress Committee that visited Panjab for an enquiry into the matter. It was an Arya Samajist again who threw all discretion to the winds and published an article on Sir Douglas Young's monkeying with the Lahore High Court even when the writer had been told that he would be sent to prison if he dared attack that despot! Ignoring even the advice of those who had made 'Satyagrah' peculiarly their own weapon, the Arya Samaj launched a successful Satyagrah against that ally of the British Government, His Exalted Highness the Nizam, and delivered such a shattering blow to his prestige that he was never able to recover his former status, at least in the eyes of his own subjects. Earlier, it had similarly braved danger in Malabar in order to bring back to the Hindu fold those who had been forcibly converted to Islam by the rebellious Moplahs.

Unlike the Brahmo Samaj, the Prarathana Samaj, and several other ninteenth-century reformist movements, the Arya Samajists never cut themselves aloof from the main stream of Hindu thought. As Dayanand had done, they rather claimed to be the true Hindus basing themselves, as they did, on the *Vedas* which every Hindu sect equally respected. Dayanand never claimed to have any message of his own, he assumed the more humble role of a lifter of the veil who uncovers what was always there but had lain hidden. He did not even claim to be a Guru in the medieval tradition, he was prepared, as he says in his introduction to the *Satyarath Prakash* to admit any error if it was pointed out to him. Here he went back to the Upanishadic tradition when the teacher on admitting a pupil in residence boldly told the pupil to follow his teacher in what was good in him not in what was bad. Here was a call to independent judgment, an insistence on scepticism which alone can form the bedrock of truth.

BIBLIOGRAPHY

BOOKS IN ENGLISH

1. Swami Dayanand, *The Satyarath Prakash*, English translation, Pandit Ganga Prashad, M.A.
2. Swami Dayanand, *Introduction to the Commentary on the Rig and the other Vedas*, English translation, Dr. Parma Nand.
3. Swami Dayanand, *Samskar Vidhi* (A Manual of Vedic Rituals), English translation.
4. Pandit Ganga Prashad, *Swami Dayanand and His Philosophy*.
5. Pandit Bahadur Mal, *Dayanand, A Study in Hinduism*.
6. Lala Diwan Chand, *The Arya Samaj*.
7. Gokal Chand Narang, *The Message of the Vedas*.
8. Swami Dayanand, *Sam Veda*, Translation and Commentary; English translation mostly based on Dayanand's system of translation by Lala Devi Chand.
9. Lala Devi Chand, *Yajur Veda*.
10. Works of Pandit Gurudatta Vidyarthi.
11. Lala Hansraj, *The Great Seer*.
12. Lala Mulraj, *A Lecture on the Arya Samaj*.
13. Lala Munshi Ram, *Lectures on the Arya Samaj*.
14. Sri Ram Sharma, *Mahatma Hansraj: A Maker of Modern Punjab*.
15. *Lajpat Rai*: Works, Vol. I, Autobiographical Writings.
16. Ganga Prashad, *Fountain-head of Religion*.
17. Diwan Chand, *Fundamentals of Religion*.
18. *Swami Dayanand*, Ganesh and Co., Madras.
19. *Swami Dayanand* (Eminent Men of India Series).
20. *Sri Ram, The Revolutionist*.
21. Ramsay Macdonald, *Awakening of India*.
22. *Annual Reports* of the D.A.V. College, Trust and Management Society.
23. N. W. Nevinson, *The New Spirit in India*.
24. Munshi Ram and Ram Dev, *The Arya Samaj and Its Detractors*.
25. *Annual Reports* of the Gurukul.
26. Sri Ram Sharma, *Our Educational Mission*.
27. Sri Ram Sharma, *Conversion and Reconversion to Hinduism during the Medieval Period*.

28. D. R. Bhandarkar, *Foreign Elements in the Hindu Population.*
29. D. A. V. College, *Golden Jubilee Commemoration Volume.*
30. *Dayanand Commemoration Volume,* Editor, H. B. Sarda.
31. Chhajju Singh, *Teachings of the Arya Samaj.*
32. *Christian Intelligencer,* March, 1820.
33. Max Muller, *Biographical Essays.*
34. *Sacred Books of the East,* Vol. XXXII.
35. Max Muller, *History of Ancient Sanskrit Literature.*
36. Max Muller, *Six Systems of Indian Philosophy.*
37. Sir Herbert Risley, *People of India.*
38. Max Muller, *Physical Religion.*
39. V. Chirol, *Indian Unrest.*
40. Sister Nivedita, *Aggressive Hinduism.*
41. Ganga Prashad, *The Caste System.*
42. Max Muller, *Chips from a German Workshop.*
43. Wintermitz, *Indian Literature.*
44. Bhagwan Das, *Science of Social Obligation.*
45. *Reports of the Dayanand Salvation Mission,* Hoshiarpur.
46. *Reports of the Dayanand Dalituddhar Mandal,* Hoshiarpur.
47. H. B. Sarda, *Swami Dayanand Sarasvati.*
48. Madame Blavatsky, *From the Caves and Jungles of Hindustan.*
49. Aurobindo Ghosh, *Dayananda.*
50. K. P. Jayaswal, *Hindu Polity.*
51. *Encylopaedia of Religion and Ethics.*
52. *Administrative and Economic Development in India,* Editors, Braibanti and Spengler.
53. Albert Schweitzer, *Indian Thought and Its Development.*
54. Burn, *Census Report for the United Provinces* (1901).
55. Blunt, *Census Report for the United Provinces* (1911).
56. Edward Maclagan, *Census Report for the Punjab* (1901).
57. Hari Krishan Kaul, *Census Report for the Punjab* (1911).
58. Morley, *Speeches.*
59. Lady Minto, *India, Minto and Morley.*
60. S. N. Das, *India Under Morley and Minto.*
61. Gokhale, *Speeches.*

INDEX

A

Acts, makers of destiny, 63
Adam, Mr., American Missionary, 99, 100
Agnihotra, 63, 147
Aitraya Brahmana, 63, 116
Ajmere, death of Dayanand at, 45
Akbar, 103
Allahabad, 32
Anatomy, Hindu, tested by Dayanand, 19
Ancestor-worship, not practised by Aryas, 95
Andrews, Rev. C.F., on Dayanand's courage and love of truth, 187; expansive powers of the Arya Samaj, 185; on militant character of Arya Samaj, 182
Angas, the Six, 61
Anglo-Vedic College, the Dayanand, 135-45, 152-5
Antesthi, or death ceremony, 42, 63
Apasthamba, 81
Aravali, 16
Aristhta Shena, 116
Arjuna, 173
Arnot, Mr., 99
Arsha Granthas, 42
Arya Samaj, the, all supposedly disaffected persons dubbed Arya Samajists, 175; ancestor-worship, does not practise, 95; appeals to intellectual Hindus, 184, 185; Assemblies, 158, 194, 195; Brahmo Samaj, main differences, 38; British officials attest non-political character of Arya Samaj, 169-72; caste system, opposes, 113-16, 122-7, 192; cathocity, 58, 59, 80, 84, 85; child marriage, opposes strongly, 119; Chirol, Sir V., attacks Samaj on political grounds, 164-6; Chirol, Sir V., his indictment categorically answered, 166-9; Christianity, predicted collapse into, 178; Christianity, Samaj styled chief modern hindrance to, in India, 178; common religion promulgated, 84; conciliated by Government since 1910, 176; creed, a definite, found necessary for propaganda, 87-89; creed, main articles of, 79, 80, 89-96; crisis in its history, 175, 176, 183; dangers and mistakes to avoid, 185-7; definiteness a source of strength, 89; deportation of Lajpat Rai, an attack on, 175; difficult, 202, 203; educational work, 102, 135-56, 196, 197; famine relief, first non-Christian agency to organize, 129; fate, not believed in by Samaj, 95; female education and status of women, views on, 116-19, 150, 151; foreigners' attitude towards, 2, 3; founded at Bombay, 40, 79; future bound up with Hinduism, 183; future difficult but hopeful, 179, 180; Gaurakshini movement supported, 172; girls' college, 150, 151; God, exalted idea of, 89-94; government recognition not sought by, 2; greatest modern religious movement in India, 177; Gurukula, 143-50; Hindu Church militant, 182; "Hindu", objection to the term, 183; Hinduism, orthodox, increasing friendship with, 184, 185; impact on contemporary India, 188-203; infallibility of any human being not accepted, 95; intolerance, 201, 202; Karma an article of faith, 95; Mahayajnas, the five 96, 97; meeting-places of, 158, 159; members and officers, 156, 157; militancy, 182; monotheistic, 89; nationalising force, 108; Niyoga, 86; no ordained priests in, 91; open in all things, 174; opposed alike to Christianity, Islam, and orthodox Hinduism, 172; organization, 156-9; orphanages, Hindu, first to organize, 129; outcome of conditions imported from the West, 108; parent of unrest, 108-10; patriotism, 198; persecuted by official, 163, 164, 175, 178; persecution found to be baseless, 173; philanthropic activities, 129-34; principles and rules, 40-43, 79, 80, 82, 83, 84, 85, 86, 185; propagation of, 191, 192; prophets recognized, but not minor gods or mediators, 94; publicity, reasons for greater, 2, 3; reclamation work, 120-8; reconstituted at Lahore, 43, 79; reformation on Vedic lines, the aim, 106,

180; religious propaganda, successful, 120, 121; religious services, open to all, 157; repentance the sole expiation, 95; ritual, 96-98; salvation, views on, 95; Sannyasi, Arya Samaj collectively a, 170; Sanskars, the sixteen, 97-98; self-reliance, its, 199; social service, and, 198; shuddhi work, 120-8; social ideals, 113-19, 198; social service, pioneer work in, 133, 134, 198, 200; souls, transformation of, 95; split in 1892, 83, 144; spread of Hindi by, 200; strength in Northern India, 123; strife, internal, better than stagnation, 182; suspected by Government, 108, 175, 176; swadeshi, 198; united front shown by Aryas in time of peril, 183; unrest, a preliminary to betterment, 108; unrest, Samaj a centre of, 108; Vedas, held to be infallible and universal, 96; Vedic glories recalled, 108; vindicated by its leaders, 169-72; virtues to cultivate, 196; Widow Homes, Hindu, Samaj first to organize, 129; worship, forms of, 95; young men, provision for, 161

Atharva-Veda, quotations from, relating to God, 93, 94

Athithi Yajna, 97

Atta Fund for D. A. V. College, 152

B

Bali Vaishwadeva yajna, 97
Banaras, 14, 28
Banaras, Raja of, 28, 31, 36
Banprastha (retirement), 17
Beliefs, Dayanand's, summarized by himself, 59-65
Bentinck, Lord William, 100
Bhagwat, not a Purana, 63
Bhakti, doctrine of, 181
Bharadwaja, Chiranjiva, 1
Bhoga doctrines of the West, warning against, 112
Bhurtpore, Prince of, 31
Bjornstjerna, Count, 90n.
Blavatsky, Madame, on Dayanand's great qualities, 45, 46
Blunt, Mr., I.C.S., on the Arya Samaj movement, 167; appreciates its bold, straightforward monotheism, 98n.; charges Aryas with partial study of other religions, 107, 172; defends the Arya Samaj from charge of being political, 170, 171, 172; on Aryas and Hindus, 184; on Christianity and Hinduism, 98n.; on Dayanand's interpretation of the Vedas, 58; on the autocracy of the Brahmins, 50, 51; on the strength of the Arya Samaj, 177
Bombay, 39, 40, 79, 80, 83, 188
Bondage of the soul caused by ignorance, 62
Bose, Professor J. C., discovers that all matter has life, 111
Brahmanas (Vedic commentaries), 61
Brahmcharya, 8, 17
Brahma Yajna, 96
Brahminhood attained by non-Brahmins, ancient instances, 116
Brahminism, degree of, 12
Brahminism, the pivot of orthodox Hinduism, 52
Brahmin organization, 51
Brahmins, in general ignorant of the Vedas, 53
Brahmins, the Popes of India, 50
Brahmin worship, the official test of Hinduism, 51
Brahmo Samaj, Dayanand's difference with, 38, 48, 80, 82, 203; early faith in the Vedas, 81; retarded by eclecticism; 89; torn by dissensions, 101, 102; weak opponent of Christianity, 101, 102
British Government, itself a source of unrest, 108; suspicious of Arya Samaj, 160
British Rule in India, Dayanand on, 172
Bryce, Rev. J., 9n.
Buddha, 14, 82
Buddhaghosh, 110
Buddhists, non-believers in the Vedas, 81
Burn, Mr., I.C.S., on Aryas not being necessarily politicians, 170; on importance of Arya Samaj in United Provinces, 177; on the conversion ceremony of the Arya Samaj, 121; on the political importance of Christianity, 180; sceptical of the Aryas ever becoming Christians, 179, 181

C

Canon of Hindu Scriptures, Dayanand's, 32, 33
Caste, Arya Samaj's attitude to, 113-16; changes of, ancient instances, 115, 116; changes of, Manu's rules

INDEX

or, 114; Dayanand's views on, 35, 36, 63
Caste System, the curse and the salvation of Hinduism, 113; hereditary, based on misunderstanding of the Vedas, 114, 115; hereditary, proved not to date from Vedic times, 114, 115, 116
Castes, low, efforts of Arya Samaj to upraise, 120-8
Chaddha, Lala Dewan Chand, 3, 130, 131, 142
Chamars, reclamation of, by Arya Samaj, 126, 127
Chand, Lal, 139
Chand, Lala Dewan, 3
Chand, Mehar, 142
Charvakas (atheists), against the Vedas, 81
Child marriage and the Arya Samaj, 119
Chirol, Sir Valentine, charges the Arya Samaj with disloyalty, 164-6; disingenuous framing of his indictment, 166; full answer on behalf of the Arya Samaj, 166-9; investigates Indian unrest, 164; on education in East India Company's days, 99; special correspondent of *The Times*, 164
Christian and Hindu teachings on salvation, 95
Christian Intelligencer, The, on Dayanand, 4, 28-38
Christianity, acceptance of, urged for political reasons, 180; appeals chiefly to lower classes, 180; attacks on, not attacks on British rule, 172; critically studied by Dayanand, 106; in India, powerful influences in favour of, 180; irreconcilable with Hinduism, 98n; political importance of, 180; spread of, in India, admittedly obstructed by Arya Samaj, 178; strength of, as against Hinduism, 87
Church Missionary Society, 4
Churumani, Lala, 131
Coleman, Mr. Charles, 90n.
College, Dayanand Anglo-Vedic, 83, 139-43, 152-5
College, Gurukula, 143-50
Colleges of the Arya Samaj, 155
Compromise, 186
Contemplation, communion and prayer, the Arya Samaj's only approved worship, 95, 96
Cotton, Sir Henry, on Arya Samaj, 177

Counsels and warnings to Aryas, 182-7
Creation, 62
Creed, Dayanand's, 60-65
Curzon, Lord, educational policy, 143

D

Darshans, 20
Dara Shikoh, 103
Dass, Lala Dwarka, 3
Dass, Lala Sain, 142
Dat, Pandit Ram Bhaj, 126
Datta, Rai Thakar, 3
Dayanand Anglo Vedic College, Lahore, aim: all-round education, especially in classical Sanskrit, 138, 153; begins a movement, 153; college, opened in 1889, 142, 153; English education made safe, 153; enthusiastically supported, 138, 152; example of community development, 152; fairly treated, on the whole, by Government, 141; fees as low as possible, 141; finance, 142; founded in memory of Dayanand, 138; general results, 143; government by committee, 154; guiding principles, 140, 141; Hansraj, Lala, organizer and honorary principal, 139, 140; Honorary and Life Members, 153, 154; novelty of the enterprise, 138, 139; principles designed to develop self-reliance, 141; school opened in 1886, 139, 140; subjects taught, 140; success of students, 141; state aid not sought, 141; teachers exclusively Indian, 140; under Hindu management, 140; under Indian management, 152
Dayanand, Swami, adopts Hindi, 199; aggressive propaganda, 109; Arya Samaj, founded at Bombay, 40, 79; Arya Samaj reconstituted at Lahore, 79; Arya Samaj stamped with his own character, 187; Banaras, Dayanand's ambition to study at, 14; Banaras, scene of famous debate (Nov. 17th, 1869), 36-38, Banaras, unsuccessful mission at, 30; Bhakti, attitude to, 191, boldness and force, 27; born A.D. 1824 (1881 Bikram), 8; Brahmin by birth, 7; Brahminism, regards as acquired, not native, 115, 116, Brahmo Samaj, differs from, 38, 80; Calcutta, visit to, 38; caste, accepts as a political institution only, 35; Christianity,

opposes energetically, 107; Christianity, studies critically, 106; commentaries on Vedas, 188; cry of 'Back to the Vedas', 190, 191; death, encounters problem of, in youth, 13; debate at Banaras, described by Christian missionary, 31, 32, 36, 39; debate at Banaras, after-effects of, 38; devotion, his attitude to, 190; early life, 7-25; education on Brahmin lines, 9; education began at five, 8; education completed with Virjananda Saraswati, 25; enlightenment, 11, 12; enmity of Brahmins excited, 26, 32; father, Dayanand's, 7, 9,, 10, 11, 12, 15 firmness of aim, 19; first years of public life, 26-34; flight from home, 14,15; forces arrayed against Dayanand, 105; foundation of Hinduism, according to, 189; Furruckabad, successful mission at, 38; God and His service, conception of, 34, 35, 60, 62, 64, 65; greatness and moderation, 86; Hindus, English-educated, influenced Dayanand, 38, 43; Hindus, may unite in the truth discovered by Dayanand, 112; Hindu thought, revolutionized, 137; idolatry or image-worship, repudiates, 34, 35; impact on contemporary India, 188-203; India, a regenerated, Dayanand's dream, 111; India's part, according to, 197; Islam, opposes energetically, 108; Islam, studies critically, 106; Jodhpur, illness at, 44. 45; knowledge thirst for, 19; later years, 44; liberty, love of, 20; marriage, refused by Dayanand, 14; ministry, short, 189; monotheism, 60, 79, 89-94; monism rejected, 192; Morvi, born at, 7; mother, Dayanand's, 7, 15; murderously attacked, 26, 45; mythology, Hindu, rejection of, 34; nature, communion with, 21; objects, Dayanand's, Christian criticism of, 29, 30; orthodoxy, his onslaughts on, 27; pamphlet propaganda, 32; parentage, 7; patriot, a true and great, 65, 174; personality described by a Christian missionary, 28; plan of campaign, on behalf of Hinduism, 111, 112; polytheism, rejects, 34; programme, practical, 191; public life, preparatory years, 26-38; Puranas, puzzling question on, 37; pursuit of knowledge, 16-21; questions his father on image-worship, 11; rebel, a born, 9, 19; reformer, a social, 65; reformer, in religion, not innovator, 60, 82, 83, 85; sacred thread, invested with, 8; Sadhu, becomes a, 15; Sannyasi, initiation as, 18; Sanskrit and Vedic learning, his strength, 26; scepticism, awakened by a mouse, 10; Self-government, Dayanand on, 197, 198; Shastras, Dayanand's list of, 32; Shiva fast, young Dayanand deliberately breaks, 11, 12; Shivaratri, his father insisted on his observing, 9; spiritual world-conquest, Dayanand's ultimate aim, 106; teacher, placed with a learned, 15; teacher, searches for a, 19-22; teacher, Virjananda Saraswati becomes his, 24; teaching, Dayanand's, Sir V. Chirol's strange criticism of, 164, 165; teachings of, 49-65; tolerant to the views of others, 86; tributes from friend and foe, 45-48; 86; Vedas, claims for, substantially founded, 71-78, 110; Vedas for the people, not for Brahmins only, 54, 55; Vedas, interpretation of, by Vedic grammar only, 55; Vedas, interpretative canons of, to be strictly observed, 55; Vedas, lost, possibility of, denied by Dayanand, 33; Vedas, study of, the duty of every Arya, 54, 79; Vedas, translation of, by, 66-78; Vedas, unique knowledge possessed by, 29; Vedicism, his, 189; wander years, 1845-60, 16-21; works of, 189; Yajur-Veda, learns by heart, 12

Dead, worship of, not sanctioned by Dayanand, 63, 95, 96

Death, problem of, how regarded by the Pandits, 13

Delhi, Durbar, 82

Depressed Classes, have no desire to leave Hinduism, 124; in danger of conversion by missionaries, 124; uplift of, a work of national self-preservation, 122, 123; uplift of, methods of the Arya Samaj, 125; uplift of, opposed by Hindu orthodoxy, 125

Design in the universe, involves a Creator, 62

Destiny, the consequence of action, 63

Deva, Professor Ram, 170

Devapi, 116

Devapuja, 63

Devas, 63

INDEX

Devatas, word misunderstood by European Vedic students, 56
Deva Yajna, or Homa, 96
Dharma and adharma, 61
Dharma, Vedic, not merely a creed, but a philosophy, 174
Diet, meat, Dayanand opposed to, 83
Domes, reclamation of, 126, 127
Duff, Dr. Alexander, authority of, great both at home and in India, 101; influences introduction of English language in India as a preliminary to Christianization, 100; inspires prohibition of Suttee, 100; opens an English school in 1830, 101; proselytizes brilliant pupils, 101
Durga Prasad, 1
Dutt, R. C., on absence of caste in Vedic times, 113

E

Earthquake in Kangra Valley, Aryas first to the rescue, 134
Educational work of the Arya Samaj, 152-55, 196, 197
Education, Brahmin, 12; current, in India, defects of, 104; Godless, increases Hindu apathy to religion, 104; Hindu, free, 22; Hindu, how maintained, 23, 97; not much encouraged by East India Company, 99; of Hindu women, ancient, 117; of Hindu women, modern, 116, 117
Energy and activity preferable to passive acquiescence, 63
English, introduction of, opposed by Carey and other early missionaries, 99
English domination of the Hindus, 103
Englishmen, tribute to, by Lala Hansraj, 103
Eternal things, three, 61
European study of Sanskrit, revealed treasures of Indian literature, 103; strengthened missionaries against Hinduism, 103, 104
Exportation, of foodstuffs, a cause of famine in India, 129, 130

F

Faizi, 243
Famine, relief work of the Arya Samaj, about 250 children rescued in 1897-8, 130; about 1,700 children rescued in 1890-1900, 132; agent sent into Rajputana in 1899, 130, 131; appeals liberally answered by Hindus and Aryas, 130; beneficial results of the work, 132; co-operation of Hissar Arya Samaj and Bhiwani Hindu Orphanage, 131; difficulties in Rajputana and Bombay, 131; general relief measures in 1908, 133; high native officials approached, 131; pioneer non-Christian agency in this work, 131; protests against proselytism by Christian missionaries, 131; tribute to helpers, 132, 133
Famines, Indian, causes of, 129
Fatalism, condemned by Dayanand and the Arya Samaj, 63, 95
Ferozepur Hindu Orphanage, 129, 130
Forces against Dayanand, apathy and fatalism of the Hindus, 105; Brahmins and the caste system, 105; Christian missions, 105; ever-active propaganda of Islam, 105; Hindu collapses before Christianity and Science, 105
Four Vedas, God's infallible Word, 60
Furruckabad, 30

G

Gait circular, the, 124
Ganges, banks of, home of learned and holy men, 16, 17, 22, 23, 27; holy river, the, 22; purity of its water, 22
Gaurakshini movement, essentially and in the main religions, 172; strongly supported by the Arya Samaj, 170
Girls' college for, at Jullundhar, 150, 151
God, and the soul, as Father and Son, 61; Dayanand's conception of, 34, 60, 61, 79; free as well as just, 64; Vedic presentation of, 90-94
Government of the Arya Samaj, 157, 158
Grihastha, 17
Griswol, Mr., differs from Yaska, 58n.
Gurdaspur, 126
Guru and Chela (teacher and pupil), relations of, 24
Gurukula college at Kangri, account of, by Mr. Myron Phelps, 144-50; aims: study and training on strict Vedic lines, 144, 145; brotherhood and self-sacrifice inculcated, 146; Chirol, Sir V., on, 150; comparison of standard attained with other colleges, 148, 149; curriculum: English, Western learning and

science included, 148; founded in 1902, 145; founded through dissatisfaction with the D. A. V. system, 144; founded to carry out Dayanand's ideas, 144, 145; Government co-operation not invited, 149; misrepresented by Christian missionaries and by Mahomedans, 149, 150; modelled on the great universities of ancient India, 145; moral and ethical instruction based on Vedas, 147, 148; personal efforts of its founder, 145, 146; programme of the day, 149; Ram, L. Munshi, describes its foundation, 145; rules and discipline, 146; Sanskrit, the first language, 149; self-sacrifice of the teacher, 146; Suggested by Dayanand's *Satyarath Prakash*, 144; suspected by Government, 149, 150; visited and commended by Sir James Meston, 150
Gurukul Section, 2, 3, 143, 144

H

Hansraj, Lala, association with the D. A. V. College, 140, 141; first Indian honorary headmaster and principal, 152; on Hindu helplessness before European science and criticism, 103, 104; tribute to his character and work, 140, 141, 152, 195
Hardinge, Lord, inaugurates policy of conciliation towards the Arya Samaj, 176
Haridwara, or Hardwar, a sacred place of the Hindus, 22, 145
Himalayas, 16, 17
Hinduism, aggressive possibilities of, 107, 109, 110; Brahmin worship, the chief test of, 50, 51; Brahmin worship, its collapse, 105; confounds means with ends, 186; Dayanand, World apostle of, 58; defences of, 185; facile comprehensiveness of, 88; friendliness with Arya Samaj increasing, 184, 185; future bound up with that of Arya Samaj, 183, 184; missionaries' declaration of war, on, 108; monotheism, its exalted, 89, 90n.; need for stiffening and consolidation, 109, 110, 111, 112; not yet moribund, 181; not yet seriously threatened, 180, 182; portals of, opened by Dayanand, 59; orthodox, too apt to lead to irreligion, 98n.; plight of, when Dayanand appeared, 50-55, 105, 109, 182; regenerative aims and methods of the Arya Samaj for, 111; revival of, by Arya Samaj, 176; salvation attainable by different paths, 59; sketch of, in Dayanand's time, 50-59; strong against Mahomedan bigotry, weak against European science, 103, 180; vagueness and vastness of, its chief weakness, 87, 89
Hindu life, four stages of, 17; Dayanand's ideals for, 112; dominated by English, but not by Mahomedans, 103; showing signs of progress, 112
Hindu thought revolutionised by Dayanand, 137
"Hindu," word disliked by Aryas, 183
Holland, Rev., predicts collapse of Arya Samaj into Christianity, 178
Homa, or Deva Yajna, 8, 63
Hoshiarpur, 126

I

Ignorance, cause of soul's bondage, 62
Image-worship (idolatry), devotee's explanation, 11; repudiated by Dayanand, 34
India, ancient, glories of, 109
Indian character, too yielding, 112
Indian unrest, diagnosed by Sir V. Chirol, 164, 165 diagnosis examined, 166-9; not antagonistic to Western ideas, 165
Infallibility, of human beings : not accepted by Arya Samaj, 83; of Vedas : accepted by Arya Samaj, 79, 80, 81, 82, 83; of Vedas : Dayanand's views on, 32, 33, 40, 60, 61
Institutions, only means to ends, not ends in themselves, 186
Islam, ever-active propaganda of, 105; studied critically by Dayanand, 106
Itihas (history), 63

J

Jains, against the Vedas, 81
Jamuna (Jumna) river, 16
Jehangir, 103
Jodhpur, Dayanand contracts his last illness at, 44
Jones, Sir William, 102
Jullundher, 145, 151
Jummu and Kashmere, 126
Just man, Dayanand's definition of a, 86

K

Kalpa, the history so-named, 63
Kangra, earthquake in, 134
Kanya Mahavidyala, 151
Karachi (Sindh), 122
Karma, doctrine of, held by Arya Samaj, 6, 64, 95, 123; suggests explanation of Hindu decline, 123
Kashi (Benares), 27
Kathiawar, Gujarat, 3
Kaul, Pandit Hari Keshan, on the improved relations between Arya Samajists and orthodox Hindus, 184, 185
Kavasha, 116
Kennedy, Colonel, 117n.
Kidnapping charge, against an Arya president dismissed, 183
Krishna, 29, 173

L

Lahore, 4, 43, 79, 82, 83, 84, 126, 130, 135, 138
Lal, Lala Chandu, 131
Lillington, Mr. Frank, on Christianity of the Brahmo Samaj 102; predicts cessation of Arya Samaj's hostility to Christianity, 173; suggests tactful policy to missionaries, 174
Lyell, Sir Alfred, on Hinduism, 59, 181
Lytton, Lord, 82

M

Macaulay's hope belied, 153
Maclagan, Sir Edward, describes the Arya Samaj as a religious body, 170; recognizes its importance in the Punjab, 177; remark on the dislike of the stricter Aryas to be classed as "Hindus", 183
Madhavacharya, questions Dayanand, 48, 49
Madras, 44, 47
Mahayajnas, the five daily, 96, 97
Mahomedanism, 173
Mahidhar's commentary on the Vedas, rejected by Dayanand, 55
Man, Dayanand's ideal, 63
Manu, 20, 32; on the caste system, 114; on the duty of husband and wife, 118, 119, on reverence due to the mother, 118
Marriage, ancient Hindu ideas on, 118; customs, Hindu, in a state of flux, 118, 119; child, strongly, opposed by Arya Samaj, 119; Dayanand's definition of, 64; laws, ancient Hindu, fairness of, 118; traditional remedy for asceticism, 14; marriageable age, Hindu, 117, 118; marriages, second and third, disapproved by the Rishis, 118
Mathura (Muttra), abode of Virjananda, 24; Gurukula College, founded at, 150
Maurice, 90n.
Meat diet, Dayanand condemns, 83
Mediators, religious, rejected by Arya Samaj, 20, 130, 193
Meghs, reclamation of, 26
Meston, Sir James, lays foundation stone of Gurukula College at Mathura, 150; promotes conciliatory policy towards (Arya Samaj), 173; regards Arya Samaj as nonpolitical, 150; visits and commends Gurukula College at Kangri, 150
Middleton, 100
Minto, Lord, 174, 175
Missionaries, Christian, in India, activities of, favour the Arya Samaj, 182; admit influence of the Arya Samaj, 178; assisted by Hindu apathy towards religious instruction, 103; attribute English superiority to Christianity, 103, 104; early, oppose establishment of English language as preliminary to Christianizing India, 99; efforts to convert Raja Ram Mohan Roy, 100; influence of, exemplified by work of Dr. Duff, 99, 100, 101; influence, vast political, wielded by, 100, 101; offer material inducements to converts, 100, 101, 105; progress of, Dayanand's birth year, 99, 100; progress of, by first year of Dayanand's public life, 101; ruthlessly attack Hinduism, 107, 108; study Hinduism partially, 107
Monogamy, the Hindu ideal of marriage, 117
Monotheism, Dayanand's, 34, 60,192
Monotheism of the Arya Samaj, 79, 89, 98n.
Monotheism of the Vedas, 90-94
Morley, Lord, withdraws accusations against Lajpat Rai, 167
Mothers, rights of, under Hindu law, 118
Muller, Professor Max, argument, as to lost Vedas, 33, 34; argument, controversial, 34; conclusions of, criticized, 68, 73; on absence of

caste from the Vedas, 115; on Dayanand, 46, 47; on Ram Mohan Roy, 81n., 82n.; on Vedic interpretation, 55, 56, 66, 67, 69, 70; on Vedic names, 56; reference to, Yajna, 82n.

Mulraj, 84-86

Mulshankar, Dayanand, originally named, 9

Multan, 138

Muradabad, 127

Mythology, Hindu, rejected by Dayanand, 34, 35

N

Nabhga, 116

Nanak, 14, 103

Narashansi, the history so-named, 63

Narbadda, 16, 17, 24

Narak (hell), 64

Nivedita, Sister, on aggressive Hinduism, 109, 110

Noble, Miss, 109, 110

O

Oxford, 14

P

Parasara, 81

Politics, Arya Samaj not concerned in, 160-76; part of the duties of Grihasthas, 170

Polytheism, rejected by Dayanand, 34

Poona, 43

Porter, Mr., 4

Poverty, chronic in India, 13

Prakriti, 61, 62

Prarthana, or prayer for God's gifts, 64

Parthana, Sagun and Nirgum, distinguished, 64

Prayer, does not dispense with efforts, 64

Puranas, 29, 33, 35, 36, 37, 63, 81

Puranas, the word, problem of its meaning, 36, 37

Pusey, Dr., Dayanand compared to, 46

R

Raddi Fund 152

Rai, Lala Lajpat, accusations against 165, 174, 175; accusations found baseless, 167, 168, 175, 176; accusations held baseless by Minto, 175; accusations withdrawn by Lord Morley, 167; deported without assigning any reason for, 167; long connection with Arya Samaj, 5; Minto on, 174, 175; Nevinson on, Lajpat Rai, 175; on the Dayanand Anglo-Vedic College, 4, 188; on the Gurukula College, 4; on the motive and scope of this book, 2, 4; on the uplifting of the depressed classes, 122, 123-7; organizes famine relief measures, 130, 132; position in relation to the Colleges, 4; Robertson memorandum, on the Punjab unrest, 177

Raja, Lala Deva, 173

Rakshas, 86

Ram, L. Munshi, founder of the Gurukula College at Kangri, 144, 150; leader of the Gurukula section of the Arya Samaj, 2, 3, 4; on the foundation of the Gurukula College, 145; on the management of the Gurukula College, 145; on the pacific character of the Arya Samaj, 169, (with Professor Ram Deva) on the patriotic but non-political character of the Vedic Church, 170, 171

Ram, Lala Ralla, 3,195

Rama, 173

Ranade, Mr Justice, 169

Rattan, B. Ram, 142

Rawalpindi, riots in 1907, 165, 166, 167

Regeneration of India, Dayanand's dream, 111; not to be realized by imitation, 112; to be achieved worthily, 112

Relief to famine-stricken areas, 195

Religion, West has yet much to learn from East, 110

Rig-Veda, quotations from, relating to God, 90, 91

Risley, Sir Herbert, on Hinduism, 107; on the Arya Samaj's revival of Hinduism, 177, 178; on the assimilative powers of Hinduism, 181

Ritualism, 193, 194

Roth, Professor von, 66

Roy, Raja Ram Mohan, attitude towards the Vedas, 105n.; Bishop Middleton's strange appeal to, 100, 101; champion of Hinduism against Christianity, 100; denies spiritual superiority of the West, 102; no effort spared for his conversion, 100

S

Sacred thread, or Hindu baptism, 8

INDEX

Sadhu, Dayanand becomes a, 15
Salvation, the emancipation of the soul, 62, 63
Sannyasis, the order of, 18
Sanskar, or sacrament, 63, 97, 98
Sanskar Vidhi, Dayanand's book of ritual, 98
Sanskrit, classical, ignored in Government schools and colleges, 136; classical, taught at the Arya colleges, 138
Saraswati, Swami Virjananda, 21-5
Satyarath Prakash, text-book of Dayanand, 1, 2, 59, 188
Satya Kama Jabala, 116
Sayena's commentary on the Vedas, rejected by Dayanand 55; by European scholars, 55n.
Saviours, 2
Schlegel, 89n.
Schopenhauer, on the Upanishads, 81n.
Science, physical, achievements of Indians in, 111
Science, physical, Europeans far in advance of ancient Indians, 111
Seeley, Sir John, on Hinduism, 88
Sen, Babu Keshub Chunder, almost becomes a Christian, 101; cause of dissension in Brahmo Samaj, 102; discusses an All-India Church with Dayanand and others, 82; leader of the Brahmo Samaj, 39; weakens position of Hinduism by Christian leanings, 101
Shankaracharya, 81
Shivaratri, fast of Shiva, 9, 10, 11; anniversary of Dayanand's enlightenment, 10
Shiva worship, 6
Suddhi, or reclamation, work of the Arya Samaj, active and aggressive proselytizism, 120; conversion ceremony, simplicity of the, 121, 125, 126; grave importance of the uplift of the depressed classes, 122; methods and success of the uplift work, 125, 126; question of national self-preservation, 122; success in reclaiming Christian and Mahomedan converts, 120, 121; success in upraising depressed Hindu classes and retaining them for Hinduism, 120; upraising of the lower castes and "untouchables", 121, 12
Sialkote, 126
Sindhudwipa, 116
Singh, Ajit, accused of violent propaganda, 165; not an Arya, 165
Singh, Bawa Chhajju, 1, 4, 5

Singh, Maharaja Pratap, a disciple of Dayanand, 45
Singh, Maharaja Sajjan, pupil of Dayanand, 44, 87
Singh, Udey Vir, 121
Sister, Dayanand's, effect on him of her death, 13
Sita, 173
Social problems, ancient Indian solutions of, as good as modern, 110
Social service, pioneer work in, of the Arya Samaj, 134
Soul, the, Dayanand's definitions of, 61; distinct from God, 61; free to act, but dependent on God's grace, 64; in bondage through ignorance, 62; salvation of, followed by reincarnation, 64
Split, in the Arya Samaj, 83-88, 143, 144
Substance and force, inseparable, 62
Suspicion of the Arya Samaj, found to be baseless, 170-2; reasons for, 160
Suttee, prohibition of, inspired by Dr. Duff, 100
Swarga (Heaven), 64
Syed Ahmad Khan, 46, 82

T

Tagore, Maharishi Debendranath, firmly supports Hindu theism, 102; meets Dayanand, 39
Tagore, Rabindranath, 39
Tantrikas, accept the Vedas, 81
Taracharana, Pandit, 36
Taxilla, ancient University of, 145
Theism, Vedic held by Dayanand superior to its competitors, 106
Theosophist, the, on Dayanand's work and death, 47, 48
Tradition of independent thought and action, 154
Truth, the five tests of, 64

U

Udaipur, Maharana of, pupil of Dayanand, 44, 87
Uncle, Dayanand's: Dayanand's only sympathiser in youth, 11; death of, 12
Universities, ancient Indian, 145
Unrest, Arya Samaj, a parent of, 108; British Government, a source of, 108; Indian, Sir V. Chirol on, 164, 165; inevitable consequence of modern conditions, 108; no progress without, 108

INDEX

"Untouchables", 120-8, 192
Upanishadas, Schopenhauer's appreciation of, 173
Upasna, or realizing God, 64; Sagun and Nirgun, distinguished, 64, 65
Upangas, the six, 61
Up-Vedas, the six, 61

V

Varma, Shyamji Krishna, quoted by Sri V. Chirol against the Arya Samaj, 166; Sir V. Chirol's quotation shown not to be evidence, 169
Vasishta, 116
Vedas, four, 20, 60
Vedas, lost (?), 43
Vedas, the, Dayanand's translation of, accomplished almost single handed, 69; accomplished in seven years, 68; a first attempt, 68; a pioneer effort, 70; Aurobindo Ghosh on, 71-8; best and most scholarly yet given, 70; handicap of language, 66, 67; inherent difficulties, 66, 67; no time for revision, 69; one of many current activities, 68; thoroughness of his methods, 69
Vedas, the four accepted almost universally-by Hindus, 104; admitted as Shastras by Dayanand, 32; Aurobindo Ghosh on, 71-8; Brahminical text-books, 12; Brahmins of Deccan classified by, 12; Canons of, interpretation of, 55, 56, 71-8; created by God, 33; Dayanand's claims for, substantially founded, 71-8, 110, 111; Dayanand's claims for, why made, 110; Dayanand's unique knowledge of, 29; Dayanand's work on, his chief claim to greatness, 68; discredited by European scholars, 67, 104; dissentients from, 81; errors in interpretation of, due to neglect of canons of interpretation, 56, 57; independent interpretation, 96; infallibility of, Dayanand's views on, 96; monotheism of, 90-4; open formally to Brahmins only, 53; quotations from, showing the Hindu conception of God, 90-94; right of interpretation demanded by Dayanand, 55; to be studied in the light of Vedic grammar, 55, 56; translation, a work of next century, 66; unfairly dealt with by missionaries, 67
Vedic Church, older than its rivals, 170; undoubtedly universal, 169, 170

Vedic Dharma, not only a creed, but a philosophy, 171
Vedic Theism, superior to its competitors, 106
Vegetarianism, 83, 84
Vidyarthi, Pandit Gurudatta, criticises European translations of the Vedas, 56; on the Vedic word, devatas, 57; on Vedic interpretation, 56, 57; tracts on the Arya Samaj,
Vidhya, 16
Virjananda Saraswati, Swami, becomes learned and a sannyasi, 23, 24; blindness, 22; character and learning, 24; chastises Dayanand, 24; Dayanand becomes his pupil, 24, 88; goes to Haridwara, 23; hard upbringing, 21, 22; migrates to Mathura, 23; teacher of princes, 24
Vishudananda Gour Swami: a great orthodox Vedantist, 31; debates with Dayanand, 36, 37
Vishvamitra, 116
Viyass, 116
Voysey, Rev. Charles, on Keshub Chunder Sen's leaning to Christianity, 101

W

Ward, Rev. Mr., 90n.
Warnings and counsels for Aryas, 158-7
Water of the Ganges, virtues of, 22
Webb, Sidney, 6
Weber, on absence of caste in Vedic age, 113
Westbrook, W.F., 6
Widow Homes, Hindu, first established by the Arya Samaj, 129
Williams, Sir Monier, 68
Women, Hindu, deplorable condition at foundation of Arya Samaj, 110; deplorable condition due to fall from old ideals, 111; education of, improved under British rule, 116, 117; improved education of, assisted by Arya Samaj, 117; high position in ancient India, 117, 118
Worship, summary of Dayanand's views on, 35, 64, 65

Y

Yajna, performance of, most commendable, 63, 69, 92, 98, 98n
Yajnyavalka, 20, 81
Yajur-Veda, quotations from relating to the conquest of death, 13, 14; relating to God, 91-3

Yaska, greatest authority on the Vedas, 56
Yaugika, all Vedic terms said to be, 56
Yoga, Dayanand's studies in, 16, 17
Yogabhyas, the Key to overcome death, 13

Young Men's Arya Samajes, 153

Z

Zoroastrianism, 170